Cooking
Healthy
Easy Recipes with 4 Ingredients

Dr. Sally N. Hunt, Ph.D.

Cooking Healthy

1st Printing   November 2003

ISBN 1-931294-61-5

Library of Congress Number: 2003113196

Illustrated by Nancy Murphy Griffith
Art Direction by Liz Reinken
Graphic Design by Fit to Print

Manufactured in China
Edited, Designed and published in the United States of America by
Cookbook Resources, LLC
541 Doubletree Drive
Highland Village, Texas 75077
Toll free 866-229-2665
www.cookbookresources.com

A Word to the Reader:

The recipes in this cookbook are designed as a guide for making healthful food choices by emphasizing the reduction of calories, fat, cholesterol, sodium and sugar. Recipes are modifications of traditional and classic cooking and have been simplified to require just four ingredients.

Additions, deletions and revisions of certain products may be made to meet individual dietary needs.

This cookbook is not intended as a weight-loss program or as a substitute for the advice of a doctor. Always consult your doctor before making significant changes in your daily food intake.

Nutritional analysis software was used to determine the nutritional value of a single serving of each recipe. Analyses do not include optional ingredients, garnishes or sauces, unless specifically stated in the recipe. When two or more ingredient choices are given, the ingredient listed first is the one used in nutritional analysis.

The artificial sweeteners in these recipes may not be tolerated by every reader, and should be used with care. (For example, people with the rare disease phenylketonuria cannot metabolize aspartame.) See your doctor for individual guidelines on fat, sodium and sugar intakes.

CONTENTS

CONTENTS

Dr. Sally Hunt

Dr. Sally Hunt

Asked about the important roles in her life, Dr. Sally Hunt readily identifies those of wife, mother and grandmother as most significant. Always ready to tackle new challenges, she welcomed the opportunity to try out the role of cookbook author.

Developing healthy recipes with only four ingredients drew on both her culinary experience and educational background in nutrition and food preparation.

Dr. Hunt's early life was spent in West Texas and New Mexico, where the cultures, cuisine and traditions of the Southwest influenced her culinary tastes and interests. Her enthusiasm and enjoyment of cooking and good food comes naturally from a family tradition of "good cooks." Having lived in Louisiana nearly 30 years, she is also influenced by the flavorful and delicious Cajun and Creole cuisines.

Nutrition and food studies were a special focus as she pursued degrees in Home Economics Education. Her undergraduate degree was awarded by the University of Oklahoma; the master's degree was granted by Northwestern State University of Louisiana; and the doctorate degree was awarded by Texas Woman's University.

Dr. Hunt's professional career as a university teacher and administrator provided her the opportunity to work with many classroom teachers and teacher education majors, both at the graduate and undergraduate levels. Over the years, she authored and administered numerous educational grants that helped classroom teachers strengthen their teaching skills and pursue national certification. Educational technology in classrooms was an early and ongoing area of interest and research.

Varied educational and personal experiences have contributed to Dr. Hunt's interests and preferred pastimes. Love and appreciation of the performing and visual arts has been a lifetime pursuit. She also recently discovered the pleasure of the quilting arts, and is delighted to find that skilled, experienced quilters enthusiastically share their expertise with novice quilters such as herself.

In the early 90's, Dr. Hunt began participating in competitive chili cookoffs in Louisiana and Texas. She even won the state championship chili competition in Louisiana in 1992 and traveled to Terlingua, Texas, for the international chili cookoff. Her chili cooking continues to attract attention from friends and family. Always looking to improve her skills, she recently attended a Southwestern cuisine workshop in Albuquerque, New Mexico, conducted by Jane Butel, cookbook author and television personality.

Dr. Hunt plans to continue her study of healthy eating and the innovative preparation of foods.

The Good News About This Cookbook

Four Ingredient Recipes

Many of today's cookbooks have recipes that require a long list of expensive ingredients, special utensils or equipment, complicated cooking techniques and/or lengthy preparation times. As wonderful as these recipes may be, they just aren't practical for busy people.

Today's cooks want quality, even luxury, from their food, yet they don't have hours to spend preparing it. That's why the four-ingredient recipe is good news.

Four-ingredient cooking is "back-to-basics" cooking. With just four food products in each recipe, the quality, flavor retention and careful preparation of each ingredient becomes important. Cooking techniques are generally basic and simple, with a focus on retaining the nutrients, flavors, colors and textures of foods.

The ingredients in these recipes have been carefully selected to result in a flavorful and satisfying cooked product. Fresh, natural and high quality ingredients are emphasized throughout.

Water, salt or salt substitute, pepper and nonstick cooking spray have been used as "free" ingredients – those essential to preparation but not counted as one of the four ingredients. "Flavor Perks" and "Variations" allow the cook to add flavors, textures, colors or garnishes that enhance the dish, or even to choose a different cooking technique.

The Good News About This Cookbook

Healthier Cooking

Dietary intake affects many Americans who suffer from health problems—heart disease, hypertension, osteoporosis, cancer and obesity. This cookbook targets the reduction of many foods or ingredients linked to these health problems.

Generally, foods used in these recipes are lower in calories; lower in fat, saturated fat and cholesterol; lower in sodium and salt; and lower in sugar. Many ingredients are substitutes for the foods that have been linked to health problems. Most recipes use sugar substitutes, for example, to replace calorie-dense sugars.

Each recipe features a nutritional analysis of ingredients, including the number of calories; grams of protein, carbohydrate, fat, sugar, and fiber; and milligrams of cholesterol, sodium, and calcium.

The Good News About This Cookbook

Smart New Products

Increasing consumer demand for healthier foods has brought many smart new products to store shelves. Supermarkets now stock hundreds of food products designed to make healthful cooking easier and more convenient.

The recipes in this cookbook take advantage of many of these new products and encourage the reader to explore the wide variety of food options available.

For most of us, eating is one of the great pleasures in life, associated with family, friends and celebrations. Although our busy lifestyles afford precious little time for cooking, we can still make daily food choices that lead to better health.

Hopefully, this cookbook will provide a smarter, simpler approach to healthier cooking and eating–four ingredients at a time.

-Sally N. Hunt, Ph.D

Healthful Cooking FAQs

What is a Healthful Food?

In this cookbook, a healthful food is one that is low in fat, saturated fat, cholesterol, simple sugars, sodium and overall calories, yet provides a balance of nutrients. Fresh, natural, unprocessed and frozen foods are generally considered better choices than are canned, pre-packaged and processed foods.

What kinds of products should I buy to help me reduce calories, sugar, fat, cholesterol and/or sodium?

Look for the following labels on prepackaged foods.

To reduce calories:
 calorie free
 low calorie
 reduced calorie

To reduce fat, saturated fat
and cholesterol:
 fat free
 low fat
 less fat
 low saturated
 less saturated
 cholesterol free
 low cholesterol
 less cholesterol
 extra lean
 lean
 light
 lite

To reduce simple sugars
(sugars that contribute only calories,
such as table sugar):
 sugar free
 lite sugar free
 low sugar
 no sugar added
 sugar substitutes or replacements
 artificial sweeteners

To reduce salt/sodium:
 no salt
 salt free
 light or lite
 sodium free
 low sodium
 light in sodium
 very low sodium

Healthful Cooking FAQs

How much food should I be eating?

Here are some recommended servings sizes of common foods.

Breads, cereals, grain products
- 1 slice bread
- ½ cup cooked cereal, rice or pasta
- 1 cup ready-to-eat cereal
- 1 bun, bagel, English muffin
- 1 small roll, biscuit or muffin
- 3-4 small or 2 large crackers

Vegetables
- ½ cup cooked or raw vegetables
- 1 cup leafy raw vegetables
- ¾ cup vegetable juice

Fruits
- 1 medium apple, banana or orange
- ½ grapefruit
- 1 melon wedge
- ¾ cup fruit juice
- ½ cup berries
- ½ cup diced, cooked or canned fruit
- ¼ cup dried fruit

Meat, Poultry, Fish and Beans
- 2-3 ounces (about the size of a deck of cards) lean, cooked meat, poultry or fish
- 1 egg
- ½ cup cooked beans
- 4 ounces tofu
- 2 tablespoons nuts, seeds or peanut butter (count as 1 ounce or ⅓ of a 3-ounce portion of meat)

Milk, Cheese and Yogurt
- 1 cup milk or yogurt
- 2 ounces processed cheese
- 1½ ounces natural cheese (Best low fat or fat free choices are nonfat and 1% milk, buttermilk, cottage cheese, yogurt and fortified soy milk.)

Fats and Sweets
- Use these sparingly, since they contribute calories or food energy but few nutrients.

Beverages
- 8 ounces or 1 cup for all beverages

Healthful Cooking FAQs

What is on a food label?

Serving size
Servings per container
Calories (food energy) per serving (grams)
Calories from fat (grams)
Saturated fat (grams)
Cholesterol (milligrams)
Sodium (milligrams)
Total carbohydrate (grams)
Dietary Fiber (grams)
Sugars (grams)
Protein (grams)

On a typical label, the percentages listed beside each nutrient compare the amount of that nutrient to a standard 2000-calorie diet to determine the Percent (%) Daily Values. This measurement indicates what percentage of a person's daily nutrients the food supplies.

So what's the big deal?

Reading food labels is the best way to determine what – and how much – we are eating. It helps us "get real" about serving sizes and nutrition. Pay special attention to these final points when studying food labels:

- Serving size – Be sure to check the actual serving size of one serving as compared to the number of servings in the entire package. When we grab a package of nuts for a snack, 170 calories per serving doesn't seem like a lot until we realize there are actually 3 servings in the bag.

- Nutrient content – Look for products that provide nutritional value instead of empty calories.

- Order of ingredients – Manufacturers list ingredients by weight. Keep this in mind when sugar is listed as the first ingredient in ready-made cereals, snacks and sweets.

APPETIZERS

Americans love appetizers and snacks, which are now an accepted part of everyday eating—from simple "dips and chips" to elaborately planned and prepared all-appetizer parties. Choosing healthy snacks and appetizers is simply a matter of selecting wisely from the huge assortment of prepared and fresh foods available. The recipes in this section offer some simple and easy-to-prepare foods that trim down calories, fat, sugar, and salt.

SWISS CHEESE MINI-QUICHES

This recipe is a healthful, single-serving variation of the traditional quiche made of eggs, cream, bacon and Swiss cheese.

**4 reduced fat flaky refrigerated biscuits
½ cup egg substitute
½ cup green onions and tops, finely chopped
½ cup reduced fat Swiss or cheddar cheese, finely shredded**

1. Preheat oven to 450°. Prepare a miniature 2-inch muffin pan for 16 muffins by coating with nonstick cooking spray. Gently separate each biscuit into four thin layers. Firmly press one layer of biscuit dough onto the bottom and up the sides of 16 muffin cups.

2. In a small bowl, combine egg substitute, green onions and cheese. Place a scant tablespoon into each prepared muffin cup. Bake 10-12 minutes or until lightly brown.

Flavor Perk: Add 1 teaspoon reduced sodium Worcestershire sauce and ½ teaspoon Dijon-style mustard.

- - - - - - - - - - - - - - - - - - -

Yield: 16 quiches
Serving size: 1 (2 inch) quiche

Calories: 42
Protein: 3 g
Carbohydrate: 3 g
Fat: 2 g
Cholesterol: 5 mg
Sodium: 94 mg
Calcium: 68 mg
Dietary Fiber: less than 1 g
Sugar: less than 1 g

SPINACH-SWISS CHEESE BITES

These bites are quick-to-fix and are similar to mini quiches.

**4 reduced fat flaky refrigerated biscuits
½ cup egg substitute
½ cup chopped spinach, cooked, drained thoroughly
½ cup reduced fat Swiss cheese, finely shredded**

1. Preheat oven to 450°. Prepare a miniature (2 inch) muffin pan for 16 appetizers by spraying with nonstick cooking spray. Gently separate each biscuit into 4 thin layers. Press one biscuit layer onto the bottom and sides of each muffin cup.

1. In a small bowl, combine egg substitute, drained spinach and cheese. Place a scant tablespoon into each sprayed muffin cup. Bake 10-12 minutes or until lightly brown. Serve hot.

Flavor Perk: Add pinch of ground nutmeg and 1 tablespoon minced onion to the egg-spinach mixture.

- - - - - - - - - - - - - - - - - - -

Yield: 16 appetizers
Serving size: 1 appetizer

Calories: 42
Protein: 3 g
Carbohydrate: 3 g
Fat: 2 g
Cholesterol: 5 mg
Sodium: 97 mg
Calcium: 74 mg
Dietary Fiber: less than 1 g
Sugar: 0 g

HOT SHRIMP CANAPÉS

1 (6 ounce) can small cooked
shrimp, drained
1 cup light mayonnaise
1 cup reduced fat shredded
cheddar cheese
10-12 slices whole-wheat bread,
trimmed, cut in squares

1. Combine shrimp, mayonnaise and cheese. Spread shrimp mixture thinly onto trimmed bread squares.

2. Preheat oven to broil. Broil squares in oven until bubbly. Serve immediately.

Flavor Perk: Add 1 tablespoon chopped fresh parsley and 1 tablespoon lemon juice to shrimp mixture.

- - - - - - - - - - - - - - - - - - - -

Yield: 20 servings (40 2-inch squares)
Serving size: 2 squares

Calories: 138
Protein: 7 g
Carbohydrate: 13 g
Fat: 7 g
Cholesterol: 25 mg
Sodium: 302 mg
Calcium: 96 mg
Dietary Fiber: 2 g
Sugar: 1 g

MARINATED SHRIMP TEASERS

⅓ cup olive oil
1 garlic clove, finely minced
1 tablespoon snipped parsley
(snip with scissors into small
pieces)
1 pound medium raw shrimp,
shelled, deveined

1. Stir together oil, garlic, parsley and ¼ teaspoon salt or salt substitute in a shallow dish. Add shrimp and coat with the marinade. Place marinated shrimp in a resealable plastic bag. Refrigerate at least 4 hours.

2. When ready to serve, preheat oven to 375°. Place the drained marinated shrimp on a broiler pan and bake about 10 minutes or until shrimp turn pink. Serve immediately.

Variation: Substitute fat free marinade or fat free Italian salad dressing for oil-garlic marinade. Another variation is to substitute reduced fat barbecue sauce for the oil-garlic marinade.

- - - - - - - - - - - - - - - - - - - -

Yield: About 30 servings
Serving size: 2-3 shrimp

Calories: 37
Protein: 3 g
Carbohydrate: less than 1 g
Fat: 3 g
Cholesterol: 23 mg
Sodium: 22 mg
Calcium: 8 mg
Dietary Fiber: 0 g
Sugar: 0 g

SAUCY CHICKEN WINGS

12 chicken wings, tips removed
½ cup brown sugar substitute
⅓ cup regular or hot ketchup
¼ teaspoon crushed red pepper flakes or hot pepper sauce to taste

1. Preheat oven to 325°. Break each wing into 2 pieces and remove any fat or excess skin. Place pieces on foil-covered shallow baking pan.

2. Mix brown sugar substitute, ketchup and pepper flakes or hot pepper sauce. Brush sparingly on both sides of chicken wings. Bake 1 hour or until chicken is fork-tender and crisp.

- - - - - - - - - - - - - - - -

Yield: 12 servings (24 pieces)
Serving size: 2 pieces

Calories: 113
Protein: 9 g
Carbohydrate: 2 g
Fat: 8 g
Cholesterol: 38 mg
Sodium: 107 mg
Calcium: 7 mg
Dietary Fiber: 0 g
Sugar: less than 1 g

CREOLE-RUB CHICKEN WINGS

12 chicken wings, tips removed
Nonstick cooking spray
Lite or salt free Creole seasoning

1. Preheat oven to 325°. Break each wing into 2 pieces and remove any fat or excess skin. Place on foil or wax paper; spray both sides with nonstick cooking spray and rub or sprinkle to taste with Creole seasoning. Place wings on foil-covered baking sheet. Bake for 1 hour or until fork-tender and crisp.

2. Serve with fat free ranch-style salad dressing or horseradish sauce and chunks of celery.

- - - - - - - - - - - - - - - -

Yield: 12 servings (24 pieces)
Serving size: 2 pieces

Calories: 107
Protein: 9 g
Carbohydrate: 0 g
Fat: 8 g
Cholesterol: 38 mg
Sodium: 29 mg
Calcium: 6 mg
Dietary Fiber: 0 g
Sugar: 0 g

QUESADILLA BASICS

The popular Southwestern quesadilla (kay-suh-DEE-ah) appetizer consists of a flour tortilla filled with cheese and jalapenos, heated until the cheese melts. The quesadilla is heated on a griddle (or Mexican comal) and eaten immediately. A variety of fillings may be added. This is an excellent party appetizer for guests to make their own quesadillas.

12 (12 inch) whole wheat flour tortillas
1½ cups shredded reduced fat cheddar or cheddar-jack cheese
1 (12 ounce) jar sliced jalapeño peppers, drained

1. Spray a skillet or griddle with nonstick cooking spray, or follow directions for an electric quesadilla maker. Preheat griddle to medium high temperature and place one tortilla on griddle. Sprinkle with cheese and sliced jalapenos to taste. Place another tortilla on top.

2. Cook until bottom tortilla is lightly brown. Carefully turn over and brown lightly on other side. Serve immediately, uncut or cut into wedges.

3. Serve with chopped tomatoes, chopped green onions and tops, chopped black olives, salsa and/or a topping of fat free sour cream.

Variation: To make fold-over quesadillas, use one flour tortilla and add filling to one side. After quesadilla is lightly browned, turn over to other side.

- -

Yield: 12 servings (6 whole or 36 wedges)
Serving size: ½ quesadilla or 3 wedges

Calories: 158
Protein: 9 g
Carbohydrate: 14 g
Fat: 6 g
Cholesterol: 20 mg
Sodium: 894 mg
Calcium: 227 mg
Dietary Fiber: 10 g
Sugar: 0 g

GREEN CHILE-CHEESE SQUARES

4 cups shredded reduced fat
cheddar cheese
1 cup egg substitute
1 (4 ounce) can chopped green
chiles, drained
4 green onions and tops, chopped

1. In a mixing bowl, combine cheese,
   egg substitute, green chilies and
   onions. Mix thoroughly and
   spread mixture into a sprayed 8 x
   8-inch square baking pan.

2. Bake 30 minutes. Cut into 1½-inch
   squares and serve hot.

3. Serve with salsa.

*Variation: Substitute 1-2 seeded, finely chopped
fresh jalapeño peppers for the green
chiles.*

- -

Yield: About 25 squares
Serving size: 1 square

Calories: 122
Protein: 10 g
Carbohydrate: 1 g
Fat: 8 g
Cholesterol: 26 mg
Sodium: 338 mg
Calcium: 265 mg
Dietary Fiber: less than 1 g
Sugar: less than 1 g

CHEDDAR CHEESE-SESAME LOGS

1 (8 ounce) package reduced fat
cream cheese, softened
2 (8 ounce) packages reduced fat
cheddar cheese, finely shredded
2 tablespoons green onions and
tops, finely chopped
3 tablespoons toasted sesame seeds

1. Thoroughly mix cream cheese,
   cheddar cheese and green onions.
   Cover and refrigerate at least 4
   hours.

2. To toast sesame seeds, place the
   seeds in a dry skillet over medium
   heat. Stir constantly (will easily
   burn) until evenly golden brown
   and fragrant. Remove from heat
   and cool.

3. Divide cheese mixture and form 2
   logs. Roll all sides in toasted
   sesame seeds. Refrigerate until
   firm. Serve with a sharp knife for
   cutting slices.

4. Serve with round Melba toast, reduced sodium whole grain round
   crackers or round raw vegetable
   slices such as cucumber, zucchini
   and yellow squash.

- -

Yield: 36 servings (About 2½ cups)
Serving size: 1 tablespoon

Calories: 60
Protein: 4 g
Carbohydrate: less than 1 g
Fat: 4 g
Cholesterol: 13 mg
Sodium: 133 mg
Calcium: 97 mg
Dietary Fiber: less than 1 g
Sugar: less than 1 g

BACON-WRAPPED WATER CHESTNUTS

This is a healthful variation of Rumaki, an appetizer with chicken livers, water chestnuts and bacon. The name Rumaki is Japanese, although the appetizer is thought to have originated in Hawaii. Guests will flock to the tantalizing aroma of this appetizer.

¼ cup light (reduced sodium)
  soy sauce
¼ teaspoon cayenne pepper
1 (8 ounce) can whole water
  chestnuts, drained, rinsed
½ pound reduced sodium bacon or
turkey bacon, sliced, cut in thirds

1. Combine soy sauce and cayenne pepper in shallow bowl. Add water chestnuts and marinate at least 1 hour.

2. Wrap ⅓ slice bacon around each water chestnut and fasten with a toothpick. Place on a rack in a shallow pan. Preheat oven broiler and broil the appetizers 5-7 minutes, turning once. Serve hot.

Flavor Perk: Add 1 small garlic clove, minced, and 6 thin slices fresh ginger root to the soy sauce marinade.

- - - - - - - - - - - - - - - - - -
Yield: About 30 appetizers
Serving Size: 2 chestnuts

Calories: 87
Protein: 6 g
Carbohydrates: 4 g
Fat: 5 g
Cholesterol: 16 mg
Sodium: 362 mg
Calcium: 1 mg
Dietary Fiber: less than 1 gram
Sugar: less than 1 gram

CREOLE PARTY MIX

4 cups bite-size crispy rice cereal
  squares
4 cups bite-size corn cereal squares
4 cups bite-size shredded wheat
  or bran squares
Salt free Creole seasoning

1. Preheat oven to 300°. Combine cereals in a large bowl.

2. Spread mix onto foil-covered shallow baking sheets. Spray evenly with butter-flavored nonstick cooking spray and sprinkle with salt free Creole seasoning to taste.

3. Bake 45 minutes, stirring every 15 minutes. Remove baking sheets from oven. With the cereal still in the foil, fold sides of foil toward middle and lift off baking sheet to cool.

4. Store cereal mix in airtight container.

Variation: Substitute 4 cups round oat cereal for one of the cereals.

- - - - - - - - - - - - - - - - - -
Yield: 24 servings (About 12-13 cups)
Serving Size: ½ cup

Calories: 52
Protein: 1 g
Carbohydrate: 12 g
Fat: 0 g
Cholesterol: 0 mg
Sodium: 86 mg
Calcium: 32 mg
Dietary Fiber: less than 1 g
Sugar: less than 1 g

BAGEL CRISPS

These are a delicious alternative to calorie-laden chips.

4 large whole grain or whole wheat unsliced bagels
Butter-flavored cooking spray

1. Preheat oven to 275°. Using a thin-bladed sharp knife or a serrated bread knife, slice each bagel horizontally into ¼-inch slices. Quarter the slices, making flat wedges.

2. Place the wedges on wax paper or parchment, and spray on both sides with cooking spray. Place on a baking sheet and bake 30-45 minutes or until golden brown and very crisp. Depending on the size of the bagel, each bagel makes about 24 wedges.

3. Store in an airtight container.

Flavor Perk: Sprinkle with crushed dried herbs or other salt free seasoning blends.

- -

Yield: 12 servings (About 96 wedges)
Serving size: 8 wedges

Calories: 57
Protein: 2 g
Carbohydrate: 12 g
Fat: less than 1 g
Cholesterol: 0 mg
Sodium: 67 mg
Calcium: 67 mg
Dietary Fiber: 2 g
Sugar: 1 g

BAKED TORTILLA CRISPS

This recipe for baked reduced fat, no-salt tortilla wedges will provide a healthier tortilla chip to offer to your family and guests for dipping into salsas and dips.

12 fresh corn or flour tortillas, 6-8 inches
Nonstick cooking spray

1. Preheat oven to 325°. In batches, stack and cut tortillas into 6 wedges. Place on wax paper or parchment paper and spray with nonstick cooking spray on both sides.

2. Transfer the sprayed wedges to a cookie sheet and bake 20-30 minutes or until crisp and lightly browned. Store in an airtight container.

Variation: Sprinkle wedges with chile powder or low sodium Mexican seasoning blend before baking.

- -

Yield: 12 servings (70 wedges)
Serving size: 4-6 wedges

Calories: 58
Protein: 1 g
Carbohydrate: 12 g
Fat: less than 1 g
Cholesterol: 0 mg
Sodium: 42 mg
Calcium: 46 mg
Dietary Fiber: 1 g
Sugar: less than 1 g

LAZY PITA CRISPS

4 whole wheat pita breads

1. Preheat oven to 350°. With a sharp knife, cut pita breads in half to form 2 pockets. Then split each pocket into halves. Cut each of the halves into 3 triangles or wedges. Each whole pita should make 12 wedges. Spray wedges lightly with nonstick cooking spray, if desired.

2. Place the wedges on a baking sheet without overlapping the edges. Bake 8-10 minutes or until wedges are crisp and lightly browned. Serve immediately or store in an airtight container.

Flavor Perk: Sprinkle with herb or spice of your choice.

- - - - - - - - - - - - - - - - - - - -

Servings: 16 servings (48 wedges)
Serving size: 3 wedges

Calories: 43
Protein: 2 g
Carbohydrate: 9 g
Fat: less than 1 g
Cholesterol: 0 mg
Sodium: 85 mg
Calcium: 2 mg
Dietary Fiber: 1 g
Sugar: less than 1 g

TASTY PARMESAN WEDGES

4 whole wheat pitas
1½ cups reduced fat grated Parmesan topping

1. Preheat oven to 350°. Cut pitas in half; then split each half. Sprinkle each half with cheese and cut into 4 wedges. There should be a total of 16 wedges from each pita.

2. Place on baking sheet and bake 12-15 minutes or until crisp and golden brown.

- - - - - - - - - - - - - - - - - - - -

Yield: 16 servings (64 wedges)
Serving size: 4 wedges

Calories: 128
Protein: 4 g
Carbohydrate: 17 g
Fat: 5 g
Cholesterol: 0 mg
Sodium: 404 mg
Calcium: 2 mg
Dietary Fiber: 1 g
Sugar: less than 1 g

WONTON CRISPS

These crisps are an easy alternative to calorie-laden, high-sodium chips.

8 fresh wonton wrappers
Nonstick cooking spray
Salt or salt substitute (optional)

1. Preheat oven to 350°. Lightly coat a baking sheet with nonstick cooking spray. Cut each wonton wrap into 6 triangles and place in a single layer on the baking sheet. Sprinkle to taste with salt or salt substitute, if desired.

2. Bake 5-7 minutes or until the wontons just begin to brown.

- - - - - - - - - - - - - - - - - - -

Yield: About 12 servings
Serving size: 3-4 crisps

Calories: 15
Protein: less than 1 g
Carbohydrate: 3 g
Fat: 0 g
Cholesterol: less than 1 mg
Sodium: 31 mg
Calcium: 3 mg
Dietary Fiber: 0 g
Sugar: 0 g

CHIHUAHUA SALSA DIP

This spicy, salsa-flavored dip is fast and easy for last-minute entertaining.

1 (8 ounce) carton fat free or light sour cream
½ cup hot salsa
½ teaspoon salt free seasoning blend
½ teaspoon prepared Dijon-style mustard

1. Combine all ingredients. Chill at least 1 hour for flavors to blend.

2. Serve with baked tortilla chips or reduced fat whole grain crackers.

- - - - - - - - - - - - - - - - - - -

Yield: 8 servings (About 1 cup)
Serving size: 2 tablespoons

Calories: 24
Protein: 1 g
Carbohydrate: 5 g
Fat: 0 g
Cholesterol: 3 mg
Sodium: 76 mg
Calcium: 38 mg
Dietary Fiber: less than 1 g
Sugar: 0 g

ZESTY CREAMY ONION DIP

1 (8 ounce) package reduced fat cream cheese, softened
1 (8 ounce) carton fat free sour cream
½ cup hot and spicy ketchup or chili sauce
1 (1⅜ ounce) packet dry onion soup mix

1. Beat cream cheese until smooth. Stir in remaining ingredients and mix well.

2. Cover and chill at least 1 hour.

3. Serve with healthful grain snacks or raw vegetables.

Flavor Perk: Add 1 tablespoon lemon juice.

- -

Yield: 20 servings (About 2½ cups)
Serving size: 2 tablespoons

Calories: 49
Protein: 2 g
Carbohydrate: 5 g
Fat: 2 g
Cholesterol: 8 mg
Sodium: 194 mg
Calcium: 15 mg
Dietary Fiber: 0 g
Sugar: 2 g

SPICY CURRY DIP

Curry powder, widely used in Indian cooking, has a pungent, recognizable flavor; however, curry powder will lose its pungency after 2 months on the shelf. To extend the life of curry powder, store tightly covered in the refrigerator.

1 cup light sour cream
⅓ cup light mayonnaise
½ teaspoon curry powder
Pinch ground cayenne

1. Stir ingredients together. Cover and refrigerate at least 4 hours. Stir again before serving.

2. Serve with healthful grain snacks or raw vegetables.

Flavor Perk: Add 1 finely minced garlic clove, ¼ teaspoon Worcestershire and/or 1 tablespoon ketchup.

- -

Yield: 10 servings (About 1½ cups)
Serving size: 2 tablespoons

Calories: 59
Protein: less than 1 g
Carbohydrate: 2 g
Fat: 6 g
Cholesterol: 12 mg
Sodium: 57 mg
Calcium: 26 mg
Dietary Fiber: 0 g
Sugar: less than 1 g

HOT CHEESY CRAB DIP

1 (16 ounce) package light
   Velveeta cheese
2 (6.5 ounce) cans crabmeat,
   drained, flaked
6 fresh green onions and tops,
   chopped
2 cups light mayonnaise

1. Melt cheese in saucepan over low heat.

2. Stir in remaining ingredients and serve warm.

3. Serve with whole wheat or whole grain crackers.

Flavor Perk: Add 1 tablespoon lemon juice or ½ teaspoon low-sodium herb or spice seasoning.

- - - - - - - - - - - - - - - - - - - -

Yield: About 40 servings (5 cups)
Serving size: 2 tablespoons

Calories: 71
Protein: 3 g
Carbohydrate: 3 g
Fat: 5 g
Cholesterol: 18 mg
Sodium: 317 mg
Calcium: 5 mg
Dietary Fiber: less than 1 g
Sugar: 1 g

ROYAL ORLEANS SHRIMP DIP

1 (8 ounce) package reduced fat
   cream cheese, softened
½ cup light mayonnaise
1 (6 ounce) can shrimp, drained,
   chopped
1½ teaspoons lite or salt free
   Creole seasoning

1. Blend cream cheese and mayonnaise. Stir in shrimp and seasoning. Chill at least 1 hour before serving.

Flavor Perk: Add 1 tablespoon lemon juice and 2 teaspoons chopped fresh parsley. Garnish with sprig of fresh parsley or whole shrimp.

- - - - - - - - - - - - - - - - - - - -

Yield: 18 servings (about 2¼ cups)
Serving size: 2 tablespoons

Calories: 65
Protein: 4 g
Carbohydrate: 1 g
Fat: 5 g
Cholesterol: 27 mg
Sodium: 146 mg
Calcium: 6 mg
Dietary Fiber: 0 g
Sugar: less than 1 g

"SHOUT ABOUT IT" SHRIMP DIP

2 cups cooked, deveined shrimp, finely chopped
2 tablespoons prepared horseradish
½ cup chili sauce
¾ cup fat free mayonnaise

1. Combine all ingredients and season to taste with salt or salt substitute and freshly ground black pepper. Refrigerate.

2. Serve with cucumber or zucchini slices.

Flavor Perk: Add 1 tablespoon lemon juice

- - - - - - - - - - - - - - - - - - -

Yield: 20 servings (About 2½ cups)
Serving size: 2 tablespoons

Calories: 41
Protein: 5 g
Carbohydrate: 4 g
Fat: less than 1 g
Cholesterol: 35 mg
Sodium: 311 mg
Calcium: 13 mg
Dietary Fiber: 0 g
Sugar: 2 g

CREAMY PESTO DIP

1 (8 ounce) carton light sour cream
¼ cup refrigerated basil pesto
Fresh basil leaves or parsley leaves

1. Stir sour cream and pesto until well blended. Place in serving bowl and garnish with sprigs of fresh basil leaves or 1 teaspoon chopped fresh parsley.

2. Serve with healthful grain snacks or raw vegetables.

- - - - - - - - - - - - - - - - - - -

Yield: 10 servings (about 1¼ cups)
Serving size: 2 tablespoons

Calories: 60
Protein: 2 g
Carbohydrate: 2 g
Fat: 5 g
Cholesterol: 8 mg
Sodium: 59 mg
Calcium: 59 mg
Dietary Fiber: 0 g
Sugar: 2 g

HOLY GUACAMOLE

A new combination kitchen product – an avocado scoop and slicer – makes preparation faster and easier.

2 large ripe Haas avocados
1 garlic clove, finely minced
2-3 tablespoons finely minced onion
1 fresh tomato, coarsely chopped

1. Cut avocados in half. Spear the pits with a small knife and twist to remove pits. Scoop out pulp and coarsely mash, leaving small chunks of avocado.

2. Stir in garlic, onion and tomato. Season to taste with salt or salt substitute.

3. Spoon mixture into a serving bowl. Place plastic wrap directly on surface and seal tightly. Refrigerate until ready to serve. Guacamole is best served same day.

Flavor Perk: Add one or more of the following: 1 teaspoon (or to taste) finely minced fresh jalapeño; 1-2 teaspoons fresh lime juice; 2 teaspoons fresh cilantro leaves, coarsely chopped.

Variation: Substitute chunky salsa for tomato.

- - - - - - - - - - - - - - - - - - -

Yield: 8-10 servings (About 1½ cups)
Serving size: 2 tablespoons

Calories: 78
Protein: 1 g
Carbohydrate: 4 g
Fat: 7 g
Cholesterol: 0 mg
Sodium: 7 mg
Calcium: 7 mg
Dietary Fiber: 2 g
Sugar: less than 1 g

GREEN CHILE DUNK

Scoop up this green chile dip with Baked Tortilla Crisps (p. 20) or Lazy Pita Crisps (p. 21).

1 (8 ounce) package reduced fat cream cheese, softened
6 tablespoons light mayonnaise
1 (4 ounce) can diced green chiles, drained
3 tablespoons minced onion

1. In a mixing bowl, combine cream cheese and mayonnaise, blending until smooth. Add chiles and onion and place in serving bowl. Refrigerate at least 1 hour for flavors to blend.

Flavor Perk: Add 1 teaspoon fresh lemon juice to the mixture. Garnish with a sprinkling of paprika.

- - - - - - - - - - - - - - - - - - -

Yield: 10 servings (About 1¼ cup)
Serving size: 2 tablespoons

Calories: 89
Protein: 2 g
Carbohydrate: 2 g
Fat: 8 g
Cholesterol: 19 mg
Sodium: 182 mg
Calcium: 9 mg
Dietary Fiber: less than 1 g
Sugar: less than 1 g

YIPPEE SOUTHWESTERN TOMATO DIP

1 (10 ounce) can Mexican-style diced tomatoes with lime juice and cilantro, drained
1 (8 ounce) carton fat free or light sour cream
1½ teaspoons salt free seasoning blend
2 teaspoons prepared horseradish

1. Combine all ingredients. Chill at least 1 hour for flavors to blend.

2. Serve with healthful grain snacks or raw vegetables.

Variation: Substitute a 10-ounce can diced tomatoes and green chiles in sauce for Mexican-style tomatoes.

- - - - - - - - - - - - - - - - - - -

Servings: 16 servings (About 2 cups)
Serving size: 2 tablespoons

Calories: 19
Protein: less than 1 g
Carbohydrate: 4 g
Fat: less than 1 g
Cholesterol: 2 mg
Sodium: 113 mg
Calcium: 30 mg
Dietary Fiber: less than 1 g
Sugar: 1 g

HI-O SILVER VEGETABLE DIP

Ranch-style dips and dressings are guaranteed to please.

1 (8 ounce) package reduced fat cream cheese, softened
1 cup light mayonnaise
1 (1 ounce) package dry reduced calorie ranch-style dressing mix
½ onion, finely minced

1. In mixing bowl, combine cream cheese and mayonnaise and beat until creamy.

2. Stir in remaining ingredients. Refrigerate at least 1 hour for flavors to blend.

3. Serve with fresh baby carrots, broccoli and cauliflower florets, celery sticks, zucchini slices or other fresh vegetables.

Flavor Perk: Garnish with parsley and ¼ teaspoon paprika.

- - - - - - - - - - - - - - - - - - -

Yield: About 16 servings (about 2¼ cups)
Serving size: 2 tablespoons

Calories: 90
Protein: 2 g
Carbohydrate: 3 g
Fat: 8 g
Cholesterol: 15 mg
Sodium: 274 mg
Calcium: less than 1 mg
Dietary Fiber: 0 g
Sugar: less than 1 g

SPINACH-VEGGIE DIP

There are many variations of spinach dip – an indication of its popularity. Four different recipes are included here. Try them all to find your favorite.

1 (10 ounce) package frozen chopped spinach, thawed
6 green onions and tops, chopped
1 (.9 ounce) package dry vegetable soup mix
2 (8 ounce) cartons light sour cream

1. Drain spinach thoroughly in a wire mesh strainer to remove excess water.

2. Combine spinach with green onions, soup mix and sour cream. Season to taste with salt or salt substitute and freshly ground black pepper.

3. Cover and chill at least 1 hour before serving.

4. Serve with reduced fat whole grain crackers.

Flavor Perk: Add 1 tablespoon lemon juice to spinach mixture.

- - - - - - - - - - - - - - - - - - - -

Yield: 24 servings (About 3 cups)
Serving size: 2 tablespoons

Calories: 21
Protein: 1 g
Carbohydrate: 2 g
Fat: less than 1 g
Cholesterol: 3 mg
Sodium: 87 mg
Calcium: 31 mg
Dietary Fiber: less than 1 g
Sugar: 1 g

TANGY SPINACH DIP

1 (10 ounce) package frozen chopped spinach
⅓ cup green onions and tops, chopped
1 tablespoon lemon juice
1 cup light sour cream

1. Drain spinach and squeeze out as much liquid as possible. Place in a blender or food processor and add green onions, lemon juice and sour cream. Process until blended.

2. Season to taste with salt or salt substitute and freshly ground black pepper. Cover and refrigerate at least 2 hours before serving.

3. Serve with baked chips or an assortment of reduced fat whole grain crackers.

- - - - - - - - - - - - - - - - - - - -

Yield: 16 servings (About 2 cups)
Serving size: 2 tablespoons

Calories: 23
Protein: 1 g
Carbohydrate: 2 g
Fat: 1 g
Cholesterol: 5 mg
Sodium: 34 mg
Calcium: 42 mg
Dietary Fiber: less than 1 g
Sugar: 1 g

CRUNCHY SPINACH DUNK

1 (10 ounce) package frozen
chopped spinach, thawed
2 (8 ounce) packages reduced fat
cream cheese, softened
1 (1.2 ounce) package dry
vegetable soup mix
1 (8 ounce) can water chestnuts,
drained, chopped

1. Drain spinach thoroughly and
squeeze to remove excess water.

2. Beat cream cheese until smooth.
Fold in spinach, soup mix and
water chestnuts.

3. Cover and chill for at least 1 hour
before serving.

4. Serve with baked chips or an assortment of reduced fat whole
grain crackers.

- -

Servings: 24 servings (About 3 cups)
Serving size: 2 tablespoons

Calories: 59
Protein: 3 g
Carbohydrate: 3 g
Fat: 4 g
Cholesterol: 13 mg
Sodium: 183 mg
Calcium: 9 mg
Dietary Fiber: less than 1 g
Sugar: less than 1 g

CREAMY SPINACH DIVE

1 (10 ounce) package frozen
chopped spinach, thawed
1 (.9 ounce) package dry vegetable
soup mix
1 cup light mayonnaise
1 cup fat free or light sour cream

1. Drain spinach thoroughly and
squeeze to remove excess water.

2. Combine all ingredients and mix
well. Cover and chill 6-8 hours.

3. Serve with baked chips or an assortment of reduced fat whole
grain crackers.

*Flavor Perk: Add ½ cup finely minced onion to
the spinach mixture.*

- -

Yield: 24 servings (About 3 cups)
Serving size: 2 tablespoons

Calories: 45
Protein: less than 1 g
Carbohydrate: 4 g
Fat: 3 g
Cholesterol: 4 mg
Sodium: 150 mg
Calcium: 20 mg
Dietary Fiber: less than 1 g
Sugar: less than 1 g

SOUTHERN CUCUMBER DIPPIN'

1 cucumber, peeled, seeded, finely
  chopped or grated
2 cups nonfat plain yogurt
1 clove garlic, finely minced
1½ teaspoons chopped fresh mint
or ½ teaspoon dried mint, crushed

1. Place cucumber in a wire mesh
   strainer and press firmly with fingers to remove excess liquid. Mix
   with yogurt, garlic and mint. Place
   in serving bowl and garnish with
   2-3 springs of fresh mint.

2. Chill at least 1 hour before serving. Dip is best served the same
   day.

3. Serve with healthful grain snacks
   or raw vegetables.

- - - - - - - - - - - - - - - - - - - -

Yield: 15 servings (about 2 cups)
Serving size: 2 tablespoons

Calories: 21
Protein: 2 g
Carbohydrate: 3 g
Fat: 0 g
Cholesterol: less than 1 mg
Sodium: 26 mg
Calcium: 68 mg
Dietary Fiber: less than 1 g
Sugar: 2 g

GREEN CHILI-ARTICHOKE SCOOP

*Scoop up this smooth chile-spiced dip
with Melba toast rounds or crunchy
bread sticks.*

2 (8½ ounce) cans artichoke hearts
  in water, drained, chopped
1 (4 ounce) can diced green chiles,
  drained
6 tablespoons light mayonnaise
1½ cups finely shredded reduced
  fat cheddar cheese

1. Preheat oven to 350°. Place
   chopped artichokes in a sprayed
   11 x 7 x 2-inch square baking dish.

2. Scatter chiles on top; then carefully spread mayonnaise. Sprinkle
   with cheese; cover and bake 15
   minutes or until hot and bubbly.
   Serve immediately.

- - - - - - - - - - - - - - - - - - - -

Yield: 20 servings (About 2½ cups)
Serving size: 2 tablespoons

Calories: 70
Protein: 6 g
Carbohydrate: 4 g
Fat: 4 g
Cholesterol: 11 mg
Sodium: 173 mg
Calcium: 138 mg
Dietary Fiber: 1 g
Sugar: less than 1 g

"BASIL RHYMES WITH DAZZLE" DIP

Basil has a robust flavor and pleasing pungent aroma. The popular pesto sauce has basil leaves as the main ingredient. Tomato dishes are particularly enhanced by this herb. Fortunately, fresh basil is readily available and is also easy to grow.

2 cups light or fat free cottage cheese
¼ cup green onions and tops, sliced
2 tablespoons fresh parsley, stemmed
6-8 fresh basil leaves, coarsely chopped

1. Place all ingredients in a food processor or blender and mix until creamy. Add salt or salt substitute and freshly ground black pepper to taste. Chill before serving.

2. Serve with raw vegetables.

- -

Yield: 16 servings (About 2½ cups)
Serving Size: 2 tablespoons

Calories: 21
Protein: 4 g
Carbohydrate: less than 1 g
Fat: less than 1 g
Cholesterol: 1 mg
Sodium: 115 mg
Calcium: 19 mg
Dietary Fiber: 0 g
Sugar: less than 1 g

SPRING FRESH VEGETABLE DIP

1 cup reduced fat cottage cheese, drained
1 cup light mayonnaise
1 (1 ounce) package dry ranch-style dressing mix
¼ cup green onions and tops, finely chopped

1. Combine all ingredients in blender or food processor. Blend until smooth. Refrigerate until ready to serve.

2. Serve with fresh vegetable pieces, sticks, or slices.

- -

Yield: 16 servings (About 2 cups)
Serving size: 2 tablespoons

Calories: 68
Protein: 2 g
Carbohydrate: 4 g
Fat: 5 g
Cholesterol: 6 mg
Sodium: 272 mg
Calcium: 11 mg
Dietary Fiber: less than 1 g
Sugar: 1 g

FESTIVE CHEESE BALL

2 (8 ounce) packages reduced fat
cream cheese, softened
1 (10 ounce) package frozen
chopped spinach, thawed, well
drained
1 (1.2 ounce) packet dry vegetable
soup mix
1 (8 ounce) can water chestnuts,
drained, rinsed, chopped

1. In mixing bowl, beat cream cheese
until smooth. Fold in remaining
ingredients.

2. Shape into a ball and cover with
plastic wrap. Chill in refrigerator
before serving.

3. Serve with healthful grain snacks,
raw zucchini or yellow squash
slices.

- - - - - - - - - - - - - - - - - - - -

Yield: About 24 servings
Serving size: 2 tablespoons

Calories: 55
Protein: 2.5 g
Carbohydrate: 3 g
Fat: 4 g
Cholesterol: 13 mg
Sodium: 182 mg
Calcium: 9 mg
Dietary Fiber: less than 1 g
Sugar: less than 1 g

FRESH ROASTED GARLIC-CANELLINI SPREAD

1 whole garlic head, roasted
3 cups canned canellini or navy
beans, drained
⅓ cup nonfat plain yogurt
3 tablespoons green onions and
tops, chopped

1. To a blender or food processor, add
garlic, beans, yogurt and green
onions. Add to the blender ½ teaspoon freshly ground black pepper.
Process until blended, and serve.

2. This dish may be stored in the refrigerator about 3 days.

3. Serve with whole wheat pita crisps,
red or green bell pepper strips and
large celery sticks.

*Heads of garlic, also called bulbs, are made
up of sections known as cloves. Garlic cloves
have become as basic to cooking as salt and
pepper.*

*To roast a garlic head, preheat oven to 325°.
Slice ½ inch off the top of the garlic head
and discard the loose papery skin, while
keeping cloves intact. Spray with nonstick
cooking spray (or rub with 1 teaspoon of
olive oil) and place in a small baking pan.
Cover with foil and bake until garlic feels
soft, about 40-45 minutes. Cool. Remove
the garlic from the skins by pinching or
squeezing the pulp from the skins.*

- - - - - - - - - - - - - - - - - - - -

Yield: 8 servings (about 4 cups)
Serving size: ½ cup

Calories: 121
Protein: 8 g
Carbohydrate: 22 g
Fat: less than 1 g
Cholesterol: less than 1 mg
Sodium: 13 mg
Calcium: 94 mg
Dietary Fiber: 5 g
Sugar: less than 1 g

OLIVE-ONION SPREAD

The zesty flavors of black olives and green onions are complemented by the smooth flavor and texture of cream cheese.

1 (8 ounce) package reduced fat cream cheese, softened
½ cup light or fat free mayonnaise
1 (4 ounce) can chopped black olives, drained
3 green onions and tops, finely chopped

1. Beat cream cheese until smooth. Stir in mayonnaise, olives and green onions.

2. Cover and chill at least 1 hour.

3. Serve with healthful grain snacks or raw vegetables.

- - - - - - - - - - - - - - - - - - -

Yield: 24 servings (About 1½ cups)
Serving size: 1 tablespoon

Calories: 44
Protein: 1 g
Carbohydrate: 1 g
Fat: 4 g
Cholesterol: 8 mg
Sodium: 95 mg
Calcium: 4 mg
Dietary Fiber: less than 1 g
Sugar: less than 1 g

ZIPPY RICOTTA SPREAD

1 (5½ ounce) carton part-skim ricotta cheese
¼ cup ketchup
1 tablespoon prepared horseradish
1 tablespoon onion flakes or dried minced onion

1. Combine all ingredients and mix well. Serve immediately or cover and refrigerate.

Flavor Perk: Add 1 tablespoon fresh parsley or fresh herb of your choice.

- - - - - - - - - - - - - - - - - - -

Servings: 16 servings (About 1 cup)
Serving size: 1 tablespoon

Calories: 19
Protein: 1 g
Carbohydrate: 2 g
Fat: less than 1 g
Cholesterol: 3 mg
Sodium: 60 mg
Calcium: 29 mg
Dietary Fiber: less than 1 g
Sugar: less than 1 g

EASY CHEESE SPREAD

⅓ cup light mayonnaise
2 cups grated reduced fat Swiss cheese
2 tablespoons fresh parsley, finely chopped

1. Mix mayonnaise and Swiss cheese, using just enough mayonnaise to achieve spreading consistency. Refrigerate until serving time.

2. Before serving, mold the spread into a mound and sprinkle with parsley.

- -

Servings: 18 servings (About 2¼ cups)
Serving size: About 1 tablespoon

Calories: 95
Protein: 7 g
Carbohydrate: 2 g
Fat: 7 g
Cholesterol: 19 mg
Sodium: 58 mg
Calcium: 223 mg
Dietary Fiber: 0 g
Sugar: less than 1 g

GREEN BELL PEPPER CHOP

½ cup grated reduced fat Swiss cheese
½ cup low fat cottage cheese
¼ cup chopped green bell pepper
½ teaspoon dried dill weed

1. Combine ingredients and add salt/salt substitute and freshly ground black pepper to taste.

2. Serve immediately or refrigerate.

Variations: Substitute reduced fat Monterey jack cheese for the Swiss; substitute ½ teaspoon Dijon-style mustard and 1 tablespoon snipped chives or green onion tops for bell pepper and dill weed.

Substitute reduced fat cheddar for the Swiss cheese; substitute ½ chopped, drained, rinsed onion and 1 teaspoon chili powder for bell pepper and dill weed.

Substitute chopped roasted red pepper and ½ teaspoon dried basil leaves, crumbled, for bell pepper and dill weed.

- -

Yield: 3 servings (About ¾ cup)
Serving size: About ¼ cup

Calories: 151
Protein: 15 g
Carbohydrate: 3 g
Fat: 8 g
Cholesterol: 28 mg
Sodium: 200 mg
Calcium: 360 mg
Dietary Fiber: less than 1 g
Sugar: 1 g

RICOTTA FRUIT SPREAD

Low in fat, cholesterol and sodium, this delicious spread can be served as an appetizer or as a breakfast spread.

1 (5½ ounce) carton part-skim ricotta cheese
2 tablespoons orange juice, plus ½ teaspoon grated orange peel
1 teaspoon brown sugar substitute or sugar substitute equal to 1 teaspoon sugar
½ teaspoon ground cinnamon

1. Blend all ingredients in blender or food processor. Serve immediately or refrigerate.

2. Serve with Bagel Crisps (p. 20) or Lazy Pita Crisps (p. 21).

Flavor Perk: Stir in ⅓ cup raisins and/or 2 tablespoons finely chopped pecans or walnuts.

- - - - - - - - - - - - - - - - - -

Yield: About 12 servings (¾ cup)
Serving size: 1 tablespoon

Calories: 19
Protein: 2 g
Carbohydrate: 1 g
Fat: 1 g
Cholesterol: 4 mg
Sodium: 16 mg
Calcium: 37 mg
Dietary Fiber: 0 g
Sugar: less than 1 g

PINEAPPLE-CHEESE MARVEL

This spread is always a crowd pleaser with its combination of cream cheese, pineapple and bell pepper.

2 (8 ounce) packages reduced fat cream cheese, softened
1 (8 ounce) can crushed pineapple in juice, drained
¼ cup finely chopped sweet red or green pepper
1 teaspoon salt free seasoning blend

1. Combine all ingredients and mix well. Place in serving bowl and chill until ready to serve.

2. Serve with selected whole grain reduced fat and low sodium crackers.

- - - - - - - - - - - - - - - - - -

Yield: 30 servings (About 2½ cups)
Serving size: About 1 tablespoon

Calories: 42
Protein: 2 g
Carbohydrate: 2 g
Fat: 3 g
Cholesterol: 11 mg
Sodium: 64 mg
Calcium: 1 mg
Dietary Fiber: 0 g
Sugar: 1 g

SUMMERTIME PLEASER

1 large cucumber
⅛-¼ cup grated onion
1 (8 ounce) package reduced fat cream cheese, softened
½ cup light mayonnaise

1. Use a vegetable peeler or sharp knife to pare a thin, even peel from around cucumber to use as curl for garnish. Continue paring peel from cucumber, then cut in half lengthwise and use a small spoon to scoop out seeds.

2. Chop or grate cucumber and place in wire mesh strainer. Add onion and firmly press with fingers to remove excess liquid. In mixing bowl, beat cream cheese and mayonnaise until smooth. Stir in well-drained cucumber and onion and garnish with cucumber peel.

3. Serve immediately or cover and refrigerate. Spread is best served the same day.

Flavor Perk: Add ¼ teaspoon garlic powder and 1 teaspoon salt-free herb seasoning blend or ¼ teaspoon lite or salt free Creole seasoning.

- -

Yield: About 12 servings
Serving size: 2 tablespoons

Calories: 83
Protein: 2 g
Carbohydrate: 2 g
Fat: 7 g
Cholesterol: 17 mg
Sodium: 141 mg
Calcium: 4 mg
Dietary Fiber: less than 1 g
Sugar: less than 1 g

EGGPLANT APPETIZER

1 eggplant (about 1½ pounds), unpeeled
4 green onions and tops, finely chopped
3 tablespoons fresh parsley, chopped
4 tablespoons fat free Italian salad dressing or vinaigrette dressing

1. Preheat oven to 350°. Bake eggplant for 1 hour in a shallow baking pan. When the eggplant is cool enough to handle, peel eggplant and chop coarsely.

2. Mix green onion, parsley and salad dressing in a large mixing bowl. Add the eggplant and stir to blend. Season to taste with salt/salt substitute and freshly ground black pepper.

3. Serve chilled or at room temperature.

Flavor Perk: Add 2 cloves garlic, finely minced or pressed.

Variation: Place green onion, parsley and salad dressing in a blender or food processor. Pulse 2-3 times or until well-blended, then mix with eggplant.

- -

Yield: 12 servings
Serving size: About 2 tablespoons

Calories: 19
Protein: less than 1 g
Carbohydrate: 4 g
Fat: 0 g
Cholesterol: 0 mg
Sodium: 63 mg
Calcium: 8 mg
Dietary Fiber: 1 g
Sugar: 2 g

STUFFED GRAPE TOMATOES

This is an attractive and fun appetizer for entertaining or anytime.

12 grape or cherry tomatoes
1 (8 ounce) package reduced fat cream cheese, softened
½ onion, finely chopped
1½ teaspoons chopped fresh parsley, plus parsley for garnish

1. Beat cream cheese until fluffy. In a small bowl, combine cream cheese, onion and 1½ teaspoons parsley.

2. Cut tomatoes in half, stem end to stem end, and drain on paper towels. Scoop out tomato pulp with a small spoon and stir pulp into cream cheese mixture. Mound cream cheese mixture onto tomato halves. Garnish with tiny sprigs of parsley.

3. Cover and refrigerate at least 1 hour.

- - - - - - - - - - - - - - - - - - -

Yield: 24 servings
Serving size: 1 cherry tomato half

Calories: 26
Protein: 1 g
Carbohydrate: less than 1 g
Fat: 2 g
Cholesterol: 7 mg
Sodium: 41 mg
Calcium: 1 mg
Dietary Fiber: less than 1 g
Sugar: less than 1 g

GRANDMOTHER'S CUCUMBERS

4 cucumbers, peeled, thinly sliced
6 green onions and tops, thinly sliced
½ teaspoon dill seed or a few sprigs of fresh dill
White wine vinegar to cover

1. Place cucumbers, onions and dill in a bowl and cover with white wine vinegar. Cover and refrigerate for at least 2-3 hours.

Flavor Perk: Add sugar substitute equal to ¼ teaspoon sugar.

- - - - - - - - - - - - - - - - - - -

Yield: 4 servings
Serving size: About ½ cup

Calories: 63
Protein: 2 g
Carbohydrate: 9 g
Fat: less than 1 g
Cholesterol: 0 mg
Sodium: 13 mg
Calcium: 64 mg
Dietary Fiber: 3 g
Sugar: 1 g

SUGAR SNAP PICK-UPS

Ever tried sugar snap peas? If not available fresh, look for them in the freezer section of the supermarket. They are a tasty discovery!

1 pound fresh sugar snap peas
¼ cup light sour cream
¼ cup light mayonnaise
2 tablespoons fresh mint leaves, chopped

1. Prepare a large bowl with ice water to cool the peas after cooking. Snap off top and bottom ends of peas and pull strings away from both sides.

2. Place 1-2 inches of water in a large skillet and bring to boiling over high heat. Add peas and cook, uncovered, about 30 seconds or until peas are bright green. Drain and immediately place in bowl of ice water to stop cooking; stir gently until cool. Drain ice water and use peas immediately or cover and refrigerate.

3. Combine sour cream, mayonnaise and mint and pour into a small bowl for serving. Arrange peas on a bed of ice in a rimmed serving platter to serve.

- - - - - - - - - - - - - - - - - -
Yield: 5-6 servings
Serving size: 4-6 peas with sauce

Calories: 106
Protein: 4 g
Carbohydrate: 12 g
Fat: 5 g
Cholesterol: 8 mg
Sodium: 175 mg
Calcium: 86 mg
Dietary Fiber: 3 g
Sugar: 6 g

ZUCCHINI CANAPÉS

2 zucchini squash, cut into ¼-inch slices
2 tablespoons reduced fat grated Parmesan topping
2 tablespoons finely chopped green onions and tops
1 tablespoon Italian-seasoned dry bread crumbs

1. Using a microwave-safe platter, place zucchini slices on the platter in a single layer. Cover and cook on high in microwave oven until tender-crisp, about 1 minute.

2. In a small bowl, combine cheese and green onion and sprinkle on the zucchini slices. Top with bread crumbs. Place in microwave oven on high power for 30 seconds or until hot. Serve immediately.

Flavor Perk: Add ¼ teaspoon dried oregano and dash of garlic powder to cheese mixture; sprinkle tops with paprika.

Variation: Substitute 2 tablespoons chopped mushrooms or 2 tablespoons chopped and drained fresh tomato for the green onions. Substitute herb-seasoned or plain dry bread crumbs for the Italian-seasoned bread crumbs.

- - - - - - - - - - - - - - - - - -
Yield: 10 servings (About 20 canapes)
Serving size: 2 canapes

Calories: 15
Protein: less than 1 g
Carbohydrate: 2 g
Fat: less than 1 g
Cholesterol: 0 mg
Sodium: 44 mg
Calcium: 8 mg
Dietary Fiber: less than 1 g
Sugar: less than 1 g

WILD STUFFED MUSHROOMS

The combined flavors and textures of mushrooms, wild rice and Parmesan cheese result in a savory, rich-tasting appetizer.

18 large mushrooms
1 (6.2 ounce) package long grain and wild rice mix, divided
2 teaspoons light mayonnaise
2 tablespoons reduced fat grated Parmesan topping, divided

1. Preheat oven to 375°. Prepare the long grain and wild rice according to package instructions. Measure 1½ cups cooked rice. Reserve remaining rice for later use.

2. Remove the stems from the mushrooms and finely chop the stems. In a sprayed nonstick skillet, sauté mushroom caps about 30 seconds. Remove and place stem-side up on a baking sheet. Add 2 tablespoons water to skillet, then bring quickly to a boil and add mushroom stems.

3. Over medium-high heat, cook and stir mushroom stems until most of liquid evaporates, about 2 minutes. In a mixing bowl, combine mushroom stems, 1-1½ cups rice, mayonnaise and 1 tablespoon Parmesan topping.

4. Spoon about 2 teaspoons rice mixture into each mushroom cap. Sprinkle with remaining cheese and bake about 10 minutes or until cheese is lightly brown. Serve immediately.

Flavor Perk: For color, sprinkle paprika on top of mushrooms before serving.

Variation: Substitute 1-1½ cups cooked brown rice for the wild rice mixture.

- -

Yield: 18 servings
Serving size: 1 mushroom

Calories: 43
Protein: 2 g
Carbohydrate: 8 g
Fat: less than 1 g
Cholesterol: less than 1 mg
Sodium: 181 mg
Calcium: 6 mg
Dietary Fiber: less than 1 g
Sugar: less than 1 g

FRESH FRUIT SING-ALONG

This easy-to-assemble and refreshing appetizer makes a stylish presentation served in a crystal or trifle bowl, with small crystal bowls for guests to help themselves. Substitute other fresh fruits in season as desired.

½-1 cup fresh blueberries
2 cups fresh sliced, peeled peaches
1 cup fresh diced, pared pears
¼ cup fresh-squeezed orange juice

1. Place fruits in a bowl and sprinkle the juice on top; toss gently. Refrigerate until ready to serve. Fruit is best served the same day.

Flavor Perk: Add sugar substitute equal to about ⅓ cup of sugar, or to taste.

Variation: Replace orange juice with ¼ cup lemon juice, sugar substitute to taste and dash salt or salt substitute. Mix lemon juice, sugar substitute and salt before adding to fruit.

- - - - - - - - - - - - - - - - - - - -

Yield: 5 servings
Serving Size: About ¼ cup

Calories: 62
Protein: less than 1 g
Carbohydrate: 16 g
Fat: less than 1 g
Cholesterol: 0 mg
Sodium: less than 1 mg
Calcium: 6 mg
Dietary Fiber: 3 g
Sugar: 11 g

TROPICAL FRUIT PLATE MYSTERY

Everyone loves fresh, prepared fruit. This appetizer will disappear quickly.

6 fresh pineapple spears or 1 (8 ounce) can pineapple chunks in juice
6 watermelon wedges
6 papaya wedges
3 bananas, peeled, quartered, brushed with pineapple or citrus juice

1. Arrange fruits attractively on platter. Serve with the fruit dressing or dip of your choice.

Flavor Perk: Garnish with wedges of 2 limes and 1 cup fresh strawberries.

Variation: If watermelon and papaya are not available, substitute other fruits such as mango, kiwi, kumquat and star fruit.

- - - - - - - - - - - - - - - - - - - -

Yield: 6 servings
Serving size: 1-1½ cup

Calories: 104
Protein: 1 g
Carbohydrate: 26 g
Fat: less than 1 g
Cholesterol: 0 mg
Sodium: 2 mg
Calcium: 118 mg
Dietary Fiber: 2 g
Sugar: 18 g

HONEY BLUE NANA MEDLEY

2 bananas
1 honeydew melon, halved, seeded
1 cup fresh blueberries
Fruit dressing of your choice

1. Slice bananas and sprinkle with lemon juice or fruit preservative to prevent darkening.

2. Slice honeydew melon into 2-inch wide wedges. Spoon blueberries and bananas on top of each wedge and drizzle with fruit dressing.

- -

Yield: 10-12 servings depending on size of honeydew melon
Serving size: 1 (2-inch wide) wedge of honeydew melon

Calories: 65*
Protein: less than 1 g
Carbohydrate: 17 g
Fat: less than 1 g
Cholesterol: 0 mg
Sodium: 11 mg
Calcium: 8 mg
Dietary Fiber: 1.5 g
Sugar: 13 g

*Nutritional information is for fruit only.

DYNAMIC DUO FRUIT DIP

Bananas and strawberries are a delightful flavor combination.

1 (8 ounce) package reduced fat cream cheese, softened
1 (8 ounce) carton light strawberry-banana yogurt
¼ cup light sugar free strawberry preserves
¼ cup mashed banana (⅓ whole banana)

1. In mixing bowl, beat cream cheese until smooth. Fold in yogurt, strawberry preserves and banana. Cover and chill at least 30 minutes before serving.

2. Serve with selected fresh fruit.

Flavor Perk: Garnish top with a dollop of strawberry preserves.

- -

Servings: 18 servings (About 2½ cups)
Serving size: About 2 tablespoons

Calories: 41
Protein: 2 g
Carbohydrate: 3 g
Fat: 3 g
Cholesterol: 9 mg
Sodium: 59 mg
Calcium: 15 mg
Dietary Fiber: 0 g
Sugar: 1 g

NUTTY BING CHERRY DUNK

When buying Bing cherries, look for deep red, large and plump fruit. Cherries at their best are available in June, July and August. Canned and frozen black cherries are good substitutes when fresh cherries are not available.

1 (8 ounce) package reduced fat cream cheese, softened
1 (8 ounce) carton light fat free no sugar added vanilla yogurt
⅓ cup pitted fresh Bing cherries, coarsely chopped, plus 1 whole cherry with stem
4 tablespoons finely chopped pecans

1. In mixing bowl, beat cream cheese until smooth. Fold in yogurt, chopped cherries and pecans. Place in serving bowl and garnish with a whole cherry on top.

2. Cover and chill at least 30 minutes before serving.

3. Serve with selected fresh fruits.

Flavor Perk: Add sugar substitute to taste.

- - - - - - - - - - - - - - - - - - - -

Yield: 16 servings (About 2 cups)
Serving size: 2 tablespoons

Calories: 55
Protein: 2 g
Carbohydrate: 2 g
Fat: 4 g
Cholesterol: 10 mg
Sodium: 68 mg
Calcium: 2 mg
Dietary Fiber: less than 1 g
Sugar: 1 g

ORANGE MARMALADE DELIGHT

1 (8 ounce) package reduced fat cream cheese, softened
1 (8 ounce) carton light fat free no sugar added orange yogurt
½ cup reduced sugar orange marmalade
4 tablespoons finely chopped pecans or walnuts, divided

1. In mixing bowl, beat cream cheese until smooth. Fold in yogurt, marmalade spread, and 3½ tablespoons nuts.

2. Place in serving bowl, and sprinkle remaining ½ tablespoon nuts on top. Cover and chill at least 30 minutes before serving.

3. Serve with selected fresh fruits.

Flavor Perk: Add 2 teaspoons finely grated orange peel to the nut garnish.

Variation: Substitute ⅛ teaspoon ground nutmeg for nuts.

- - - - - - - - - - - - - - - - - - - -

Yield: About 16 servings
Serving size: 2 tablespoons

Calories: 65
Protein: 2 g
Carbohydrate: 5 g
Cholesterol: 10 mg
Sodium: 55 mg
Calcium: 1 mg
Dietary Fiber: less than 1 g
Sugar: 3 g

Kitchen Helper

PINEAPPLE FRUIT BOAT

This fruit boat is attractive and festive for entertaining.

1 large or 2 small pineapples
1 large navel orange, sectioned, diced, juice reserved
1 cup seedless green grapes, whole or halved
Sugar substitute to taste

1. Using a large sharp knife and large cutting board, carefully cut pineapple (including top) in half lengthwise. Hollow out halves and remove core; dice pineapple and sprinkle with orange juice to prevent browning.

2. Gently mix together pineapple chunks, orange sections and grapes. Add sugar substitute to taste. Spoon fruit mixture into pineapple halves and serve immediately.

Flavor Perk: Garnish with fresh mint leaves.

Yield: 4-6 servings
Serving size: $\frac{1}{2}$-1 cup fruit

Calories: 103
Protein: 1 g
Carbohydrate: 28 g
Fat: less than 1 g
Cholesterol: 0 mg
Sodium: 2 mg
Calcium: 31 mg
Dietary Fiber: 3 g
Sugar: 24 g

Kitchen Helper

WATERMELON FRUIT BASKET

This watermelon boat serves a crowd and is ideal for parties or brunches.

1 large oblong watermelon, well chilled
Selected fresh fruits, chilled

1. Using a sharp knife, remove top third of watermelon, cutting in a sawtooth pattern. Use a paper pattern to make even cuts. Remove top of the watermelon; then scoop out fruit and cut into chunks.

2. Place chunks back in the watermelon bottom and add selected fruits such as whole strawberries, kiwi fruit slices and diced cantaloupe. Serve immediately.

Flavor Perk: Garnish with fresh mint.

Variation: Cut watermelon into a basket shape.

Serving size: 1 cup fruit*
*(Nutritional information will vary depending on choice of fruit.)

BEVERAGES

How much plain water do you consume daily? Since water makes up 55-60% of an adult's body weight—about 90 pounds in a 150-pound person—it goes without saying that a healthy body is maintained with a generous daily intake of water and beverages made with water.

Water is certainly the healthiest beverage of choice and, of course, regular tap water is readily available and inexpensive. If you choose to purchase bottled water, read labels to be aware of water sources and compare costs to find the best buy for your personal preference.

With healthy choices in mind, beverage recipes included in this section take advantage of a variety of fresh fruits, low fat dairy products, sugar free products and decaffeinated teas and coffees.

BANANA SMOOTHIE

1 ripe banana, peeled
1 cup skim milk
½ teaspoon vanilla extract

1. Cut banana into 1-inch pieces. Wrap in foil and freeze.

2. Place frozen banana, milk and vanilla in food processor and blend until smooth.

Flavor Perk: Add ½ cup fresh berries.

- - - - - - - - - - - - - - - - - - - -

Yield: 2 servings

Calories: 100
Protein: 5 g
Carbohydrate: 20 g
Fat: less than 1 g
Cholesterol: 2 mg
Sodium: 64 mg
Calcium: 154 mg
Dietary Fiber: 1 g
Sugar: 15 g

MERRY BERRY-BANANA SMOOTHIE

2 cups plain fat free yogurt
2 ripe bananas
1 cup sliced fresh or unsweetened frozen strawberries
1 cup fresh or frozen unsweetened berries (mixed berries, blueberries, or blackberries)

1. Combine all ingredients in blender and blend until pureed.

Flavor Perk: Garnish with fresh berries.

- - - - - - - - - - - - - - - - - - - -

Yield: 3-4 servings
Serving size: About 1½ cups

Calories: 153
Protein: 8 g
Carbohydrate: 30 g
Fat: less than 1 g
Cholesterol: 2 mg
Sodium: 96 mg
Calcium: 255 mg
Dietary Fiber: 3 g
Sugar: 20 g

BANANA SLOSH

1 cup buttermilk or soy milk
1 banana, peeled
½ teaspoon vanilla or almond
extract

1. Blend all ingredients in blender or food processor until smooth.

Variations: Substitute any of the following for the banana: 1 fresh peach, ½ cup berries or seasonal fruit, fruit combination (i.e. orange and banana).

- - - - - - - - - - - - - - - - - -

Yield: 1 serving (1½ cups)

Calories: 213
Protein: 9 g
Carbohydrate: 40 g
Fat: 3 g
Cholesterol: 9 mg
Sodium: 259 mg
Calcium: 294 mg
Dietary Fiber: 3 g
Sugar: 30 g

ISLAND SMOOTHIE

1 cup crushed pineapple in juice,
plus 1 cup pineapple juice
2 tablespoons low-sugar apricot
preserves
1 (12 ounce) package light firm
tofu, cubed
1 ripe banana, peeled, sliced

1. Combine all ingredients in blender and process until smooth. Chill until ready to serve or blend in 4-5 ice cubes and serve immediately.

- - - - - - - - - - - - - - - - - -

Yield: 2 servings

Calories: 216
Protein: 12 g
Carbohydrate: 41 g
Fat: 2 g
Cholesterol: 0 mg
Sodium: 144 mg
Calcium: 81 mg
Dietary Fiber: 2 g
Sugar: 33 g

MANGO-BANANA SMOOTHIE

1 cup peeled, cubed ripe mango
1 ripe banana, peeled, sliced
⅔ cup skim milk
1 teaspoon honey

1. Arrange mango cubes in a single layer on a baking sheet; freeze until firm.

2. Combine frozen mango, banana, milk and honey. Pour into blender or food processor and process until smooth.

Flavor Perk: Add ¼ teaspoon vanilla extract.

- -

Yield: 2 servings

Calories: 168
Protein: 4 g
Carbohydrate: 40 g
Fat: less than 1 g
Cholesterol: 2 mg
Sodium: 45 mg
Calcium: 112 mg
Dietary Fiber: 3 g
Sugar: 34 g

STRAWBERRY-BANANA SMOOTHIE

2 bananas, peeled, sliced
1 pint (2 cups) fresh strawberries, washed, stemmed, quartered
1 (8 ounce) carton fat free no sugar added vanilla yogurt
¼ cup fresh-squeezed orange juice

1. Place ingredients in blender or food processor and process until smooth.

2. Serve as is or over crushed ice.

Flavor Perk: Add sugar substitute to taste.

Variation: Substitute 8 ounces light strawberry yogurt.

- -

Yield: 4 servings
Serving size: About 1½ cups

Calories: 110
Protein: 3 g
Carbohydrate: 25 g
Fat: less than 1 g
Cholesterol: 1 mg
Sodium: 31 mg
Calcium: 15 mg
Dietary Fiber: 3 g
Sugar: 18 g

THREE-FRUIT SMOOTHIE

2 (8 ounce) cartons light vanilla
yogurt
1 cup fresh frozen blueberries
1 cup fresh peach slices
1 (8 ounce) can pineapple chunks
in juice, drained

1. Process all ingredients in a blender until smooth, stopping often to scrape down sides.

2. Serve immediately.

- - - - - - - - - - - - - - - - - -

Yield: 3 servings
Serving size: About 1½ cups

Calories: 244
Protein: 9 g
Carbohydrate: 50 g
Fat: 2 g
Cholesterol: 8 mg
Sodium: 109 mg
Calcium: 264 mg
Dietary Fiber: 4 g
Sugar: 24 g

FRUIT MEDLEY SMOOTHIE

2 cups fresh or frozen
unsweetened berries
½ banana, sliced
1¼ cups crushed pineapple (or
pineapple tidbits) in juice, drained
½ cup light firm tofu, cubed

1. In a blender or food processor, combine berries, banana and pineapple. Blend until smooth, and add tofu and 2 cups ice cubes. Process until blended and liquefied.

- - - - - - - - - - - - - - - - - -

Yield: 3 servings
Serving size: About 1½ cups

Calories: 147
Protein: 3 g
Carbohydrate: 34 g
Fat: 1 g
Cholesterol: 0 mg
Sodium: 34 mg
Calcium: 37 mg
Dietary Fiber: 4 g
Sugar: 25 g

TROPICAL HEATWAVE

1½ cups peeled, seeded, cubed
ripe papaya
1 banana, peeled, sliced
1½ cups peeled, cubed cantaloupe
1 (6 ounce) carton fat free no
sugar added coconut cream pie
yogurt

1. Place all ingredients in blender or
food processor and process until
smooth. (If mixture is too thick,
add water or skim milk to thin.)

2. Pour into glasses and serve immediately.

- - - - - - - - - - - - - - - - - - - -

Yield: 3 servings
Serving size: 1½ cups

Calories: 128
Protein: 3 g
Carbohydrate: 29 g
Fat: less than 1 g
Cholesterol: 1 mg
Sodium: 42 mg
Calcium: 29 mg
Dietary Fiber: 3 g
Sugar: 20 g

ORANGE SLUSH

2 cups orange juice
½ cup instant nonfat dry milk
½ teaspoon almond extract
8 ice cubes

1. Combine all ingredients in blender
and process on high until mixture
is smooth and thickened.

2. Serve immediately.

- - - - - - - - - - - - - - - - - - - -

Yield: 2 servings

Calories: 177
Protein: 8 g
Carbohydrate: 35 g
Fat: less than 1 g
Cholesterol: 3 mg
Sodium: 98 mg
Calcium: 242 mg
Dietary Fiber: less than 1 g
Sugar: 34 g

RASPBERRY LEMONADE

1 (.125 ounce) tub sugar free raspberry-flavored soft drink powder
1 (6 ounce) can frozen lemonade concentrate
1 (10 ounce) package frozen raspberries, partially thawed
1 (28 ounce) bottle diet lemon-lime carbonated beverage

1. Place 2 cups water, drink powder and lemonade concentrate in a 2-quart pitcher. Stir until well-blended. Add an additional 2 cups water and raspberries. Stir and chill until ready to serve.

2. Just before serving, slowly stir in carbonated beverage. Serve over ice.

- - - - - - - - - - - - - - - - - - -

Yield: 8 servings (2 quarts)
Serving size: 1 cup

Calories: 59
Protein: less than 1 g
Carbohydrate: 13 g
Fat: 0 g
Cholesterol: 0 mg
Sodium: 11 mg
Calcium: 1 mg
Dietary Fiber: less than 1 g
Sugar: 11 g

CRANBERRY-TEA REFRESHER

4 decaffeinated green tea bags
1 mint tea bag
2 cups reduced calorie cranberry juice cocktail, chilled

1. In a medium saucepan, bring 3 cups water to boiling. Remove from heat and add tea bags. Cover and let steep for 10 minutes. Remove and discard tea bags, and chill tea.

2. When well-chilled, add cranberry juice. Serve over ice.

Flavor Perk: Garnish with mint leaves or float cranberries on top.

- - - - - - - - - - - - - - - - - - -

Yield: 5 servings
Serving size: 1 cup

Calories: 19
Protein: 0 g
Carbohydrate: 5 g
Fat: 0 g
Cholesterol: 0 mg
Sodium: 13 mg
Calcium: 0 mg
Dietary Fiber: 0 g
Sugar: 5 g

LEMON-LIME TEA

3 tablespoons instant unsweetened
  decaffeinated iced tea mix
Sugar substitute equal to ½ cup
  sugar
⅓ cup fresh lime juice
3 tablespoons fresh lemon juice

1. Combine ingredients in a pitcher
   with 2 cups water. Stir until ingredients are well blended. Add an
   additional 2 cups water.

2. Serve over ice in tall glasses.

*Flavor Perk: Garnish with maraschino cherries
  and lime slices.*

- - - - - - - - - - - - - - - - - - - -

Yield: 6 servings (1½ quarts/6 cups)
Serving size: 1 cup

Calories: 16
Protein: less than 1 g
Carbohydrate: 4 g
Fat: 0 g
Cholesterol: 0 mg
Sodium: 3 mg
Calcium: 42 mg
Dietary Fiber: less than 1 g
Sugar: less than 1 g

LEMON-ORANGE TEA

4-6 tablespoons decaffeinated
lemon-flavored instant tea mix,
prepared with sugar substitute
⅓ cup unsweetened orange juice
Sugar substitute to taste
8-10 sprigs mint

1. Mix instant tea, orange juice and
   sugar substitute with 7 cups water. Garnish with mint. Serve over
   ice.

- - - - - - - - - - - - - - - - - - - -

Yield: About 7 servings
Serving size: 1 cup

Calories: 11
Protein: less than 1 g
Carbohydrate: 3 g
Fat: 0 g
Cholesterol: 0 mg
Sodium: 18 mg
Calcium: 4 mg
Dietary Fiber: 0 g
Sugar: 1 g

RASPBERRY TEA

2 cups fresh or frozen raspberries
4-5 decaffeinated tea bags

1. Place raspberries and tea bags in a heat-resistant container. Add 5 cups boiling water and cover. Let steep for 5 minutes; then remove tea bags.

2. Place a wire mesh strainer over a large bowl and strain raspberries from tea; discard berries. Cool tea and chill. Serve over ice.

Flavor Perk: Garnish with fresh raspberries.

- - - - - - - - - - - - - - - - - -

Yield: 5 servings
Serving size: 1 cup

Calories: 11
Protein: less than 1 g
Carbohydrate: 2 g
Fat: 0 g
Cholesterol: 0 mg
Sodium: 5 mg
Calcium: 7 mg
Dietary Fiber: 2 g
Sugar: 2 g

LEMON-PINEAPPLE PUNCH

1 (2 liter) diet lemon-lime soda
1 (12 ounce) can frozen lemonade concentrate
1 (46 ounce) can unsweetened pineapple juice, chilled

1. Combine all ingredients in punch bowl and mix well.

- -

Yield: 15 servings
Serving size: 1 cup

Calories: 96
Protein: less than 1 g
Carbohydrate: 24 g
Fat: less than 1 g
Cholesterol: 0 mg
Sodium: 15 mg
Calcium: 18 mg
Dietary Fiber: less than 1 g
Sugar: 21 g

CRANBERRY-PINEAPPLE PUNCH

1 (48 ounce) bottle reduced
calorie cranberry juice cocktail
1 (48 ounce) can unsweetened
pineapple juice
Sugar substitute to equal ½ cup
sugar
1 (2 liter) bottle ginger ale, chilled

1. Combine cranberry drink and
   pineapple juice; sweeten to taste
   with sugar substitute.

2. Cover and chill 8 hours.

3. When ready to serve, stir in ginger
   ale.

Flavor Perk: Add 2 teaspoons almond extract.

- - - - - - - - - - - - - - - - - - - -

Yield: 20 servings
Serving size: About 1 cup

Calories: 94
Protein: less than 1 g
Carbohydrate: 24 g
Fat: 0 g
Cholesterol: 0 mg
Sodium: 19 mg
Calcium: 28 mg
Dietary Fiber: less than 1 g
Sugar: 22 g

MOCHA YUMMY

1 cup skim milk
1 banana, frozen
1 teaspoon instant decaffeinated
coffee granules
¼ cup fat free frozen vanilla
yogurt

1. Place milk, peeled frozen banana,
   coffee granules and frozen yogurt
   in a blender or food processor.
   Blend until mixture is smooth.
   Serve immediately.

Flavor Perk: Season to taste with
sugar substitute, and garnish
with sliced banana.

- - - - - - - - - - - - - - - - - - - -

Yield: 2 servings

Calories: 119
Protein: 6 g
Carbohydrate: 24 g
Fat: less than 1 g
Cholesterol: 3 mg
Sodium: 78 mg
Calcium: 190 mg
Dietary Fiber: 1 g
Sugar: 18 g

CAFÉ AU LAIT

2 cups skim milk, heated
2 cups prepared strong
decaffeinated coffee, hot
Sugar substitute to taste

1. Combine skim milk and coffee.
Sweeten to taste. Serve hot.

- - - - - - - - - - - - - - - - - - - -

Yield: 4 servings
Serving size: 1 cup

Calories: 51
Protein: 4 g
Carbohydrate: 8 g
Fat: less than 1 g
Cholesterol: 2 mg
Sodium: 66 mg
Calcium: 153 mg
Dietary Fiber: 0 g
Sugar: 5 g

ICED COFFEE

1½ cups skim milk
Sugar substitute equal to 2
tablespoons sugar
2 tablespoons decaffeinated
instant coffee powder
1 (16 ounce) bottle diet cola,
chilled

1. Blend together milk, sugar substitute and coffee powder. Just before serving, gently stir in diet cola.

2. Serve over ice.

Flavor Perk: Add ¼ teaspoon ground cinnamon to milk mixture.

- - - - - - - - - - - - - - - - - - - -

Yield: 6 servings
Serving size: About ½ cup

Calories: 28
Protein: 2 g
Carbohydrate: 4 g
Fat: less than 1 g
Cholesterol: 1 mg
Sodium: 42 mg
Calcium: 88 mg
Dietary Fiber: 0 g
Sugar: 3 g

Kitchen Helper

SPICED COFFEE MIX

1 cup instant decaffeinated
coffee granules
4 teaspoons dried grated
lemon peel
4 teaspoons ground cinnamon
1 teaspoon ground cloves

1. In a small jar, combine all ingredients and mix well. Store
tightly covered.

2. For each serving, spoon 2 teaspoons mix into coffee cup
and stir in ¾ cup boiling water.

3. Sweeten to taste.

Yield: 5 servings
Serving size: 2 teaspoons mix

Calories: 46
Protein: 2 g
Carbohydrate: 9 g
Fat: less than 1 g
Cholesterol: 0 mg
Sodium: 6 mg
Calcium: 52 mg
Dietary Fiber: 1 g
Sugar: less than 1 g

FAVORITE HOT CHOCOLATE MIX

3½ cups nonfat dry milk
powder
Sugar substitute equal to 2
cups sugar
1 cup fat free powdered non-
dairy creamer
½ cup unsweetened cocoa
powder

1. Before mixing ingredients, sift
each ingredient to remove
lumps. Combine all sifted ingredients in a large bowl. Place
in an airtight container to
store.

2. To make one serving, place ⅓
cup mix in a mug, and add ¾
cup boiling water.

Yield: About 20 servings (16 cups
mix)
Serving size: ⅓ cup mix

Calories: 81
Protein: 5 g
Carbohydrate: 15 g
Fat: less than 1 g
Cholesterol: 2 mg
Sodium: 69 mg
Calcium: 201 mg
Dietary Fiber: less than 1 g
Sugar: 6 g

BREADS

The bread recipes found in this section make use of convenient products such as self-rising flour and bread mixes and simple, straightforward methods for making yeast and quick breads. Remember to choose whole wheat and whole grain products and avoid refined products when selecting breads and bread ingredients.

VEGGIE PIZZA

½ recipe Food Processor Pizza Crust (p. 71) or prebaked thin pizza crust
1 cup shredded reduced fat mozzarella cheese
1 (10 ounce) carton frozen chopped broccoli or spinach, thawed, squeezed dry
1 (8 ounce) package fresh sliced mushrooms

1. Preheat oven to 500° or the temperature on package directions for prebaked crust.

2. Sprinkle cheese evenly over crust. Top with broccoli or spinach and sliced mushrooms. Season to taste with salt/salt substitute and freshly ground black pepper.

3. Bake 10-15 minutes or until mushrooms are cooked through, cheese bubbles and crust is golden brown.

4. Serve immediately.

- - - - - - - - - - - - - - - - - - -

Yield: 4 servings
Serving size: ¼ pizza

Calories: 199
Protein: 20 g
Carbohydrate: 12 g
Fat: 8 g
Cholesterol: 20 mg
Sodium: 497 mg
Calcium: 562 mg
Dietary Fiber: 3 g
Sugar: 1 g

FANCY PARMESAN BREAD

1 loaf unsliced Italian or French bread
½ cup refrigerated light or fat free creamy Caesar salad dressing
⅓ cup reduced fat grated Parmesan-style topping
3 tablespoons finely chopped green onions with tops

1. Cut 24 (½-inch thick) slices from bread.

2. In small bowl, combine dressing, cheese and onion. Spread 1 tablespoon mixture onto each bread slice.

3. Place bread on baking sheet and broil 4 inches from broiler element until golden brown.

4. Serve warm.

- - - - - - - - - - - - - - - - - - -

Yield: 12 servings (24 slices)
Serving size: 2 slices

Calories: 151
Protein: 5 g
Carbohydrate: 27 g
Fat: 2 g
Cholesterol: 0 mg
Sodium: 474 mg
Calcium: 39 mg
Dietary Fiber: 2 g
Sugar: 2 g

QUICK PUMPKIN BREAD

Enjoy this recipe as a fragrant breakfast or snack bread for crisp, fall days.

1 (16 ounce) package pound cake mix
1 cup canned pumpkin
½ cup egg substitute
1 teaspoon ground allspice

1. Preheat oven to 350°. Combine all ingredients in mixing bowl. Add ⅓ cup water and blend well.

2. Bake about 1 hour or until a toothpick inserted in the center comes out clean.

3. Cool 10 minutes and turn out onto cooling rack.

- - - - - - - - - - - - - - - - - - -

Yield: 12 servings
Serving size: 1 slice

Calories: 175
Protein: 3 g
Carbohydrate: 31 g
Fat: 4 g
Cholesterol: less than 1 g
Sodium: 266 mg
Calcium: 60 mg
Dietary Fiber: 1 g
Sugar: less than 1 g

EASY LIGHT POPOVERS

This recipe yields a popover that is crisp and golden brown outside, and soft inside. It is so named because the batter expands and "pops over" the sides of the baking cup.

1 cup flour
1 cup skim milk
½ cup egg substitute

1. Heat oven to 450°. Coat 6 glass custard cups with nonstick cooking spray and place on baking sheet. Using a 2-cup lidded jar, shake flour and skim milk together just long enough to remove lumps.

2. Add egg substitute and fill custard cups about half full. Bake 20 minutes; then reduce oven temperature to 350° and bake an additional 20 minutes or until golden brown.

3. Serve immediately.

- - - - - - - - - - - - - - - - - - -

Yield: 6 servings
Serving size: 1 popover

Calories: 98
Protein: 5 g
Carbohydrate: 18 g
Fat: less than 1 g
Cholesterol: less than 1 mg
Sodium: 319 mg
Calcium: 127 mg
Dietary Fiber: less than 1 g
Sugar: 2 g

FRENCH TOAST MADEMOISELLE

This is a quickly-made breakfast treat.

¾ cup egg substitute
¾ cup skim milk
¼ teaspoon vanilla extract
8 slices whole grain bread

1. Beat egg substitute, skim milk and vanilla with wire whisk or hand beater until smooth. Add dash salt or salt substitute, if desired.

2. Preheat griddle or skillet coated with nonstick cooking spray over medium heat. To check temperature, sprinkle with a few drops of water. Temperature is hot enough if water bubbles and jumps.

3. Dip both sides bread into egg mixture and place on griddle. Cook 3-4 minutes on each side or until golden brown.

4. Serve immediately.

5. Serve with reduced calorie sugar free fat free maple syrup.

Flavor Perk: Add sugar substitute to taste to the egg mixture.

- - - - - - - - - - - - - - - - - - - -

Yield: 8 servings
Serving size: 1 slice bread

Calories: 80
Protein: 5 g
Carbohydrate: 16 g
Fat: 0 g
Cholesterol: less than 1 g
Sodium: 129 mg
Calcium: 136 g
Dietary Fiber: 5 g
Sugar: 2 g

GINGER CRAN-RAISIN MUFFINS

This recipe uses a new prepackaged mix of golden raisins and dried cranberries, now available in supermarkets.

1 (14½ ounce) box gingerbread mix
1¼ cups reduced calorie cranberry juice cocktail
¼ cup egg substitute
½ cup golden raisin-dried cranberry mix

1. Preheat oven to 350°. Place gingerbread mix in mixing bowl and break up lumps with fingers or fork. Add the cranberry juice and egg substitute; stir to blend. Stir vigorously 2 minutes, scraping sides and bottom of bowl as necessary.

2. Stir in dried fruit, and spoon mixture into a sprayed muffin pan (or paper muffin cups in pan), filling cups half full.

3. Bake 20 minutes or until a toothpick inserted in center of muffin comes out clean.

- - - - - - - - - - - - - - - - - - - -

Yield: 12 servings
Serving size: 1 muffin

Calories: 174
Protein: 3 g
Carbohydrate: 33 g
Fat: 3 g
Cholesterol: 0 mg
Sodium: 241 mg
Calcium: 30 mg
Dietary Fiber: less than 1 g
Sugar: 19 g

ORANGE-PINEAPPLE GINGERBREAD

1 (14½ ounce) box gingerbread mix
1 cup orange juice and 1 tablespoon finely grated orange peel
¼ cup crushed pineapple, drained
¼ cup egg substitute

1. Preheat oven to 350°. Add gingerbread mix to a mixing bowl and break up lumps with fingers or a fork. Add orange juice, crushed pineapple and egg substitute. Stir to blend and moisten; then vigorously stir about 2 minutes, scraping sides and bottom as necessary.

2. Pour into an 8 x 8 x 2-inch baking pan coated with nonstick cooking spray, and bake about 35 minutes or until a toothpick inserted in center comes out clean.

3. Cut into 3-inch squares. Serve warm or at room temperature.

Flavor Perk: To serve as a dessert, top servings with orange or lemon dessert sauce or fat free lemon-flavored yogurt.

- - - - - - - - - - - - - - - - - - - -

Yield: 8 (3-inch) squares
Serving size: 1 square

Calories: 245
Protein: 4 g
Carbohydrate: 45 g
Fat: 5 g
Cholesterol: 0 mg
Sodium: 355 mg
Calcium: 49 mg
Dietary Fiber: less than 1 g
Sugar: 25 g

MIXED FRUIT GINGERBREAD

1 (14½ ounce) box gingerbread mix
1¼ cups lukewarm water
¼ cup egg substitute
½ cup dried mixed fruit, chopped

1. Preheat oven to 350°. Combine gingerbread mix, water and egg substitute; mix well. Stir in mixed fruit.

2. Pour batter into an 8 x 8 x 2-inch pan coated with nonstick cooking spray.

3. Bake 30-35 minutes. Gingerbread is done when a toothpick is inserted in the center and comes out clean.

4. Cut into 3-inch squares. Serve warm or at room temperature.

Flavor Perk: Serve with dollop of fat free orange-flavored yogurt.

- - - - - - - - - - - - - - - - - - - -

Yield: 8 (3-inch) squares
Serving size: 1 square

Calories: 258
Protein: 4 g
Carbohydrate: 50 g
Fat: 5 g
Cholesterol: 0 mg
Sodium: 358 mg
Calcium: 48 mg
Dietary Fiber: 2 g
Sugar: 20 g

PEANUTTY CORNBREAD

Satisfy that craving for peanut butter.

1 (6 ounce) package corn muffin
mix
¼ cup reduced fat creamy or
crunchy peanut butter
⅔ cup skim milk
¼ cup egg substitute

1. Preheat oven to 425°. Pour muffin mix into mixing bowl and mix in peanut butter with fingers or fork until peanut butter is evenly dispersed.

2. Add skim milk and egg substitute; stir just until dry ingredients are moistened. Spoon into a hot 9-inch baking pan or skillet coated with nonstick cooking spray. If using corn stick or muffin pan, spoon batter into 6-8 hot sprayed muffin cups, filling about ⅔ full.

3. Bake 18-20 minutes or until golden brown.

- - - - - - - - - - - - - - - - - -

Yield: 12 servings
Serving size: 1 square

Calories: 98
Protein: 3 g
Carbohydrate: 13 g
Fat: 4 g
Cholesterol: less than 1 g
Sodium: 218 mg
Calcium: 28 mg
Dietary Fiber: 1 g
Sugar: 4 g

QUICK MEXICAN CORNBREAD

4 tablespoons light Velveeta
¼ cup skim milk
¼ cup egg substitute
1 (6 ounce) package Mexican-style
cornbread mix

1. Preheat oven to 425°. In a saucepan or skillet, melt cheese with milk over low heat.

2. In a mixing bowl, combine egg substitute and cornbread mix. Fold in cheese mixture, stirring just until moistened.

3. Pour into a preheated 9 x 9-inch skillet or baking pan coated with nonstick cooking spray.

4. Bake 18-20 minutes or until golden brown.

Variation: Use regular corn muffin mix and stir into the batter ¼ cup drained chopped green chilies or 1½ tablespoons seeded, minced fresh jalapeño pepper.

- - - - - - - - - - - - - - - - - -

Yield: 12 serving
Serving size: 1 square

Calories: 74
Protein: 3 g
Carbohydrate: 11 g
Fat: 2 g
Cholesterol: 3 mg
Sodium: 243 mg
Dietary: less than 1 g
Sugar: less than 1 g

TURKEY BLT'S

3 strips turkey bacon
2 slices whole grain bread, toasted,
spread with 1 tablespoon fat free
or light mayonnaise
4 slices tomato
Crisp lettuce leaves

1. With paper towels on top and bottom, place turkey bacon in microwave oven and cook until crisp, according to manufacturer's instructions. If bacon is fried in a skillet, cook until crisp and drain thoroughly on paper towels.

2. Place turkey bacon on toast slice with mayonnaise, and add slices of tomato. Season tomato to taste with salt or salt substitute and freshly ground black pepper.

3. Add lettuce and top with second toast slice.

- - - - - - - - - - - - - - - - - -

Calories: 276
Protein: 15 g
Carbohydrate: 42 g
Fat: 10 g
Cholesterol: 30 mg
Sodium: 921 mg
Calcium: 306 mg
Dietary Fiber: 7 g
Sugar: 9 g

TASTY TURKEY BURGERS

Surprisingly tasty!

½ cup onion, finely chopped
2 slices fresh whole wheat or
whole grain bread
1 pound ground turkey
1 cup grated zucchini

1. In a skillet coated with nonstick cooking spray, sauté onion until clear and tender. Remove onion from skillet and set aside. Using a food processor or blender, process the bread until crumbs are fine; measure 1 cup.

2. In a mixing bowl, lightly mix the onion, turkey, zucchini and bread crumbs. Season to taste with salt or salt substitute and freshly ground black pepper.

3. Form mixture into 5-6 flat patties. Place patties in the skillet and cook 3-4 minutes on each side or until done. Patties are done when the meat in the center is no longer pink. Do not overcook or will be dry.

4. Serve with light whole wheat buns, lettuce, tomato and red onion rings.

Flavor Perk: Add ½ teaspoon poultry seasoning and 1 tablespoon minced fresh parsley to the mixture before making patties.

- - - - - - - - - - - - - - - - - -

Yield: 5-6 patties
Serving size: 1 patty

Calories: 187	Sodium: 154 mg
Protein: 18 g	Calcium: 32 mg
Carbohydrate: 10 g	Dietary Fiber: 2 g
Fat: 8 g	Sugar: 2 g
Cholesterol: 72 mg	

SLOPPY TOMS

1 pound ground turkey
1 cup frozen seasoning blend
(onion, celery, peppers and
parsley), partially thawed
1 cup ketchup or no salt tomato
sauce
1 tablespoon Worcestershire sauce

1. In a sprayed large skillet over medium heat, sauté the seasoning
blend until water evaporates and
vegetables are tender. Add turkey
and cook until turkey is no longer
pink.

2. Stir in ketchup, Worcestershire
sauce and ⅛ teaspoon freshly
ground black pepper.

3. Simmer uncovered 5-10 minutes,
stirring occasionally.

4. Serve with toasted whole wheat
buns.

- - - - - - - - - - - - - - - - - -

Yield: 4 servings
Serving size: 1 sandwich

Calories: 251
Protein: 21 g
Carbohydrate: 20 g
Fat: 10 g
Cholesterol: 90 mg
Sodium: 877 mg
Calcium: 31 mg
Dietary Fiber: 1 g
Sugar: 9 g

KID-PLEASING TURKEY TOMS

*Cheese-stuffed, bacon-wrapped hot dogs
are fun to eat. This recipe trims the fat
and calories by using turkey bacon,
turkey franks and reduced fat cheese.*

4 slices fully cooked turkey bacon
4 turkey frankfurters
4 strips reduced fat cheddar
cheese
4 light whole wheat hot dog buns

1. Preheat oven to 400°. Cut a slit
down the middle of each frankfurter and insert cheese strips.
Wrap one slice of bacon around
each frankfurter. Place on baking
sheet and bake 10-12 minutes or
until bacon is crisp.

2. Split and toast buns. Serve bacon-
wrapped frankfurters on buns immediately.

*Flavor Perk: Provide garnishes of crushed
pineapple, sauerkraut, dill relish,
chopped onion, coleslaw or chopped
tomato.*

- - - - - - - - - - - - - - - - - -

Yield: 4 servings
Serving size: 1 frankfurter

Calories: 286
Protein: 20 g
Carbohydrate: 20 g
Fat: 16 g
Cholesterol: 73 mg
Sodium: 1192 mg
Calcium: 273 mg
Dietary Fiber: 3 g
Sugar: 4 g

GRILLED TURKEY-SALSA BURGERS

1 pound ground turkey
1 (1.25 ounce) reduced sodium taco seasoning mix
4 light whole wheat hamburger buns, split, toasted
¼ cup thick and chunky salsa

1. Heat gas grill to medium heat according to manufacturer's instructions. Mix turkey and taco seasoning and form 6 patties. Place patties 4-6 inches from heat source. Cover and grill 7-8 minutes on each side or until turkey is no longer pink in middle. Do not overcook or turkey will be dry.

2. Top cooked patties with salsa and serve with buns.

Flavor Perk: Add slices of fat free or reduced fat cheddar, Swiss or Monterey Jack cheese.

Variation: Use conventional oven for broiling turkey patties. Place on broiler pan, uncovered, and broil about 5-6 minutes on each side.

- - - - - - - - - - - - - - - - - - - -

Yield: 4 servings
Serving size: 1 burger

Calories: 281
Protein: 23 g
Carbohydrate: 25 g
Fat: 10 g
Cholesterol: 90 mg
Sodium: 872 mg
Calcium: 45 mg
Dietary Fiber: 3 g
Sugar: 7 g

GRILLED PORTOBELLO BURGERS

Try this delicious beef-less burger.

4 large Portobello mushroom caps (about 1 pound)
Fat free balsamic vinaigrette dressing
4 reduced fat whole wheat or multi-grain hamburger buns, toasted
Burger "fixin's" (lettuce, tomato slices, onion rings)

1. Preheat gas grill to medium heat or prepare charcoal grill. Brush mushroom caps with dressing and season to taste with salt/salt substitute and freshly ground black pepper.

2. Grill, turning once, about 12 minutes or until softened. Place mushrooms on toasted buns and add "fixin's." Drizzle with dressing and serve.

- - - - - - - - - - - - - - - - - - - -

Yield: 4 servings
Serving size: 1 burger

Calories: 165
Protein: 7 g
Carbohydrate: 30 g
Fat: 3 g
Cholesterol: 0 mg
Sodium: 370 mg
Calcium: 55 mg
Dietary Fiber: 3 g
Sugar: 9 g

HEALTHY WRAP IDEAS

Basic preparation:
1. **Tortilla** (Select size and type.)
2. **Spread** (Spread 1-2 tablespoons over tortilla.)
3. **Topping I** (Sprinkle to within 1 inch of edge.)
4. **Main Filling** (1-2 slices, 2-3 tablespoons. Spoon in center of tortilla.)
5. **Topping II** (Sprinkle over main filling.)
6. **Extra Topping** (Optional: use sparingly.)

Roll tortilla tightly. Serve immediately or wrap securely with plastic wrap and refrigerate. Eat within 24 hours for best quality.

1. TORTILLAS ....
6-8 inches (flour or whole wheat)
10-12 inches (flour or whole wheat)

2. SPREADS ....
Mayonnaise, fat free or light
Mustard, Dijon-style, brown deli, yellow, hot spicy
Pesto
Horseradish sauce
Cream cheese, fat free or light
Sour cream, fat free or light
Yogurt, nonfat, plain
Cottage cheese, fat free or light
Ricotta, reduced fat
Creamy salad dressing, fat free or light
Hummus (garbanzo spread)
Refried beans, fat free

3. TOPPING I ....
Iceberg lettuce leaf
Romaine leaf
Red leaf lettuce
Green leaf lettuce
Spinach leaves
Alfalfa sprouts

Bibb lettuce leaf
Butter lettuce leaf
Other lettuce leaves
Tomato slices
Cucumber slices
Zucchini slices
Avocado slices (use sparingly)

4. MAIN FILLING ....
Ham, fat free, thinly sliced
Turkey, fat free, thinly sliced
Turkey bacon, cooked
Lean roast beef, thinly sliced
Albacore tuna, chunks, salad
Salmon, chunks, salad
Crabmeat, drained, salad
Shrimp, cooked, salad
Other fish, cooked, pieces
Refried beans, fat free
Beans, mashed (black, navy, kidney, garbanzo or chick pea)
Tofu, cooked, crumbled
Egg substitute, scrambled
Peanut butter, reduced fat, chunky or creamy
Other nut butters
American cheese, fat free, sliced, thin strips
Cheddar cheese, fat free or reduced fat, sliced, thin strips

Swiss, fat free or reduced, sliced, thin strips
Mozzarella, reduced fat, sliced, thin strips
Monterey jack, sliced, thin strips
Jalapeño jack, sliced, thin strips
Other cheeses, sliced, thin strips

5. TOPPING II ....

Tomato, sliced, chopped
Cucumber, grated or sliced
Water chestnuts, chopped or sliced
Celery, sliced, chopped
Yellow, red, or green bell pepper, strips or chopped
Carrot, shredded or grated
Broccoli, chopped
Zucchini, shredded
Turnip, shredded
Yellow squash, shredded
Green onions and tops, chopped, sliced
Red onion, rings, chopped
White or yellow onion, rings, chopped
Alfalfa sprouts
Bean sprouts
     Cole slaw, fat free dressing
Salsa
Pickled jalapeno slices
Dill pickles, sliced, relish
Pickled beet slices
Roasted red pepper, sliced, chopped
Green chiles, canned, sliced, chopped
Olives, black, green, chopped (use sparingly)
Cooked snow or sugar snap peas
Cooked whole green beans
Cooked asparagus spears
Apple, chopped, sliced
Pear, chopped, sliced
Banana, chopped, sliced
Kiwi, sliced

6. EXTRA TOPPING .....

Selected Toppings I or II
Selected Spreads
Toasted pine nuts, sesame seeds, soy nuts
Chopped peanuts, pecans, walnuts, cashews, pistachios, sunflower seeds
Fresh herbs (parsley, cilantro, basil, etc.)
Hot pepper sauce
Freshly ground black pepper
Croutons, crushed
Ramen noodles, toasted, crushed
Salad dressings, fat free, light
Vinaigrette, fat free, light

LUNCHBOX TURKEY ROLLUPS

Like this recipe? See "Wrap Ideas" in this section.

4-6 (8 inch) whole wheat flour tortillas
2-3 tablespoons reduced fat cream cheese
12 thin slices 98% fat free turkey
8-10 fresh spinach leaves, washed, patted dry

1. Spread each tortilla with cream cheese, and add 2-3 slices turkey and 2-3 spinach leaves. Tightly roll up each tortilla and wrap securely in plastic wrap. Refrigerate until serving time.

Flavor Perk: Add chopped tomato and serve with Dijon-style mustard.

- -

Yield: 4-6 servings
Serving size: 1 tortilla

Calories: 109
Protein: 9 g
Carbohydrate: 14 g
Fat: 2 g
Cholesterol: 16 mg
Sodium: 680 mg
Calcium: 29 mg
Dietary Fiber: 10 g
Sugar: less than 1 g

CHICKEN SALAD FOR SANDWICHES

1½ cups chopped cooked chicken or turkey
¼-½ cup fat free or light mayonnaise
½ cup (1 stalk) celery, chopped
¼ cup dill pickle, chopped

1. Mix all ingredients and season to taste with salt or salt substitute and freshly ground black pepper.

Variation: Substitute 2 (6 ounce) cans or 2 (7 ounce) pouches albacore tuna for the chicken. Substitute 1 teaspoon lemon juice for the dill pickle.

- -

Yield: 6 servings
Serving size: About ¼ cup

Calories: 96
Protein: 11 g
Carbohydrate: 2 g
Fat: 5 g
Cholesterol: 33 mg
Sodium: 223 mg
Calcium: 14 mg
Dietary Fiber: less than 1 g
Sugar: less than 1 g

CHEESE SANDWICH SPREADS

1 cup shredded reduced fat
cheddar cheese
1-2 cups reduced fat small curd
cottage cheese
Selected ingredients from list
below

1. Mix cheeses until well blended.
   Add one or more of the following
   ingredients:
   Finely chopped celery
   Finely chopped red or green bell
   pepper
   Minced parsley
   Snipped chives or green onion
   tops
   Chopped tomatoes
   Dash paprika, dry mustard
   Sprinkle dill weed
   Chopped roasted red pepper, pi-
   miento
   Chopped green chiles
   Minced jalapeño or Serrano pep-
   per
   Finely chopped onion, green,
   white, yellow, red

- -

Yield: 2-4 cups

SPECIAL SANDWICH SPREAD

*This is a Middle Eastern spread called
hummus and may be used as a spread
for wrap sandwiches or as an appetizer.*

1 (15 ounce) can garbanzo beans
or chick peas, drained, liquid
reserved
¼ cup toasted sesame seeds
3 tablespoons fresh lemon juice
1 large clove garlic, peeled, halved

1. Place garbanzos in a food processor or blender. Add sesame seeds,
   lemon juice, garlic and ¼ cup reserved garbanzo liquid. Pulse, adding more liquid if needed, until
   mixture is smooth and the consistency of a thick batter.

2. Season to taste with salt/salt substitute and freshly ground black
   pepper.

3. Serve with pita bread or whole
   wheat tortillas.

*Flavor Perk: Add 1-2 tablespoons olive oil to the
food processor or blender.*

*Variation: Prepare spread using black beans,
pine nuts and orange juice.*

- -

Yield: 6 servings (12 tablespoons)
Serving size: 2 tablespoons

Calories: 153
Protein: 7 g
Carbohydrate: 22 g
Fat: 5 g
Cholesterol: 0 mg
Sodium: 6 mg
Calcium: 96 mg
Dietary Fiber: 6 g
Sugar: 4 g

WATERCRESS TEA SANDWICHES

20 slices thin-sliced whole wheat
bread, trimmed
1 (3 ounce) package reduced fat
cream cheese, softened
1 bunch watercress, washed, finely
chopped

1. Spread cream cheese on bread slices. Place chopped watercress on half of the bread slices; then cover with remaining bread slices.

2. Cut each sandwich into 3 bars. Garnish each with tiny springs of watercress.

- - - - - - - - - - - - - - - - - - - -

Yield: 30 servings (30 bars)
Serving size: 1 bar

Calories: 86
Protein: 3 grams
Carbohydrate: 14 grams
Fat: 2 grams
Cholesterol: 2 milligrams
Sodium: 209 milligrams
Calcium: 17 milligrams
Dietary Fiber: 2 grams
Sugar: 1 gram

CUCUMBER TEA SANDWICHES

These appealing sandwiches are a long-time favorite for receptions and parties.

1 (8 ounce) package reduced fat
cream cheese, softened
2 cucumbers, peeled, seeded,
grated, drained
1 loaf whole wheat bread,
trimmed
¾ teaspoon salt free seasoning
blend

1. Beat cream cheese until smooth. Add cucumber and seasoning blend; mix well.

2. Combine cream cheese, cucumber and seasoning blend; mix well. Spread on bread slices to make sandwiches.

3. Cut sandwiches in triangles or bars.

Flavor Perk: Add 1 teaspoon finely minced onion.

- - - - - - - - - - - - - - - - - - - -

Yield: 12 servings
Serving size: About 3 sandwiches

Calories: 171
Protein: 6 g
Carbohydrate: 23 g
Fat: 7 g
Cholesterol: 14 mg
Sodium: 376 mg
Calcium: 29 mg
Dietary Fiber: 3 g
Sugar: 2 g

Kitchen Helper

FOOD PROCESSOR PIZZA CRUST

This crust is a fresh and delicious start to homemade pizza.

3 cups flour
2 teaspoons rapid-rise dry yeast
4 teaspoons olive oil
2 tablespoons cornmeal

1. In food processor, place flour, yeast and 1 teaspoon salt. Pulse briefly to blend. With processor running, add 1 cup warm (105°-115°) water and oil through feed tube. Process about 10 seconds or until mixture forms a ball.

2. Turn dough out onto lightly-floured surface and knead until smooth. Place dough in a mixing bowl sprayed with nonstick cooking spray. Cover lightly with plastic wrap and let rise in a warm place 45-60 minutes or until dough doubles in size.

3. Turn dough out onto lightly-floured surface. Divide in half, and knead each half until dough forms a smooth ball. Spray 2 large bowls with nonstick cooking spray and put a dough ball in each. Cover lightly again and let rise 10-15 minutes.

4. To prepare pizza, preheat oven to 500°. For one crust, lightly spray a 12-inch pizza pan and dust with 1 tablespoon cornmeal. Turn dough out again on a lightly-floured surface and shape into a round, flat shape. Let rest 3-4 minutes; then pat and gently stretch in the pizza pan to desired shape. Sprinkle with toppings of your choice and bake about 15 minutes or until crust is crisp and golden brown.

Yield: 8 servings (2 12-inch pizza crusts)
Serving size: ¼ pizza crust

Calories: 195
Protein: 5 g
Carbohydrate: 37 g

Fat: 3 g
Cholesterol: 0 mg
Sodium: 620 mg
Calcium: 166 mg
Dietary Fiber: 2 g
Sugar: less than 1 g

Kitchen Helper

BASIC WHITE OR FRENCH BREAD

This recipe requires a bread machine.

1⅛ cups warm water or skim milk
1½ tablespoons vegetable oil (optional)
*3 cups bread flour
2 teaspoons active dry yeast

*Add 1½ teaspoons salt to the bread machine
following the addition of the flour.*

1. Place ingredients into the bread pan in the following order: water or skim milk, oil, bread flour, 1½ teaspoons salt and yeast.

2. Following manufacturer's instructions for the bread machine, select "Basic Bread" setting and desired crust setting; start the machine. (The cycle takes about 2½ hours.)

3. When bread is done, remove from machine and cool slightly before removing paddle.

4. Use within 2-3 days or freeze.

Yield: 8 slices (1-1½ pound loaf)
Serving size: 1 slice

Calories: 188
Protein: 7 g
Carbohydrate: 38 g
Fat: less than 1 g
Cholesterol: 0 mg
Sodium: 2 mg
Calcium: 8 mg
Dietary Fiber: 1 g
Sugar: less than 1 g

Kitchen Helper

LITE PANCAKE MIX (16-18 PANCAKES)

1½ cups sifted enriched self-rising flour
Sugar substitute equal to 2 tablespoons sugar
¼ cup egg substitute
1⅓ cups skim milk
3 tablespoons vegetable oil

1. Sift flour and sugar substitute together into a mixing bowl. In another bowl, blend together egg substitute, milk and oil. Add egg mixture all at once to flour mixture, stirring only until flour is moistened (batter may be lumpy).

2. For each pancake, pour about ¼ cup batter onto preheated skillet or griddle coated with nonstick cooking spray. Bake until small bubbles appear; then turn over and bake until golden brown.

Variations:
Stir ½ cup fresh or frozen (thawed, well drained) blackberries, blueberries or raspberries into batter.
Sprinkle nuts, chopped fresh or dried fruit on pancakes before turning over to bake second side.

Yield: 16 servings
Serving size: 1 pancake

Calories (mix only): 74
Protein: 2 g
Carbohydrate: 10 g
Fat: 3 g
Cholesterol: less than 1 mg
Sodium: 166 mg
Calcium: 70 mg
Dietary Fiber: less than 1 g
Sugar: 1 g

LITE BISCUIT MIX

2¼ cups sifted enriched self-rising flour, divided
¼ cup stick margarine
½-¾ cup skim milk

1. Preheat oven to 450°. Place 2 cups flour in mixing bowl. With pastry blender or fingers, cut margarine into flour until mixture resembles coarse crumbs. Blend in just enough milk to make a soft dough.

2. Turn out onto lightly floured board and knead gently 30 seconds. Roll out ½-inch thick. Cut out biscuits with floured 2-inch biscuit cutter or sharp knife. Place on ungreased baking sheet.

3. Bake 10-12 minutes or until lightly browned.

Variations: Drop Biscuits: Increase skim milk to 1 cup and blend in enough milk to make a thick drop batter. Drop by rounded tablespoonfuls onto ungreased baking sheet.

Buttermilk Biscuits: Substitute buttermilk for skim milk.

Poppy Seed Biscuits: Spray tops of unbaked biscuits with nonstick cooking spray and sprinkle on poppy seeds.

Yield: 12 biscuits
Serving size: 1 biscuit

Calories: 120
Protein: 3 g
Carbohydrate: 18 g
Fat: 4 g
Cholesterol: less than 1 mg
Sodium: 347 mg
Calcium: 93 mg
Dietary Fiber: less than 1 g
Sugar: less than 1 g

Kitchen Helper

LITE MUFFIN MIX

2 cups sifted enriched self-rising flour
Sugar substitute equal to 3 tablespoons sugar
¼ cup egg substitute
1 cup skim milk
3 tablespoons vegetable oil

1. Preheat oven to 400°. Stir flour and sugar together in a mixing bowl. In another bowl, mix egg substitute, milk and oil. Add egg mixture all at once to flour mixture, stirring just until flour is moistened.

1. Fill sprayed nonstick muffin cups ⅔ full. Bake 20-25 minutes or until a toothpick inserted in center comes out clean.

Variations:
Add ½ cup chopped apple.
Add ¼ cup grated carrot and ¼ cup chopped raisins.
Add ¼ teaspoon lemon extract or 1 tablespoon lemon juice plus 1 teaspoon grated lemon peel.
Add ¼ teaspoon orange extract or 2 tablespoons orange juice
*   plus 1 teaspoon grated orange peel.*
Add ½ cup mashed banana.
Add ¼ cup dried cranberries.
Add ½ cup raisins and pinch of cloves or nutmeg.
Surprise Muffins: Fill muffin cups ⅓ full; place teaspoonfuls sugar free
*   low calorie preserves or fruit-only spread over batter. Cover with remaining batter*
*   to make muffin cups ⅔ full.*

Yield: 12 servings
Serving size: 1 muffin

Calories (mix only): 114
Protein: 3 g
Carbohydrate: 17 g
Fat: 4 g
Cholesterol: less than 1 mg
Sodium: 283 mg
Calcium: 105 mg
Dietary Fiber: less than 1 g
Sugar: 1 g

Kitchen Helper

LITE CORNBREAD MIX

This recipe yields 1 (8-inch) square cornbread, 12 muffins or 14 corn sticks.

2 cups enriched self-rising cornmeal
Sugar substitute equal to 2 tablespoons sugar
½ cup egg substitute
1-1¼ cups skim milk
¼ cup vegetable oil

1. Preheat oven to 425°. Combine cornmeal and sugar substitute in mixing bowl. In another bowl, mix together egg substitute, 1 cup milk and oil. Add egg mixture all at once to corn meal mixture, mixing until well blended. If necessary, add more milk to make a medium-thick batter.

2. For cornbread, pour batter into an 8-inch square pan coated with nonstick cooking spray. For muffins, pour ⅔ cup batter into sprayed muffin cups. For corn sticks, spray corn stick sections generously with nonstick cooking spray. Fill sections with batter, level with top of pan. Bake cornbread 25-30 minutes or until golden brown. Bake corn muffins or sticks 15-20 minutes or until golden brown.

3. For crisper crusts on muffins or corn sticks, place sprayed muffin or corn stick pans in oven to heat while preparing batter.

Variation: Bacon-Chive Muffins - Stir 6 slices chopped cooked turkey bacon into cornmeal mixture, and 2 tablespoons chopped chives or green onion tops into egg mixture.

Yield: 12 servings
Serving size: ¹/₁₂ mix

Calories: 152
Protein: 4 g
Carbohydrate: 22 g
Fat: 5 g
Cholesterol: less than 1 mg
Sodium: 401 mg

SALADS
A Short Guide to Greens

Greens are truly bonus foods for reducing calories and increasing the nutrient value, variety, color and texture of our meals. Eating a hearty portion of greens daily is a healthful and smart choice.

Use greens in a tossed salad, as part of a sandwich or as a base for other salads. Here is a list of popular greens, with suggestions on how to purchase:

Bok choy: 1 head (1¼ pounds) yields 7 cups shredded leaves and sliced stems.

Butterhead (Bibb or Boston) lettuce: 1 head (8 ounces) yields 6 cups torn, bite-size portions.

Cabbage: 1 head (2 pounds) yields 12 cups shredded or 10 cups coarsely chopped.

Iceberg lettuce: 1 head (1¼ pounds) yields about 10 cups torn; 12 cups shredded or chopped.

Leaf lettuce: 1 head (12 ounces) yields about 10 cups torn leaves.

Napa cabbage: 1 head (2 pounds) yields about 12 cups shredded leaves and sliced stems.

Romaine: 1 head (1 pound) yields about 10 cups torn leaves.

Savoy cabbage: 1 head (about 2 pounds) yields 12 cups coarsely shredded.

Spinach: 1 pound yields about 12 cups torn leaves, stems removed.

Most of these greens can be pre-washed and stored, reducing preparation time for salads. Cabbage, iceberg lettuce, leaf lettuce, butterhead lettuce and Savoy cabbage can be washed and, if stored properly, will stay fresh about 5 days in the refrigerator.

Store greens in a plastic bag or airtight container lined with paper towels to keep lettuce from being too wet. For best results, use dry greens for salads. Use a salad spinner or clean, dry dishtowels or paper towels for patting dry individual leaves.

MARINATED CUCUMBER SLICES

Before slicing cucumbers, run the tines of a fork down the length of each cucumber.

2 cucumbers, unpeeled, thinly
sliced
½ onion, sliced
¼ cup cider or white vinegar
Sugar substitute equal to ⅓ cup
sugar

1. Place cucumbers and onion in a shallow bowl. Combine vinegar and sugar substitute. Pour over cucumbers and onions.

2. Cover and chill 2-3 hours before serving.

- - - - - - - - - - - - - - - - - - - -

Yield: 6 servings
Serving size: About ½ cup

Calories: 25
Protein: less than 1 g
Carbohydrate: 6 g
Fat: less than 1 g
Cholesterol: 0 mg
Sodium: 4 mg
Calcium: 42 mg
Dietary Fiber: less than 1 g
Sugar: 1 g

MARINATED BRUSSELS SPROUTS

Although fresh Brussels sprouts have great flavor and texture, frozen sprouts are very acceptable and quick-to-fix for this salad.

2 (10 ounce) packages frozen
Brussels sprouts
1 cup light or fat free Italian salad
dressing
1 cup chopped green or red bell
pepper
½ cup chopped onion

1. With fork, pierce packages of frozen Brussels sprouts and cook in microwave for 7 minutes. Drain and place in shallow dish.

2. In a small bowl, mix dressing, bell pepper and onion.

3. Pour over sprouts and marinate at least 24 hours. Drain to serve.

- - - - - - - - - - - - - - - - - - - -

Yield: 6 servings
Serving size: About ⅔ cup

Calories: 71
Protein: 4 g
Carbohydrate: 15 g
Fat: less than 1 g
Cholesterol: 0 mg
Sodium: 250 mg
Calcium: 30 mg
Dietary Fiber: 4 g
Sugar: 2 g

STUFFED TOMATO CUPS

For a main-dish salad, fill tomato cups with this cottage cheese mixture or a low-calorie chicken, tuna or salmon salad. Garnish with sprigs of fresh herbs.

To make tomato cups, select firm-fleshed, round, brightest-red tomatoes. Cut off a ¼-inch slice from the stem of each tomato. Using a spoon, scoop out the tomato pulp, leaving a ¼ to ½-inch thick shell. Save the pulp to add to a sauce or soup.

2 cups reduced fat cottage cheese, drained
⅓ cup green onions and tops, finely chopped
2 tomatoes, chopped
4 large tomatoes, hollowed

1. Combine first 3 ingredients and mix well. Spoon mixture into tomato shells.

2. Serve immediately or refrigerate.

- - - - - - - - - - - - - - - - - -

Yield: 4 servings
Serving size: 1 tomato

Calories: 123
Protein: 16 g
Carbohydrate: 12 g
Fat: 2 g
Cholesterol: 5 mg
Sodium: 478 mg
Calcium: 84 mg
Dietary Fiber: 2 g
Sugar: 7 g

HERB-MARINATED TOMATOES

Look for firm, vine-ripened bright red tomatoes for best results.

4 tomatoes, cut in ¼-inch slices
½ cup light or fat free red wine vinaigrette dressing
Lettuce leaves (romaine, iceberg or leaf)
2 teaspoons fresh chopped basil leaves or ½ teaspoon dried basil leaves

1. Place sliced tomatoes in a shallow bowl and spoon dressing evenly over the top. Cover and chill at least 1 hour, basting tomatoes with dressing 2-3 times.

2. To serve, place lettuce leaves on salad plate. Top with tomatoes and sprinkle with basil.

- - - - - - - - - - - - - - - - - -

Yield: 4 servings
Serving size: 1 sliced tomato

Calories: 49
Protein: 1 g
Carbohydrate: 11 g
Fat: less than 1 g
Cholesterol: 0 mg
Sodium: 184 mg
Calcium: 11 mg
Dietary Fiber: 1 g
Sugar: 7 g

GREEN BEAN-TOMATO SALAD

Seeding tomatoes before chopping will help keep them firm.

2 (16 ounce) packages frozen cut green beans
5 Roma or small tomatoes, chopped, drained
6-8 green onions with tops, thinly sliced
1 cup fat free Italian salad dressing

1. Cook green beans in microwave oven according to package instructions. Drain and chill.

2. Just before serving, combine tomatoes and onions in salad dressing in a small bowl. Add green beans and toss lightly.

3. Serve immediately.

- -

Yield: 6 servings
Serving size: About ⅔ cup

Calories: 105
Protein: 3 g
Carbohydrate: 24 g
Fat: less than 1 g
Cholesterol: 0 mg
Sodium: 504 mg
Calcium: 91 mg
Dietary Fiber: 6 g
Sugar: 9 g

GREEN BEAN MEDLEY

1 (16 ounce) package frozen whole green beans
1 cup fresh mushrooms, thinly sliced
½ cup thinly sliced red onion
⅓ cup light or fat free red wine vinaigrette salad dressing

1. Cook green beans according to package instructions; drain and chill.

2. In salad bowl, combine chilled green beans, mushrooms and red onion.

3. Toss lightly with salad dressing.

Flavor Perk: Add 2 teaspoons fresh or dried herbs of your choice.

- -

Yield: 6 servings
Serving size: About ½ cup

Calories: 39
Protein: 2 g
Carbohydrate: 8 g
Fat: less than 1 g
Cholesterol: 0 mg
Sodium: 84 mg
Calcium: 42 mg
Dietary Fiber: 3 g
Sugar: 5 g

CREAMY EGG SALAD

Serve this salad only occasionally if you crave "real" eggs.

4 eggs, hard-cooked, chopped
1 (8 ounce) package reduced fat cream cheese, softened
½ cup fat free mayonnaise
2 tablespoons minced onion

1. Combine all ingredients, mixing well. Serve immediately or refrigerate.

Flavor Perk: Add ½ teaspoon fresh or dried herbs of your choice.

- -

Yield: 6 servings
Serving size: About ½ cup

Calories: 158
Protein: 8 grams
Carbohydrate: 5 grams
Fat: 12 grams
Cholesterol: 168 milligrams
Sodium: 381 milligrams
Calcium: 17 milligrams
Dietary Fiber: 0 grams
Sugar: 2 grams

RED HOT ONIONS

Serve this dish as a condiment or as a perk-up for salads or vegetables.

3 large red onions, thinly sliced
2 tablespoons hot pepper sauce
1⅓ tablespoons olive oil or vegetable oil
3 tablespoons red wine vinegar

1. Place onions in medium bowl. Pour 1 cup boiling water over onions and let stand 1 minute; drain.

2. Mix pepper sauce, oil and vinegar in a small bowl. Pour over onion rings.

3. Cover and refrigerate at least 3 hours. Drain to serve.

- -

Yield: 6 servings
Serving size: About ½ cup

Protein: less than 1 g
Carbohydrate: 3 g
Fat: 3 g
Cholesterol: 0 mg
Sodium: 33 mg
Calcium: 8 mg
Dietary Fiber: less than 1 g
Sugar: 2 g

POBLANO CHILE SALAD OLÉ

Originating in the Puebla region, Central Mexican Valley, the red or green poblano chile pepper is larger and much milder than the jalapeño. Poblanos are best known for making chiles rellenos. They can also be cut into strips and used as a garnish. Diced poblanos are known as ancho chiles.

2 poblano chile peppers, rinsed, stemmed, seeded
1 red bell pepper, rinsed, stemmed, seeded
1 cucumber, rinsed, peeled, seeded
1 cup chopped green onions and tops

1. Cut chiles, bell pepper and cucumber into ¼ inch pieces. Add green onions, salt/salt substitute and freshly ground black pepper to taste.

2. Serve with Cilantro Salad Dressing (p. 82).

Flavor Perk: Add ½ cup cooked frozen whole kernel corn or ½ cup rinsed black beans. Squeeze 2-3 tablespoons lime juice over salad before serving.

- - - - - - - - - - - - - - - - - - - -

Yield: 30
Protein: 1 g
Carbohydrate: 7 g
Fat: less than 1 g
Cholesterol: 0 mg
Sodium: 6 mg
Calcium: 29 mg
Dietary Fiber: 1 g
Sugar: less than 1 g

CILANTRO SALAD DRESSING

¾ cup light sour cream
¼ cup light or fat free mayonnaise
¼-½ cup snipped fresh cilantro leaves
¼-½ cup chopped fresh parsley

1. Stir ingredients until well blended. Season to taste with salt/salt substitute.

- - - - - - - - - - - - - - - - - - - -

Yield: 8 servings (About 1 cup)
Serving size: 2 tablespoons

Calories: 59
Protein: 2 g
Carbohydrate: 3 g
Fat: 4 g
Cholesterol: 10 mg
Sodium: 68 mg
Calcium: 58 mg
Dietary Fiber: less than 1 g
Sugar: 2 g

TANGY ORANGE SALAD

This unique salad complements spicy hot or Mexican foods.

1 cup fresh alfalfa sprouts
2 large navel oranges, peeled, sliced
8 thin red onion slices
Lime-Honey Salad Dressing (p. 83)

1. Place ¼ cup sprouts on each of 4 salad plates. Arrange orange slices and red onion rings on sprouts.

2. Spoon ½-1 tablespoon Lime-Honey Salad Dressing on each salad. Serve immediately.

- - - - - - - - - - - - - - - - - - - -

Yield: 4 servings

Calories (without dressing): 45
Protein: 1 g
Carbohydrate: 11 g
Fat: less than 1 g
Cholesterol: 0 mg
Sodium: 2 mg
Calcium: 36 mg
Dietary Fiber: 2 g
Sugar: 8 g

LIME-HONEY SALAD DRESSING

4 tablespoons lime juice and ½ teaspoon finely grated lime peel
3-4 tablespoons honey
¼ teaspoon ground coriander
¼ teaspoon ground nutmeg

1. Mix all ingredients until well blended.

- - - - - - - - - - - - - - - - - - - -

Yield: 4 servings (About ½ cup)
Serving size: 2 tablespoons

Calories: 53
Protein: less than 1 g
Carbohydrate: 14 g
Fat: 0 g
Cholesterol: 0 mg
Sodium: less than 1 mg
Calcium: 3 mg
Dietary Fiber: less than 1 g
Sugar: 13 g

RED CABBAGE SLAW

Finely shredded red cabbage has been a salad basic for years, long before radicchio appeared in produce sections.

1 large head red cabbage, shredded
1 onion, finely chopped
½ cup light mayonnaise
1 tablespoon rice vinegar

1. Combine shredded cabbage and onions in large bowl. In small bowl, stir together mayonnaise and vinegar.

2. Toss salad dressing and cabbage-onion mixture. Serve immediately or refrigerate until serving time.

Variation: Substitute green cabbage or coleslaw mix for red cabbage.

- - - - - - - - - - - - - - - - - -

Yield: 6 servings
Serving size: About ⅔ cup

Calories: 81
Protein: less than 1 g
Carbohydrate: 6 g
Fat: 8 g
Cholesterol: 7 mg
Sodium: 123 mg
Calcium: 16 mg
Dietary Fiber: less than 1 g
Sugar: 2 g

RED ONION FLOWER SALAD

1 head lettuce (iceberg, romaine or leaf), torn into bite-size pieces
4 cups cauliflower florets
1 cup thinly sliced red onion
¾ cup light or fat-free creamy salad dressing of your choice

1. Combine lettuce, florets and onion in a salad bowl. Toss lightly with salad dressing.

Flavor Perk: Sprinkle salad with ⅓ cup reduced calorie Parmesan cheese.

Variation: Use ¾ cup reduced calorie or fat free mayonnaise. In one layer, place lettuce, then cauliflower, then red onions in salad bowl. Spread mayonnaise over top to seal in the salad. Refrigerate overnight. Just before serving, toss salad to combine ingredients.

- - - - - - - - - - - - - - - - - -

Yield: 10 servings
Serving size: About ⅔ cup

Yield: 140
Protein: 2 g
Carbohydrate: 10 g
Fat: 11 g
Cholesterol: 0 mg
Sodium: 329 mg
Calcium: 36 mg
Dietary Fiber: 3 g
Sugar: 6 g

CRUNCHY BROCCOLI SLAW

Now widely available, prepackaged broccoli slaw has expanded vegetable salad choices.

1 cup sunflower seeds
2 (3 ounce) packages chicken-flavored Ramen noodles, uncooked, crushed
1 (16 ounce) package broccoli slaw
1 cup fat free Italian salad dressing

1. In a dry skillet over medium heat, toast sunflower seeds and noodles, stirring constantly until lightly browned.

2. Combine slaw, toasted seeds and noodles. Toss with salad dressing to taste or serve dressing on the side.

3. Chill before serving.

- - - - - - - - - - - - - - - - - - - -

Yield: 10 servings
Serving size: About ½ cup

Calories: 190
Protein: 5 grams
Carbohydrate: 21 grams
Fat: 10 grams
Cholesterol: 0 milligrams
Sodium: 782 milligrams
Calcium: 31 milligrams
Dietary Fiber: 3 grams
Sugar: 3 grams

CHICKEN CAESAR SALAD

Convenient, precooked chicken breast strips will speed preparation, but read the nutrition label to check for high-sodium seasonings.

4 boneless skinless chicken breasts, grilled
1 head romaine lettuce, torn into bite-size pieces
½ cup reduced fat grated Parmesan topping
1 cup fat free herb seasoned croutons

1. Cut chicken breasts into strips.

2. Combine chicken with lettuce, cheese and croutons.

Flavor Perk: When ready to serve, toss salad with reduced fat Caesar Italian dressing to taste.

- - - - - - - - - - - - - - - - - - - -

Yield: 8 servings
Serving size: About 1 cup

Calories: 160
Protein: 23
Carbohydrate: 5 g
Fat: 5 g
Cholesterol: 60 mg
Sodium: 197 mg
Calcium: 18 mg
Dietary Fiber: less than 1 g
Sugar: less than 1 g

SIMPLE YOGURT SALAD DRESSING

½ cup plain nonfat yogurt
1 tablespoon chopped fresh
parsley (or 2 teaspoons dried
parsley) or chopped fresh dill (or
1 teaspoon dill seed)

1. Combine ingredients and serve.
Store in refrigerator.

- - - - - - - - - - - - - - - - - - - -

Yield: 4 servings
Serving size: 2 tablespoons

Calories: 17
Protein: 2 g
Carbohydrate: 2 g
Fat: 0 g
Cholesterol: less than 1 g
Sodium: 24 mg
Calcium: 62 mg
Dietary Fiber: 0 g
Sugar: 2 g

SIMPLE CHICKEN SALAD

*The Simple Yogurt Salad Dressing
complements the chicken-celery-raisin
combination in this salad.*

1 cup cooked cubed chicken
breast
1 cup sliced celery
¼ cup raisins or dried cranberries
Simple Yogurt Salad Dressing
(p. 86)

1. Mix chicken, celery and raisins in
large mixing bowl. Add ½ cup
salad dressing and toss lightly. Season to taste with salt or salt substitute and freshly ground black
pepper.

- - - - - - - - - - - - - - - - - - - -

Yield: 4 servings
Serving size: About ½ cup

Calories: 94
Protein: 12 g
Carbohydrate: 9 g
Fat: 1 g
Cholesterol: 30 mg
Sodium: 76 mg
Calcium: 32 mg
Dietary Fiber: 1 g
Sugar: 7 g

BROCCOLI-CHICKEN SALAD

Buy broccoli crowns for easiest and most economical preparation.

3-4 boneless skinless chicken breasts, cooked, cubed
2 cups fresh broccoli florets
1 red bell pepper, seeded, chopped
1 cup chopped celery

1. Place all ingredients in a large mixing bowl; toss lightly.

Flavor Perk: At serving time, toss salad with fat free salad dressing of your choice.

- - - - - - - - - - - - - - - - - - - -

Yield: 6 servings
Serving size: ⅔ cup

Calories: 156
Protein: 27 g
Carbohydrate: 4 g
Fat: 3 g
Cholesterol: 70 mg
Sodium: 102 mg
Calcium: 43 mg
Dietary Fiber: 2 g
Sugar: less than 1 g

CHICKEN SALAD VERONIQUE

Curry powder is a fragrant blend of up to 20 spices. For freshest, best flavor, buy small amounts to use up quickly, as curry powder does not keep well over 2-3 months.

⅔ teaspoon curry powder
1-2 tablespoons light mayonnaise
2 cups cooked, sliced chicken breast
1 cup seedless red or green grapes, halved

1. Combine curry powder with 1 tablespoon mayonnaise. In medium bowl, stir mayonnaise mixture, chicken and grapes until coated. Use remaining 1 tablespoon mayonnaise only if needed to moisten ingredients.

Flavor Perk: Toasted slivered almonds.

- - - - - - - - - - - - - - - - - - - -

Yield: 6 servings
Serving size: About ½ cup

Calories: 104
Protein: 15 g
Carbohydrate: 5 g
Fat: 3 g
Cholesterol: 40 mg
Sodium: 50 mg
Calcium: 10 mg
Dietary Fiber: less than 1 g
Sugar: 5 g

FIESTA CHICKEN SALAD

Garbanzos or chickpeas provide a different flavor and texture to this main-dish salad.

3-4 boneless skinless chicken breasts, cooked, cubed
1 (15 ounce) can chickpeas (garbanzo beans), rinsed, drained
2 red bell peppers, seeded, diced
1 cup chopped celery

1. Combine chicken, chick peas, peppers and celery. Toss with Fiesta Chicken Salad Dressing (p. 88) and serve immediately or refrigerate until serving time.

- - - - - - - - - - - - - - - - - - -

Yield: 6 servings
Serving size: About 1 cup

Calories: 183
Protein: 23 g
Carbohydrate: 15 g
Fat: 3 g
Cholesterol: 56 mg
Sodium: 224 mg
Calcium: 44 mg
Dietary Fiber: 4 g
Sugar: 3 g

FIESTA CHICKEN SALAD DRESSING

1½ cups light sour cream
2 tablespoons salsa
1-2 teaspoons ground cumin
1 tablespoon snipped fresh cilantro leaves

1. Combine all ingredients. Season to taste with salt or salt substitute and freshly ground black pepper.

- - - - - - - - - - - - - - - - - - -

Yield: 10 servings (About 1½ cups)
Serving size: 2 tablespoons

Calories: 48
Protein: 2 g
Carbohydrate: 3 g
Fat: 3 g
Cholesterol: 12 mg
Sodium: 31 mg
Calcium: 72 mg
Dietary Fiber: 0 g
Sugar: 2 g

CHICKEN-CRANBERRY SALAD

Dried cranberries add a sweet tartness to this main-dish salad.

1 cup cooked cubed chicken
1 cup sliced celery
¼ cup sweetened dried cranberries
½ cup nonfat plain yogurt

1. Mix chicken, celery and cranberries in large mixing bowl. Add ½ cup yogurt and toss lightly.

2. Season to taste with salt or salt substitute and freshly ground black pepper.

- - - - - - - - - - - - - - - - - - - -

Yield: 4 servings
Serving size: About ½ cup

Calories: 140
Protein: 20 g
Carbohydrate: 10 g
Fat: 2 g
Cholesterol: 49 mg
Sodium: 92 mg
Calcium: 81 mg
Dietary Fiber: less than 1 g
Sugar: 8 g

CHICKEN-WALDORF SALAD

Chicken and fruit are a delicious combination.

3 boneless skinless chicken breasts, cooked, cubed
1½ cups seedless red grapes, halved
2 red delicious apples, unpeeled, diced
½ cup light mayonnaise

1. Combine all ingredients and serve immediately or cover and refrigerate. To prevent browning, sprinkle apples with lemon juice or powdered ascorbic acid.

Flavor Perk: Add 1 cup diced celery.

- - - - - - - - - - - - - - - - - - - -

Yield: 6 servings
Serving size: About ⅔ cup

Calories: 239
Protein: 22 g
Carbohydrate: 17 g
Fat: 10 g
Cholesterol: 67 mg
Sodium: 173 mg
Calcium: 18 mg
Dietary Fiber: 2 g
Sugar: 14 g

MANDARIN SPINACH SALAD

2 cups fresh spinach, torn into pieces
⅓ cup slivered almonds, toasted
1 (11 ounce) can mandarin oranges, drained
Reduced fat red wine vinaigrette salad dressing to taste

1. Lightly toss spinach, almonds and oranges together. Add dressing to taste and toss gently.

2. Serve immediately.

Variation: Substitute romaine or other lettuce for the spinach.

- - - - - - - - - - - - - - - - - - - -

Yield: 6 servings
Serving size: About ½ cup

Calories (without dressing): 107
Protein: 2 g
Carbohydrate: 18 g
Fat: 4 g
Cholesterol: 0 mg
Sodium: 19 mg
Calcium: 34 mg
Dietary Fiber: 3 g
Sugar: less than 1 g

SPINACH SALAD WITH SHRIMP BITES

Try this main dish salad with no salad dressing – just a squeeze of lemon.

1 cup medium shrimp, cooked, drained
3 cups fresh spinach, stemmed, torn into bite-size pieces
½ cup sliced celery
Light or fat free Thousand Island salad dressing

1. Combine first three ingredients and toss lightly.

2. Add salad dressing and gently toss.

3. Serve immediately.

- - - - - - - - - - - - - - - - - - - -

Yield: 6 servings
Serving size: About ⅔ cup

Calories (without dressing): 45
Protein: 8 g
Carbohydrate: 1 g
Fat: less than 1 g
Cholesterol: 57 mg
Sodium: 91 mg
Calcium: 40 mg
Dietary Fiber: 2 g
Sugar: less than 1 g

STRAWBERRY HILL SPINACH SALAD

2 (10 ounce) packages fresh baby spinach, stemmed, torn into pieces
1 quart fresh strawberries, halved
¼ cup slivered almonds, toasted
Light or fat free poppy seed salad dressing to taste

1. In a large bowl, lightly toss spinach, strawberries and almonds. Add salad dressing to taste and toss lightly.

2. Serve immediately.

Variation: Substitute romaine or leaf lettuce for the spinach.

- - - - - - - - - - - - - - - -

Yield: 6 servings
Serving size: About 1 cup

Calories (without dressing): 85
Protein: 5 g
Carbohydrate: 11 g
Fat: 3 g
Cholesterol: 0 mg
Sodium: 228 mg
Calcium: 122 mg
Dietary Fiber: 5 g
Sugar: 6 g

BOSTON BIBB BITES

1 head Boston bibb lettuce, torn into bite-size pieces
1 (11 ounce) can mandarin oranges, drained
⅓ cup sunflower seeds, toasted
Fat free poppy seed dressing

1. Combine lettuce, oranges and sunflower seeds in salad bowl. Serve immediately or refrigerate until serving time.

2. Just before serving, toss lightly with dressing.

- - - - - - - - - - - - - - - - -

Yield: 6 servings
Serving size: About ⅔ cup

Calories: 74
Protein: 2 g
Carbohydrate: 10 g
Fat: 4 g
Cholesterol: 0 mg
Sodium: 179 mg
Calcium: 19 mg
Dietary Fiber: 1 g
Sugar: less than 1 g

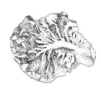

SWEET-SOUR BEAN SALAD

SWEET-SOUR SALAD DRESSING

This is an easy and different type of bean salad.

1¾ cups frozen wax beans
1 (14 ounce) can bean sprouts, rinsed, drained
¼ cup diced red bell pepper
Sweet-Sour Salad Dressing (p. 92)

1. Cook wax beans according to package directions. Mix wax beans, bean sprouts and bell pepper. Place in a shallow dish or large resealable plastic bag.

2. Pour Sweet-Sour Salad Dressing over vegetables. Cover and chill at least 2 hours.

Flavor Perk: Add ½ cup each sliced radishes and sliced celery.

Variation: Substitute 3 tablespoons diced pimiento for the red bell pepper.

- - - - - - - - - - - - - - - - - - - -

Yield: 4 servings
Serving size: About ⅔ cup

Calories (without dressing): 29
Protein: 2 g
Carbohydrate: 5 g
Fat: 0 g
Cholesterol: 0 mg
Sodium: 39 mg
Calcium: 23 mg
Dietary Fiber: 2 g
Sugar: 3 g

½ cup white wine vinegar
1 tablespoon reduced sodium soy sauce
2 tablespoons olive or vegetable oil
Sugar substitute to taste

1. Mix ingredients until well blended.

- - - - - - - - - - - - - - - - - - - -

Yield: 6 servings (About ¾ cup)
Serving size: 2 tablespoons

Calories: 49
Protein: less than 1 g
Carbohydrate: less than 1 g
Fat: 5 g
Cholesterol: 0 mg
Sodium: 85 mg
Calcium: 2 mg
Dietary Fiber: 0 g
Sugar: less than 1 g

SUNFLOWER SALAD

To reduce calories, add half the package of Swiss cheese.

1 large head romaine lettuce
6 green onions and tops, chopped
1 (8 ounce) package shredded reduced fat Swiss cheese
¼ cup sunflower seeds, toasted

1. Tear the lettuce into bite-size pieces.

2. Add remaining ingredients and toss.

3. Serve with low calorie balsamic or raspberry vinaigrette dressing.

- - - - - - - - - - - - - - - - - -

Yield: 6 servings
Serving size: About ⅔ cup

Calories: 158
Protein: 12 g
Carbohydrate: 4 g
Fat: 11 g
Cholesterol: 27 mg
Sodium: 92 mg
Calcium: 355 mg
Dietary Fiber: 1 g
Sugar: less than 1 g

FRESH CRUNCHY ROMAINE SALAD

1 head romaine lettuce, torn into bite-size pieces
1 zucchini, sliced
1 (8 ounce) can sliced water chestnuts, rinsed, drained
⅓ cup fat free Italian salad dressing or fresh low calorie dressing of choice

1. Toss lettuce, zucchini and water chestnuts.

2. When ready to serve, add salad dressing and toss lightly.

Variation: Substitute mixed salad greens for the romaine lettuce.

- - - - - - - - - - - - - - - - - -

Yield: 6 servings
Serving size: About ⅔ cup

Calories: 27
Protein: 1 g
Carbohydrate: 8 g
Fat: 0 g
Cholesterol: 0 mg
Sodium: 164 mg
Calcium: 12 mg
Dietary Fiber: 1 g
Sugar: 2 g

ITALIAN ASPARAGUS SPEARS

Fresh asparagus, with its bright color and unique flavor, makes this a special salad.

1 pound fresh asparagus spears, cleaned, trimmed
Romaine lettuce leaves (to serve as a salad base), rinsed, dried
2 fresh tomatoes, sliced
Light or fat free Italian salad dressing

1. Cook fresh asparagus in boiling water for 5-6 minutes or steam until tender and drain. Chill asparagus. Arrange lettuce on 4 salad plates. Place chilled asparagus spears and tomato slices over lettuce.

2. Drizzle with salad dressing and serve immediately.

- - - - - - - - - - - - - - - - - -

Yield: 4 servings

Calories (without dressing): 39
Protein: 3 g
Carbohydrate: 5 g
Fat: less than 1 g
Cholesterol: 0 mg
Sodium: 20 mg
Calcium: 17 mg
Dietary Fiber: 2 g
Sugar: 4 g

CHILLED CRANBERRY SUNSHINE

2 cups fresh cranberries
1 small orange, peeled, chopped
Sugar substitute to equal 6 teaspoons sugar
2 (4 serving) packages sugar free orange or cranberry gelatin

1. In food processor or blender, combine cranberries, orange and sweetener and process until finely chopped.

2. Dissolve gelatin in 2 cups boiling water; cool at least 10 minutes. Stir cranberry mixture into gelatin, and add ½ cup cold water.

3. Transfer to a 6-cup serving dish. Refrigerate until firm.

- - - - - - - - - - - - - - - - - - -

Yield: 12 servings (About 6 cups)
Serving size: ½ cup

Calories: 16
Protein: less than 1 g
Carbohydrate: 4 g
Fat: 0 g
Cholesterol: 0 mg
Sodium: 8 mg
Calcium: 11 mg
Dietary Fiber: 1 g
Sugar: 1 g

ABOUT GELATIN SALADS

The gelatin salad recipes you'll find in this cookbook are made with flavored, sugar free low calorie gelatin mixes. A .3 ounce package of gelatin mix yields 4 (½ cup) servings. Many recipes call for 2 (4 serving) packages of gelatin mix.

A general rule of thumb is to add up to 1½ cups of fruits or vegetables per 4-serving size prepared gelatin. When adding ingredients, most recipes specify chilling the liquid gelatin 20-40 minutes (or to the texture of unbeaten egg whites) before folding in additional ingredients. With the gelatin salad recipes, the approximate yield in number of cups is given so that you can decide what size and type of container to use for chilling and serving the salad.

If the gelatin gels or thickens too much to stir in additions, place container over a large bowl of warm water and stir to thin. Chill again until gelatin reaches desired consistency of unbeaten egg whites.

For a gelatin mixture to fully "set" or gel, refrigerate a 4-serving recipe about 3 hours. Allow 4-6 hours or overnight for larger amounts.

To unmold a gelatin salad, gently loosen gelatin around the edges of the mold with a spatula. Dip mold in warm water to the rim for just a few seconds. Another way to loosen is to press a warm, wet towel around the mold. Once loosened, tilt and rotate the mold to let air in. Place serving platter upside down over mold. Holding platter and mold together, invert and shake gently. Carefully lift off mold.

Gelatin salads generally stay fresh 24 hours to 3 days in the refrigerator.

CHERRY-BERRY SALAD

2 (4 serving) packages sugar free cranberry or cherry gelatin
1 (8 ounce) carton light sour cream
1 (16 ounce) can whole berry cranberry sauce
1 (8 ounce) can crushed pineapple in juice, undrained

1. In a heat resistant mixing bowl, pour 1½ cups boiling water over gelatin and stir to dissolve. Cool to room temperature. Stir in sour cream, cranberry sauce and pineapple.

2. Pour into a 6-cup serving dish. Refrigerate until firm.

- - - - - - - - - - - - - - - - - - -

Yield: 12 servings (About 6 cups)
Serving size: ½ cup

Calories: 97
Protein: less than 1 g
Carbohydrate: 19 g
Fat: 2 g
Cholesterol: 7 mg
Sodium: 23 mg
Calcium: 20 mg
Dietary Fiber: less than 1 g
Sugar: 17 g

WHIPPED PINEAPPLE FLUFF

1 (20 ounce) can crushed pineapple in juice, juice reserved
2 (4 serving) packages sugar free raspberry gelatin
1 cup reduced fat small curd cottage cheese, drained
1 (8 ounce) carton lite frozen whipped topping, thawed

1. In a saucepan, heat pineapple juice and enough water to equal 2 cups. Bring to a boil; add gelatin and mix well.

2. Transfer to a mixing bowl and refrigerate until gelatin is partially set. Fold in cottage cheese and whipped topping.

3. Pour into an 8-cup serving dish. Refrigerate until firm.

- - - - - - - - - - - - - - - - - - -

Yield: 16 servings (About 8 cups)
Serving size: ½ cup

Calories: 64
Protein: 2 g
Carbohydrate: 9 g
Fat: 2 g
Cholesterol: less than 1 mg
Sodium: 63 mg
Calcium: 14 mg
Dietary Fiber: less than 1 g
Sugar: 7 g

CREAMY PINEAPPLE WHIP

1 (20 ounce) can crushed
pineapple in juice, juice reserved
2 (4 serving) packages sugar free
lemon gelatin
1 (8 ounce) package reduced fat
cream cheese, softened
1 (8 ounce) carton lite frozen
whipped topping, thawed

1. In a saucepan, heat pineapple juice and enough water to equal 1½ cups. Bring to a boil; then pour over gelatin in heat resistant mixing bowl, stirring to dissolve. Cool to room temperature.

2. Using food processor or mixer, beat cream cheese until creamy. Add crushed pineapple and beat together until well blended. Fold in cooled gelatin mixture. Chill until partially set.

3. Fold in whipped topping and pour into an 8-cup serving dish. Refrigerate until firm.

- - - - - - - - - - - - - - - - - -

Yield: 16 servings (About 8 cups)
Serving size: ½ cup

Calories: 47
Protein: 2 g
Carbohydrate: 7 g
Fat: less than 1 g
Cholesterol: 1 mg
Sodium: 87 mg
Calcium: 33 mg
Dietary Fiber: less than 1 g
Sugar: 6 g

CHILLED ORANGE SURPRISE

Using prepackaged finely shredded (angel hair) cabbage speeds preparation time.

2 (4 serving) packages sugar free
orange gelatin
3 cups orange juice, divided
1 (8 ounce) can crushed pineapple
in juice, undrained
2 cups finely shredded cabbage

1. Sprinkle gelatin over 1 cup orange juice in a saucepan. Heat until gelatin is dissolved.

2. Stir in remaining orange juice, transfer to a mixing bowl and chill until slightly thickened.

3. Fold in pineapple and cabbage; blend well.

4. Pour into a 6 to 8-cup serving dish. Refrigerate until firm.

- - - - - - - - - - - - - - - - - - -

Yield: 12 servings (About 6 cups)
Serving size: ½ cup

Calories: 43
Protein: less than 1 g
Carbohydrate: 10 g
Fat: less than 1 g
Cholesterol: 0 mg
Sodium: 7 mg
Calcium: 15 mg
Dietary Fiber: less than 1 g
Sugar: 9 g

PINE-APPLESAUCE JELL

This is an out-of-the-pantry gelatin salad.

2 cups unsweetened Granny
  Smith or regular applesauce
2 (4 serving) packages sugar free
  lime gelatin
1 (12 ounce) can diet lemon lime
  carbonated drink
1 (8 ounce) can crushed pineapple
  in juice, undrained

1. Heat applesauce in a large saucepan.

2. Add gelatin to the hot applesauce
   and stir until dissolved. Add ½ cup
   cold water, lemon lime drink and
   crushed pineapple and juice.

3. Pour into a 6-cup serving dish.
   Refrigerate until firm.

- -

Yield: 12 servings (About 6 cups)
Serving size: ½ cup

Calories: 29
Protein: less than 1 g
Carbohydrate: 8 g
Fat: 0 g
Cholesterol: 0 mg
Sodium: 7 mg
Calcium: 4 mg
Dietary Fiber: less than 1 g
Sugar: 3 g

APPLE CIDER CRUNCH

2 cups apple cider or apple juice
1 (4 serving) package sugar free
  lemon gelatin
1 large Red Delicious apple,
  unpeeled, diced
½ cup sliced celery

1. Bring apple cider or juice to boiling; add gelatin and stir to dissolve. Transfer to a mixing bowl
   and refrigerate until partially set.

2. Stir in apple and celery and pour
   into a 4 or 5-cup serving dish. Refrigerate until firm.

- -

Yield: 8 servings (About 4 cups)
Serving size: ½ cup

Calories: 45
Protein: less than 1 g
Carbohydrate: 10 g
Fat: 0 g
Cholesterol: 0 mg
Sodium: 18 mg
Calcium: 12 mg
Dietary Fiber: less than 1 g
Sugar: 9 g

GRANNY'S TIDBITS

Granny Smith apples give a tart, crisp flavor to this salad.

2 (4 serving) packages sugar free
lemon gelatin
1 (20 ounce) can pineapple tidbits
in juice, undrained
1 cup unpeeled, diced Granny
Smith or other tart apple
1 cup chopped celery

1. Dissolve gelatin in 1½ cups boiling water in heat resistant mixing bowl. Add pineapple and refrigerate until slightly thickened.

2. Fold in remaining ingredients. Pour into a 6-cup serving dish. Refrigerate until firm.

- - - - - - - - - - - - - - - - -

Yield: 12 servings (About 6 cups)
Serving size: ½ cup

Calories: 30
Protein: less than 1 g
Carbohydrate: 7 g
Fat: 0 g
Cholesterol: 0 mg
Sodium: 19 mg
Calcium: 8 mg
Dietary Fiber: less than 1 g
Sugar: 6 g

CALYPSO CHILL

1 (20 ounce) can crushed
pineapple in juice, juice reserved
2 (4 serving) packages sugar free
lime gelatin
1 cup reduced fat cottage cheese,
drained
1 banana, peeled, sliced

1. Combine reserved juice from crushed pineapple and enough water to equal 1 cup. Heat to boiling in saucepan.

2. Remove juice mixture from heat and pour into heat resistant mixing bowl. Add gelatin and stir to dissolve. Add ½ cup cold water. Refrigerate until partially set.

3. Gently stir in crushed pineapple, cottage cheese and banana.

4. Pour into a 6 to 8-cup serving dish. Refrigerate until firm.

- - - - - - - - - - - - - - - - - - -

Yield: 12 servings (About 6 cups)
Serving size: ½ cup

Calories: 51
Protein: 3 g
Carbohydrate: 10 g
Fat: less than 1 g
Cholesterol: less than 1 mg
Sodium: 81 mg
Calcium: 19 mg
Dietary Fiber: less than 1 g
Sugar: 9 g

CREAMY ORANGE WHIP

1 (15 ounce) can light sliced pears, drained, juice reserved
2 (4 serving) packages sugar free orange gelatin
1 (8 ounce) package reduced fat cream cheese, softened
1 (8 ounce) carton lite frozen whipped topping

1. Bring pear juice and ½ cup water to boiling. Pour over gelatin in a heat resistant mixing bowl and stir until dissolved. Refrigerate until slightly thickened.

2. In a food processor or mixer, beat cream cheese until creamy. Add pears and beat until well blended. Fold chilled gelatin mixture into pear mixture, then gently fold whipped topping into mixture.

3. Spoon into an 8-cup serving dish. Refrigerate until firm.

- - - - - - - - - - - - - - - - - -

Yield: 16 servings (About 8 cups)
Serving size: ½ cup

Calories: 83
Protein: 2 g
Carbohydrate: 7 g
Fat: 5 g
Cholesterol: 10 mg
Sodium: 68 mg
Calcium: 0 mg
Dietary Fiber: 0 g
Sugar: 5 g

DOUBLE ORANGE FAVORITE

This is a quick and easy all-time favorite gelatin salad.

1 (16 ounce) carton reduced fat cottage cheese, drained
2 (4 serving) packages sugar free orange gelatin
2 (11 ounce) cans mandarin oranges, drained
1 (8 ounce) carton lite frozen whipped topping, thawed

1. Sprinkle gelatin over cottage cheese; mix well to dissolve the gelatin. Stir in oranges. Fold in thawed whipped topping.

2. Mound into an 8-cup serving dish.

3. Refrigerate at least 1 hour before serving.

- - - - - - - - - - - - - - - - - - - -

Yield: 16 servings (About 8 cups)
Serving size: ½ cup

Calories: 46
Protein: 4 g
Carbohydrate: 6 g
Fat: less than 1 g
Cholesterol: 1 mg
Sodium: 123 mg
Calcium: 22
Dietary Fiber: less than 1 g
Sugar: 1 g

STRAWBERRY FRUIT STACK

This is an attractive layered salad.

2 (4 serving) packages sugar free
  strawberry gelatin
2½ cups or 2 (10 ounce) packages
frozen sliced strawberries, thawed
3 bananas, peeled and sliced
1 (8 ounce) carton light sour
  cream

1. Dissolve gelatin in 1¼ cups boiling water; mix well. Cool 10 minutes and stir in strawberries.

2. In a 6 or 8-cup serving dish, place
   sliced bananas. Pour ½ gelatin
   mixture over bananas. Chill until
   firm. Spread sour cream over firm
   gelatin.

3. Gently pour remaining gelatin
   mixture over sour cream. Refrigerate until firm.

- - - - - - - - - - - - - - - - - - -

Yield: 12 servings (About 6 cups)
Serving size: ½ cup

Calories: 62
Protein: 1 g
Carbohydrate: 10 g
Fat: 3 g
Cholesterol: 7 mg
Sodium: 15 mg
Calcium: 21 mg
Dietary Fiber: 1 g
Sugar: 6 g

CREAMY FRESH STRAWBERRY WHIP

1 (24 ounce) carton reduced fat
small curd cottage cheese, drained
2 (4 serving) packages sugar free
  strawberry gelatin
1 (8 ounce) carton fat free or lite
frozen whipped topping, thawed
1½ cups fresh strawberries, sliced

1. Combine cottage cheese with dry
   gelatin and mix well. Fold in
   whipped topping and strawberries.

2. Refrigerate at least 1 hour before
   serving.

- - - - - - - - - - - - - - - - - - -

Yield: 16 servings (About 8 cups)
Serving size: ½ cup

Calories: 43
Protein: 5 g
Carbohydrate: 4 g
Fat: less than 1 g
Cholesterol: 2 mg
Sodium: 180 mg
Calcium: 28 mg
Dietary Fiber: less than 1 g
Sugar: 2 g

STRAWBERRY-RHUBARB SALAD

Fresh rhubarb is available for a relatively long period of time – January through June. One pound of fresh rhubarb yields about 2 cups cooked. To prepare, discard leaves and use only the stalks.

**2 cups diced fresh or frozen rhubarb, partially thawed
Sugar substitute equal to ½ to ¾ cup sugar
1 (4 serving) package sugar free strawberry gelatin
1½ cups lite frozen whipped topping, thawed**

1. In a saucepan, bring rhubarb, sweetener to taste and ¼ cup water to a boil. Reduce heat and simmer, uncovered, 3-5 minutes or until rhubarb is soft.

2. Remove from heat; stir in gelatin until dissolved. Pour into mixing bowl and refrigerate 30 minutes or until partially set.

3. Fold in whipped topping; transfer to a 4-cup serving dish. Refrigerate until firm.

- - - - - - - - - - - - - - - - - -

Yield: 8 servings (About 4 cups)
Serving size: ½ cup

Calories: 47
Protein: less than 1 g
Carbohydrate: 7 g
Fat: 2 g
Cholesterol: 0 mg
Sodium: 6 mg
Calcium: 60 mg
Dietary Fiber: less than 1 g
Sugar: 2 g

TANGY LIME CHILL

Cucumber and onion combined with lime-flavored gelatin and sour cream result in a uniquely-flavored salad.

**1 (4 serving) package sugar free low calorie lime gelatin
2 cucumbers, peeled
1 tablespoon minced or grated onion
1 cup reduced fat sour cream**

1. Dissolve gelatin in ¾ cup boiling water; mix well. Cool to room temperature.

2. Slice cucumbers in half and remove seeds. Grate cucumbers and add to cooled gelatin along with onion and sour cream.

3. Pour into a 4 to 5-cup dish. Refrigerate until firm.

- - - - - - - - - - - - - - - - - -

Yield: 8 servings (About 4 cups)
Serving size: ½ cup

Calories: 50
Protein: 1 g
Carbohydrate: 3 g
Fat: 4 g
Cholesterol: 12 mg
Sodium: 20 mg
Calcium: 41 mg
Dietary Fiber: less than 1 g
Sugar: 0 g

GARDEN FRESH CRUNCH

Prepackaged finely shredded cabbage is a convenience in the preparation of this gelatin salad.

2 (4 serving) packages sugar free lemon gelatin
3 cups finely shredded (angel hair) cabbage or coleslaw mix
½ cup green bell pepper, finely chopped
1 cup shredded carrot

1. In a heat resistant mixing bowl, pour 2½ cups boiling water over gelatin. Stir to dissolve and refrigerate until partially set. Gently stir cabbage, bell pepper and shredded carrot into gelatin.

2. Pour gelatin mixture into an 8-cup serving dish.

3. Refrigerate until firm.

- - - - - - - - - - - - - - - - - - - -

Yield: 16 servings (About 8 cups)
Serving size: ½ cup

Calories: 7
Protein: less than 1 g
Carbohydrate: 1 g
Fat: 0 g
Cholesterol: 0 mg
Sodium: 6 mg
Calcium: 8 mg
Dietary Fiber: less than 1 g
Sugar: less than 1 g

TROPICAL CHILL

2 (4 serving) packages sugar free orange gelatin
1 cup grated carrots
1 (20 ounce) can crushed pineapple in juice, undrained
¾ cup sweetened dried cranberries

1. Dissolve gelatin in 1 cup boiling water and mix well. Cool; then add carrots, pineapple, and cranberries.

2. Pour into a 6-cup serving dish. Refrigerate until firm.

- - - - - - - - - - - - - - - - - - -

Yield: 12 servings (About 6 cups)
Serving size: ½ cup

Calories: 50
Protein: less than 1 g
Carbohydrate: 13 g
Fat: 0 g
Cholesterol: 0 mg
Sodium: 6 mg
Calcium: 5 mg
Dietary Fiber: less than 1 g
Sugar: 12 g

FAVORITE WALDORF SALAD

2 Red or Golden Delicious apples,
unpeeled, cored, diced
1 cup diced celery
¼ cup raisins or dried cranberries
2 tablespoons light or fat free
mayonnaise

1. Combine all ingredients in medium bowl and toss lightly. Serve immediately or refrigerate.

Flavor Perk: Serve as individual salads on lettuce leaves. Garnish each salad with 1 teaspoon sunflower seeds or soy nuts.

- - - - - - - - - - - - - - - - - -

Yield: 6 servings
Serving size: About ½ cup

Calories: 68
Protein: less than 1 g
Carbohydrate: 14 g
Fat: 2 g
Cholesterol: 2 mg
Sodium: 64 mg
Calcium: 21 mg
Dietary Fiber: 2 g
Sugar: 11 g

FRUIT BITES

Figs were one of the earliest cultivated fruits. Spanish missionaries first cultivated figs in California, where domestic commercial figs are still grown today due to the state's favorable climate.

Fully ripe, fresh figs should be fairly soft to the touch. They are extremely perishable; a sour odor indicates that they are overripe.

3 red apples, unpeeled
8 fresh or dried figs, quartered
3 navel oranges, peeled, sliced,
juice reserved
Fruit salad dressing of your choice

1. Core apples and cut into thin wedges. Sprinkle apple wedges with juice from sliced oranges to prevent browning.

2. Arrange apple wedges, figs and orange slices on a large serving platter or individual salad plates. Serve immediately.

Flavor Perk: Place leaf lettuce on platter or individual plates before placing fruit.

Variation: Substitute chopped dates or prunes for the figs.

- - - - - - - - - - - - - - - - - -

Yield: 6 servings
Serving size: About ⅔ cup fruit

Calories: 138
Protein: 2 g
Carbohydrate: 35 g
Fat: less than 1 g
Cholesterol: 0 mg
Sodium: 3 mg
Calcium: 69 mg
Dietary Fiber: 7 g
Sugar: 31 g

CREAMY APPLE GRAPES

Vanilla yogurt contributes a sweet, tangy creaminess to this salad.

2 Red or Golden Delicious apples, cored, unpeeled, diced
¼ cup sunflower seeds, toasted
½ cup green grapes
⅓ cup low fat vanilla yogurt

1. Combine all ingredients in a mixing bowl, and toss until well blended.

2. Transfer to serving bowl and refrigerate.

- - - - - - - - - - - - - - - - - - -

Yield: 6 servings
Serving size: About ⅔ cup

Calories: 81
Protein: 2 g
Carbohydrate: 13 g
Fat: 3 g
Cholesterol: less than 1 mg
Sodium: 52 mg
Calcium: 30 mg
Dietary Fiber: 2 g
Sugar: 11 g

SUMMERTIME APPLE CRUNCH

Delicious apples, either Red or Golden, are considered the best salad and eating-out-of-hand apples. The five knobs on the blossom end identify these all-purpose apples.

To keep apples from browning, sprinkle with lemon juice or powdered ascorbic acid.

2 Red Delicious apples, unpeeled, cored, coarsely chopped
1 cup seedless green grapes, halved
1 cup chopped celery
⅓ cup light mayonnaise

1. Combine all ingredients and chill.

Variation: Substitute Golden Delicious apples and red seedless grapes for the Red Delicious apples and green grapes.

- - - - - - - - - - - - - - - - - - -

Yield: 6 servings
Serving size: About ⅔ cup

Calories: 96
Protein: less than 1 g
Carbohydrate: 15 g
Fat: 5 g
Cholesterol: 4 mg
Sodium: 113 mg
Calcium: 21 mg
Dietary Fiber: 2 g
Sugar: 12 g

SWEET AND TART MIXED GREENS

4 cups mixed salad greens, torn
into bite-size pieces
3 fresh green onions and tops,
thinly sliced
2 Red Delicious apples, unpeeled,
coarsely chopped
½ cup light poppy seed dressing

1. Combine salad greens, onions and
apples.

2. Drizzle with dressing and toss
lightly.

- - - - - - - - - - - - - - - - - - -

Yield: 6 servings
Serving size: About ⅔ cup

Calories: 81
Protein: less than 1 g
Carbohydrate: 9 g
Fat: 5 g
Cholesterol: 2 mg
Sodium: 89 mg
Calcium: 29 mg
Dietary Fiber: 2 g
Sugar: 7 g

SUNSHINE FRUIT SLAW

*Prepackaged shredded cabbage and slaw
mixes are a great convenience for adding
this healthful and ever-popular
ingredient to salads and vegetable dishes.*

1 (8 ounce) can pineapple tidbits
in juice, undrained
3 cups finely shredded green
cabbage
1½ cups unpeeled, coarsely
chopped Red Delicious or Gala
apples
¾ cup light mayonnaise

1. Drain pineapple, reserving 3 tablespoons juice. Combine pineapple,
cabbage and apple in a large bowl.
Add dressing quickly after cutting
apple so the apple will not darken.

2. Combine reserved juice and mayonnaise; add to cabbage mixture,
tossing gently. Cover and chill.

Flavor Perk: Add ½ cup chopped celery.

- - - - - - - - - - - - - - - - - - -

Yield: 10 servings
Serving size: About ½ cup

Calories: 99
Protein: less than 1 g
Carbohydrate: 12 g
Fat: 6 g
Cholesterol: 6 mg
Sodium: 112 mg
Calcium: 15 mg
Dietary Fiber: 2 g
Sugar: 9 g

PEACHY FRUIT SALAD

Children and adults alike love this creamy, delicious fruit-marshmallow combination.

**2 (21 ounce) cans light no sugar added peach pie filling
1 (20 ounce) can pineapple chunks in juice, drained
1 (11 ounce) can mandarin oranges, drained
1 cup miniature marshmallows**

1. Combine all ingredients in large bowl and fold together gently.

2. Chill at least 1 hour before serving.

Flavor Perk: Add 1 sliced banana.

- - - - - - - - - - - - - - - - - -

Yield: 15 servings
Serving size: About ½ cup

Calories: 70
Protein: less than 1 gram
Carbohydrate: 18 grams
Fat: less than 1 gram
Cholesterol: 0 milligrams
Sodium: 5 milligrams
Calcium: 8 milligrams
Dietary Fiber: less than 1 gram
Sugar: 13 grams

CREAMY PINEAPPLE DELIGHT

Try this new variation of the traditional carrot-raisin salad.

**2 cups grated carrot
1 cup crushed pineapple in juice, drained
¼ cup plain fat free yogurt
2 tablespoons light mayonnaise**

1. Combine carrot and drained pine-apple in medium bowl. In a separate bowl, stir together yogurt and mayonnaise.

2. Pour yogurt mixture over carrot mixture and toss.

3. Cover and refrigerate at least one hour before serving.

Flavor Perk: Add 2 tablespoons raisins and 1 tablespoon lemon juice.

- - - - - - - - - - - - - - - - - - - -

Yield: 6 servings
Serving size: About ½ cup

Calories: 60
Protein: less than 1 g
Carbohydrate: 11 g
Fat: 2 g
Cholesterol: 2 mg
Sodium: 51 mg
Calcium: 6 mg
Dietary Fiber: 2 g
Sugar: 9 g

CREAMY APRICOT SALAD

1 (15 ounce) can crushed pineapple in juice, undrained
1 (8 serving) package apricot gelatin
2 cups buttermilk
1 (12 ounce) carton fat free frozen whipped topping

1. Bring pineapple and juice to a boil. Add gelatin and stir until well dissolved. Cool completely.

2. When mixture begins to thicken, add buttermilk; then fold in whipped topping.

3. Pour into a 9 x 13-inch glass dish and refrigerate.

4. Cut into squares to serve.

- - - - - - - - - - - - - - - - - - - -

Yield: 6 servings (About 12 squares)
Serving size: 2 squares

Calories: 121
Protein: 3 grams
Carbohydrate: 25 grams
Fat: less than 1 gram
Cholesterol: 3 milligrams
Sodium: 119 milligrams
Calcium: 95 milligrams
Dietary Fiber: less than 1 gram
Sugar: 19 grams

EASY FRUIT MIX

This easy salad is a good choice for potluck dinners and buffets.

2 (20 ounce) cans pineapple tidbits in juice, drained
1 (16 ounce) can whole cranberry sauce
2 (11 ounce) cans mandarin oranges, drained
1 (8 ounce) carton light frozen whipped topping, thawed

1. Combine pineapple, cranberries and oranges. Fold in thawed whipped topping.

2. Chill at least 1 hour before serving.

- - - - - - - - - - - - - - - - - - - -

Yield: 15 servings
Serving size: About ½ cup

Calories: 119
Protein: less than 1 g
Carbohydrate: 29 g
Fat: less than 1 g
Cholesterol: 0 mg
Sodium: 7 mg
Calcium: 15 mg
Dietary Fiber: 1 g
Sugar: 23 g

FUN KIWI MIX

Available year-round, kiwis are an elegant and beautiful fruit with green, velvety flesh and a sweet, tart flavor. Because they do not darken as other fruits do, they can be peeled and sliced hours before serving.

Use a vegetable peeler to remove the fuzzy brown peel, then slice crosswise.

4 kiwi fruit, peeled, sliced horizontally
1 cup seedless red grapes, halved
2 ripe bananas, sliced
Low fat poppy seed salad dressing

1. In a large bowl, combine kiwi, grapes and bananas; mix gently. Cover tightly and refrigerate ½ hour. Serve with salad dressing.

Flavor Perk: Sprinkle salad with ¼ cup finely chopped walnuts or pecans.

Variation: Substitute 1 can pineapple chunks in juice, drained, for the bananas.

- - - - - - - - - - - - - - - - - - - -
Yield: 4 servings
Serving size: About ⅔ cup

Calories: 135
Protein: 2 g
Carbohydrate: 32 g
Fat: 1 g
Cholesterol: 0 mg
Sodium: 3 g
Calcium: 38 mg
Dietary Fiber: 4 g
Sugar: 25 g

MELON BOAT PLEASURE

Serve this salad when cantaloupes are in peak season. A slice of juicy cantaloupe is always a welcome sight at breakfast, lunch or dinner.

A perfectly ripe cantaloupe should have no greenish cast. The flower end should yield slightly to pressure and give off a pleasant melon aroma. Avoid shriveled or green, hard melons.

2 just-ripe cantaloupes, chilled
4 cups red and green seedless grapes, chilled
1 cup fat free mayonnaise
⅓ cup orange juice and 2 teaspoons orange zest (finely grated orange peel)

1. Cut each melon to form 6 sections, and remove seeds and rind. Place on separate salad plates.

2. Heap grapes over and around the cantaloupe sections.

3. Combine mayonnaise, juice and zest. Mix well and drizzle over fruit.

Flavor Perk: Place green or red leaf lettuce on salad plates before adding melon and grapes.

- - - - - - - - - - - - - - - - - - - -
Yield: 12 servings
Serving size: 1 cantaloupe section

Calories: 87
Protein: 1 g
Carbohydrate: 21 g
Fat: less than 1 g
Cholesterol: 0 mg
Sodium: 169 mg
Calcium: 17 mg
Dietary Fiber: 1 g
Sugar: 19 g

LACEY MELON SALAD

2 cups romaine lettuce, washed, drained, torn into bite-size pieces
1 cup cubed honeydew melon
1 cup cubed cantaloupe
1 lime, quartered

1. Toss lettuce and melon cubes in a salad bowl. Serve immediately or refrigerate until serving time.

2. Squeeze lime juice over salad just before serving.

Variation: Substitute honey-lime dressing for lime juice.

- -

Yield: 6 servings
Serving size: About ⅔ cup

Calories: 26
Protein: less than 1 g
Carbohydrate: 7 g
Fat: less than 1 g
Cholesterol: 0 mg
Sodium: 7 mg
Calcium: 15 mg
Dietary Fiber: 1 g
Sugar: 5 g

NOTES

SALAD DRESSINGS

Which oils are healthful choices?

Oils vary in types and amounts of saturated fats, monounsaturated fats and polyunsaturated fats. According to scientific studies, oils high in saturated fats lead to health problems. On the other hand, oils high in monounsaturated or polyunsaturated fats and low in saturated fats are healthier choices.

Listed below are a few examples based on this simple comparison:

Healthful Choices
High in Monounsaturated
and/or Polyunsaturated Fats

- Canola oil
- Corn oil
- Olive oil
- Peanut oil
- Soybean oil
- Sunflower oil

Less Healthful Choices
High in Saturated Fats

- Coconut Oil
- Palm Oil

QUICK RASPBERRY VINAIGRETTE DRESSING

⅓ cup seedless low sugar raspberry preserves or raspberry all-fruit spread
½ cup red wine vinegar
¼ cup olive or vegetable oil

1. Stir ingredients together until well blended. Add ¼ teaspoon salt or salt substitute.

- -

Yield: 8 servings (About 1 cup)
Serving size: 2 tablespoons

Calories: 76
Protein: 0 g
Carbohydrate: 4 g
Fat: 7 g
Cholesterol: 0 mg
Sodium: 0 mg
Calcium: 0 mg
Dietary Fiber: 0 g
Sugar: 3 g

DIJON VINAIGRETTE

1 tablespoon olive or vegetable oil
1 tablespoon garlic-flavored red wine vinegar
2 teaspoons Dijon-style mustard
1 tablespoon fresh chopped parsley

1. Combine oil, vinegar and mustard. Add parsley, 2 tablespoons water, salt or salt substitute and freshly ground black pepper to taste.

2. Place in a container with a tightly-fitting lid and shake vigorously. Shake again before serving.

- -

Yield: 2 servings (About ¼ cup)
Serving size: 2 tablespoons

Calories: 67
Protein: less than 1 g
Carbohydrate: less than 1 g
Fat: 7 g
Cholesterol: less than 1 mg
Sodium: 29 mg
Calcium: 9 mg
Dietary Fiber: less than 1 g
Sugar: 0 g

DIJON-ONION SALAD DRESSING

1 tablespoon Dijon-style mustard
1 tablespoon minced yellow, white
   or red onion
3 tablespoons white wine or red
   wine vinegar
¼-½ cup olive or vegetable oil

1. Stir ingredients together in a small bowl to blend. Place in a shaker bottle to use and store. Olive oil will separate under refrigeration.

2. Remove from refrigerator before use and shake to blend.

Flavor Perk: Use an herb-seasoned oil; sweeten to taste with sugar substitute or honey.

Variations: Add ⅛-¼ cup honey, 4 teaspoons poppy seed and ¾ teaspoon ground mace. For spicier flavors, add ½ teaspoon Worcestershire sauce, ½ teaspoon liquid hot pepper sauce and dash freshly ground black pepper.

- - - - - - - - - - - - - - - - - -

Yield: 6 servings (About ¾ cup)
Serving size: 2 tablespoons

Calories: 85
Protein: 0 g
Carbohydrate: less than 1 g
Fat: 9 g
Cholesterol: 0 mg
Sodium: 58 mg
Calcium: less than 1 mg
Dietary Fiber: 0 g
Sugar: 0 g

BALSAMIC VINAIGRETTE DRESSING

The characteristic dark color and fruity sweetness of Italian-made balsamic vinegars result from years of aging white grape juices in wooden barrels. New types of Italian-imported balsamic vinegars now available in supermarkets include white balsamic vinegars – blends of Italian white wine vinegars and white grapes.

½ cup olive or vegetable oil
⅓ cup dark or white balsamic
   vinegar
1 tablespoon snipped fresh basil
or ½ teaspoon dried basil, crushed
1 teaspoon Dijon-style mustard

1. Add ingredients to a tightly covered container and shake vigorously. Add ⅛ teaspoon freshly ground black pepper. Shake again before serving.

Flavor Perk: Add 1 finely minced or pressed garlic clove and sugar substitute to taste.

Variation: Orange Balsalmic Vinaigrette – Reduce balsamic vinegar to 3 tablespoons and add ¼ cup fresh orange juice and ½ teaspoon finely grated orange peel.

- - - - - - - - - - - - - - - - - -

Yield: 6 servings (About ¾ cup)
Serving size: 2 tablespoons

Calories: 178
Protein: 0 g
Carbohydrate: 4 g
Fat: 18 g
Cholesterol: 0 mg
Sodium: 22 mg
Calcium: 2 mg
Dietary Fiber: 0 g
Sugar: 4 g

RED WINE VINAIGRETTE DRESSING I

1 tablespoon Dijon-style mustard
¼ cup red wine vinegar
Sugar substitute equal to 1 teaspoon sugar
⅛-¼ cup olive or canola oil

1. In a blender or food processor, place mustard, vinegar, sugar substitute, ¼ cup water and ½ teaspoon freshly ground black pepper. Process until blended; then add 2-3 drops of oil at a time until well blended.

2. Place dressing in a bottle with tightly-fitting lid. Serve immediately or store in refrigerator 2-3 days. Shake before serving.

Flavor Perk: Use a seasoned vinegar or herbed oil of your choice.

- - - - - - - - - - - - - - - - - - - -

Yield: 6 servings (About ¾ cup)
Serving size: 2 tablespoons

Calories: 43
Protein: 0 g
Carbohydrate: 0 g
Fat: 5 g
Cholesterol: 0 mg
Sodium: 58 mg
Calcium: 2 mg
Dietary Fiber: 0 g
Sugar: 0 g

RED WINE VINAIGRETTE DRESSING II

½ cup red wine vinegar
2 tablespoons olive oil
½ clove garlic, finely minced
1 tablespoon finely chopped fresh parsley or 2 teaspoons dried parsley flakes

1. Combine all ingredients in a bottle with tightly-fitting lid and shake vigorously.

Flavor Perk: Add pinch dried tarragon or oregano leaves.

- - - - - - - - - - - - - - - - - - - -

Yield: 6 servings (About ¾ cup)
Serving size: 2 tablespoons

Calories: 40
Protein: 0 g
Carbohydrate: less than 1 g
Fat: 5 g
Cholesterol: 0 mg
Sodium: less than 1 g
Calcium: 1 g
Dietary Fiber: 0 g
Sugar: 0 g

ORANGE VINAIGRETTE DRESSING

1 orange, peeled, cut up and 1 tablespoon grated orange peel
1 tablespoon olive or canola oil
1 tablespoon cider vinegar
2 tablespoons fresh parsley, finely chopped

1. Place orange, peel, oil and vinegar in blender with salt or salt substitute to taste. Process until well blended.

2. Stir in parsley.

- - - - - - - - - - - - - - - - - -

Yield: 5 servings (About ⅔ cup)
Serving size: 2 tablespoons

Calories: 37
Protein: less than 1 g
Carbohydrate: 3 g
Fat: 3 g
Cholesterol: 0 mg
Sodium: less than 1 g
Calcium: 13 mg
Dietary Fiber: less than 1 g
Sugar: 2 g

RED WINE VINEGAR DRESSING

1 tablespoon olive or vegetable oil
1 tablespoon garlic-flavored red wine vinegar
¼ cup reduced sodium fat free chicken or vegetable broth
1-2 teaspoons dried oregano, crumbled

1. Stir all ingredients together. Add salt or salt substitute and freshly ground black pepper to taste. Place in a container with a tightly-fitting lid and shake vigorously.

2. Serve immediately or cover and refrigerate. Shake again before serving.

- - - - - - - - - - - - - - - - - -

Yield: 2 servings

Calories: 64
Protein: less than 1 g
Carbohydrate: less than 1 g
Fat: 7 g
Cholesterol: 0 mg
Sodium: 78 mg
Calcium: 12 mg
Dietary Fiber: less than 1 g
Sugar: less than 1 g

RICE VINEGAR DRESSING

⅓ cup olive or vegetable oil
⅓ cup rice vinegar or distilled
white vinegar
Sugar substitute to equal 3-4
teaspoons sugar
½ teaspoon freshly ground black
pepper

1. Mix ingredients in a jar with a
tightly-fitting lid. Shake vigorously
to blend.

- - - - - - - - - - - - - - - - - - - -

Yield: 6 servings (About ¾ cup)
Serving size: 2 tablespoons

Calories: 114
Protein: 0 g
Carbohydrate: less than 1 g
Fat: 12 g
Cholesterol: 0 mg
Sodium: 1 mg
Calcium: 9 mg
Dietary Fiber: 0 g
Sugar: less than 1 g

FRUITED VINEGAR DRESSING

½ cup vegetable oil
¼ cup raspberry or other fruit-
flavored vinegar
Sugar substitute to equal 2
tablespoons sugar
½ teaspoon dry mustard

1. Combine ingredients and blend
well.

*Flavor Perk: Add ½ teaspoon paprika and 1
green onion with top, finely chopped.*

- - - - - - - - - - - - - - - - - - - -

Yield: 6 servings (About ¾ cup)
Serving size: 2 tablespoons

Calories: 162
Protein: 0 g
Carbohydrate: less than 1 g
Fat: 18 g
Cholesterol: 0 mg
Sodium: less than 1 mg
Calcium: 4 mg
Dietary Fiber: 0 g
Sugar: 0 mg

ZERO CALORIE DRESSING

½ cup vinegar (red wine, white wine, apple cider or rice)
½ clove garlic, finely minced or pressed
1 tablespoon chopped fresh parsley
⅛ teaspoon dried oregano or tarragon leaves

1. Place all ingredients in a bottle and shake to blend. Add salt or salt substitute to taste.

- - - - - - - - - - - - - - - - - -

Yield: 4 servings (About ½ cup)
Serving size: 2 tablespoons

Calories: 1
Protein: 0 g
Carbohydrate: less than 1 g
Fat: 0 g
Cholesterol: 0 mg
Sodium: less than 1 g
Calcium: 3 mg
Dietary Fiber: 0 g
Sugar: 0 g

ORANGE-BASIL DRESSING

½ cup fresh orange juice and 1 tablespoon finely grated orange peel
¼-½ cup vegetable oil
1 tablespoon fresh chopped basil leaves or 1-2 teaspoons dried basil leaves, crumbled
Sugar substitute to taste

1. Mix orange juice, peel, oil and basil until well blended. Add sugar substitute to taste.

- - - - - - - - - - - - - - - - - -

Yield: 6 servings (About ¾ cup)
Serving size: 2 tablespoons

Calories: 90
Protein: less than 1 g
Carbohydrate: 2 g
Fat: 9 g
Cholesterol: 0 mg
Sodium: less than 1 mg
Calcium: 11 mg
Dietary Fiber: less than 1 g
Sugar: 0 g

SWEET-SOUR SALAD DRESSING

⅓ cup apple cider vinegar
Sugar substitute to equal 2 tablespoons sugar
¼ cup olive or vegetable oil
2 tablespoons Dijon-style mustard

1. In a small saucepan, combine ingredients and 1 teaspoon freshly ground black pepper. Bring to boiling; remove from heat and cool to room temperature.

Flavor Perk: Add ½-1 teaspoon finely minced garlic or ⅛-¼ teaspoon hot pepper sauce.

- -

Yield: 4 servings (About ½ cup)
Serving size: 2 tablespoons

Calories: 135
Protein: 0 g
Carbohydrate: 2 g
Fat: 14 g
Cholesterol: 0 mg
Sodium: 174 mg
Calcium: 24 mg
Dietary Fiber: 0 g
Sugar: 0 g

HONEY-MUSTARD DRESSING

This is delicious over citrus fruits combined with salad greens.

¼ cup canola oil
3 tablespoons cider vinegar
1½ tablespoons Dijon-style mustard
2 teaspoons honey

1. Mix all ingredients until well blended.

Flavor Perk: Add ¼ teaspoon dried tarragon leaves.

- -

Yield: 4 servings (About ½ cup)
Serving size: 2 tablespoons

Calories: 138
Protein: 0 g
Carbohydrate: 4 g
Fat: 14 g
Cholesterol: 0 mg
Sodium: 130 mg
Calcium: less than 1 mg
Dietary Fiber: 0 g
Sugar: 3 g

ROASTED RED PEPPER DRESSING

⅓ cup olive or vegetable oil
3 tablespoons white wine vinegar
2 green onions and tops, finely chopped
2 tablespoons chopped roasted red pepper

1. Place ingredients in a tightly-covered container and shake to blend. Shake again before serving.

Flavor Perk: Add 1 tablespoon capers.

Variation: Substitute diced, drained pimiento for the roasted red pepper.

- -

Yield: 4 servings (About ½ cup)
Serving size: 2 tablespoons

Calories: 166
Protein: less than 1 g
Carbohydrate: less than 1 g
Fat: 18 g
Cholesterol: 0 mg
Sodium: 2 mg
Calcium: 7 mg
Dietary Fiber: less than 1 g
Sugar: less than 1 g

RED CHILE DRESSING

½ cup olive or vegetable oil
⅓ cup red wine or white wine vinegar
1 teaspoon chili powder
1 teaspoon snipped fresh cilantro or ⅛ teaspoon ground cumin

1. Place all ingredients in a tightly-covered container and shake to blend. Shake again before serving.

Flavor Perk: Add ½ teaspoon garlic powder and ⅛ teaspoon crushed red pepper flakes.

- -

Yield: 6 servings (About ¾ cup)
Serving size: 2 tablespoons

Calories: 162
Protein: less than 1 g
Carbohydrate: less than 1 g
Fat: 18 g
Cholesterol: 0 mg
Sodium: 5 mg
Calcium: 2 mg
Dietary Fiber: less than 1 g
Sugar: 0 g

LIME-CILANTRO DRESSING

This is a taste-as-you-go salad dressing. Start with small ingredient amounts and add larger quantities as desired.

¼-½ cup olive or vegetable oil
¼-⅓ cup fresh lime juice
2-3 tablespoons snipped fresh
   cilantro leaves
½-1 teaspoon ground cumin

1. Add ingredients to a tightly covered container. Shake vigorously until well blended. Season to taste with salt or salt substitute and freshly ground black pepper.

2. Shake again before serving.

Flavor Perk: Add ½-1 finely chopped or pressed garlic clove.

Variation: Substitute white vinegar for the lime juice.

- - - - - - - - - - - - - - - - - - - -

Yield: 6 servings (About ¾ cup)
Serving size: 2 tablespoons

Calories: 85
Protein: less than 1 g
Carbohydrate: 1 g
Fat: 9 g
Cholesterol: 0 mg
Sodium: less than 1 mg
Calcium: 5 mg
Dietary Fiber: less than 1 g
Sugar: 0 g

LEMON-BELL PEPPER DRESSING

Try this dressing mixed with hearty bean or pasta salads.

1 tablespoon olive or canola oil
2 tablespoons lemon juice and 2
   teaspoons finely grated peel
½ cup fresh parsley, chopped
1 tablespoon green or red bell
   pepper, finely chopped

1. Mix ingredients and add salt or salt substitute and freshly ground black pepper to taste.

- - - - - - - - - - - - - - - - - - - -

Yield: 4 servings (About ½ cup)
Serving size: 2 tablespoons

Calories: 35
Protein: less than 1 g
Carbohydrate: 1 g
Fat: 3 g
Cholesterol: 0 mgr
Sodium: 4 mg
Calcium: 11 mg
Dietary Fiber: less than 1 g
Sugar: less than 1 g

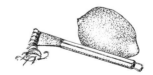

FRESH LEMON JUICE DRESSING

½ cup olive oil or canola oil
¼ cup fresh lemon juice
¼ teaspoon dry mustard
1 tablespoon fresh chopped parsley or 1 teaspoon dried parsley leaves, crumbled

1. Place ingredients in a tightly-covered container and shake vigorously. Add salt or salt substitute and freshly ground black pepper to taste. Shake again before serving.

- - - - - - - - - - - - - - - - - - - -

Yield: 6 servings (About ¾ cup)
Serving size: 2 tablespoons

Calories: 162
Protein: 0 g
Carbohydrate: less than 1 g
Fat: 18 g
Cholesterol: 0 mg
Sodium: less than 1 mg
Calcium: 2 mg
Dietary Fiber: 0 g
Sugar: less than 1 g

FRESH TOMATO SALAD DRESSING

1 ripe tomato, unpeeled
1-2 tablespoons olive or vegetable oil
1 tablespoon red wine vinegar
1-2 teaspoons fresh chopped basil or ½ teaspoon dry basil leaves

1. In a medium saucepan over high heat, bring to boiling enough water to cover tomato. Carefully drop tomato in boiling water and continue boiling until skin of tomato begins to peel back. Remove immediately and plunge into cold or ice water.

2. With a small knife, remove tomato stem and peel skin. Dice the tomato and mix thoroughly with oil, vinegar and basil.

Variation: Add a dash of dry mustard, freshly ground black pepper and 1 tablespoon fresh chopped parsley.

- - - - - - - - - - - - - - - - - - - -

Yield: 6 servings (About ¾ cup)
Serving size: 2 tablespoons

Calories: 24
Protein: less than 1 g
Carbohydrate: less than 1 g
Fat: 2 g
Cholesterol: 0 mg
Sodium: 2 mg
Calcium: 1 mg
Dietary Fiber: less than 1 g
Sugar: less than 1 g

POPPY SEED DRESSING

This dressing is delicious over fruits or salad greens.

1 tablespoon poppy seeds
¼-½ cup vegetable oil
⅓ cup honey
¼-½ cup fresh lemon juice

1. Place ingredients in a tightly covered container. Shake vigorously to blend.

2. Shake again before serving.

- - - - - - - - - - - - - - - - - - - -

Yield: 8 servings (About 1 cup)
Serving size: 2 tablespoons

Calories: 169
Protein: less than 1 g
Carbohydrate: 12 g
Fat: 14 g
Cholesterol: 0 mg
Sodium: less than 1 mg
Calcium: 17 mg
Dietary Fiber: less than 1 g
Sugar: 12 g

BLUE CHEESE SALAD DRESSING

1 ounce blue cheese, crumbled
1 tablespoon light or fat free mayonnaise
2 tablespoons reduced fat or fat free small curd cottage cheese
¼ cup buttermilk

1. Stir ingredients together and season to taste with salt or salt substitute and freshly ground black pepper.

Flavor Perk: Add pinch of garlic powder and/or snipped chives or green onion tops.

Variation: For a smoother dressing, blend mayonnaise, cottage cheese and buttermilk in a blender or food processor; add crumbled blue cheese.

- - - - - - - - - - - - - - - - - - - -

Yield: 4 servings (About ½ cup)
Serving size: 2 tablespoons

Calories: 49
Protein: 3 g
Carbohydrate: 2 g
Fat: 3 g
Cholesterol: 7 mg
Sodium: 166 mg
Calcium: 60 mg
Dietary Fiber: 0 g
Sugar: 1 g

LITE BUTTERMILK DRESSING

This is a lighter version of the ever-popular buttermilk dressing.

¾ cup light or fat free mayonnaise
½ cup buttermilk
¼ teaspoon garlic powder or 1 garlic clove, minced
¼ teaspoon onion powder or 1 teaspoon grated onion

1. Mix all ingredients thoroughly. Season to taste with salt or salt substitute and freshly ground black pepper.

2. Cover and refrigerate at least 2 hours to blend flavors.

- - - - - - - - - - - - - - - - - -

Yield: 8 servings (About 1 cup)
Serving size: 2 tablespoons

Calories: 81
Protein: less than 1 g
Carbohydrate: 4 g
Fat: 8 g
Cholesterol: 8 mg
Sodium: 151 mg
Calcium: 18 g
Dietary Fiber: 0 g
Sugar: 1 g

BUTTERMILK-GARLIC DRESSING

1-2 tablespoons vegetable oil
2 tablespoons fresh lemon juice and 2 teaspoons finely grated lemon peel
⅓ cup buttermilk
Pinch finely minced or pressed garlic clove or ⅛ teaspoon garlic powder

1. Mix ingredients together until well blended. Add pinch salt or salt substitute and freshly ground black pepper.

Flavor Perk: 2-3 tablespoons snipped chives, green onion tops, ¼ cup chopped parsley or other fresh herb.

- - - - - - - - - - - - - - - - - -

Yield: 4 servings (About ½ cup)
Serving size: 2 tablespoons

Calories: 42
Protein: less than 1 g
Carbohydrate: 2 g
Fat: 4 g
Cholesterol: less than 1 mg
Sodium: 22 mg
Calcium: 26 mg
Dietary Fiber: less than 1 g
Sugar: 1 g

BUTTERMILK-BLUE CHEESE DRESSING

¾ cup buttermilk
2 tablespoons light mayonnaise
1 tablespoon blue or feta cheese, crumbled
1 tablespoon chopped fresh parsley or fresh herb of your choice

1. Place all ingredients in a jar with a tight-fitting lid. Cover and shake well.

Variation: Use 1½ teaspoons each of feta and blue cheese, crumbled. Substitute 1 teaspoon dried parsley or other dried herb for the fresh herbs.

- - - - - - - - - - - - - - - - - - - -

Yield: 8 servings (About 1 cup)
Serving size: 2 tablespoons

Calories: 32
Protein: less than 1 g
Carbohydrate: 2 g
Fat: 2 g
Cholesterol: 2 mg
Sodium: 68 mg
Calcium: 29 mg
Dietary Fiber: 0 g
Sugar: 1 g

COTTAGE CHEESE SALAD DRESSING

¼ cup low fat or fat free cottage cheese
¼ cup buttermilk
2 teaspoons fresh lemon juice
½-1 tablespoon canola oil

1. Mix ingredients with a wire whisk or in the blender. Add a pinch salt or salt substitute and a pinch of freshly ground black pepper.

Flavor Perk: Add 1 teaspoon chopped fresh parsley or other fresh herb of your choice.

- - - - - - - - - - - - - - - - - - - -

Yield: 4 servings (About ½ cup)
Serving size: 2 tablespoons

Calories: 32
Protein: 2 g
Carbohydrate: 1 g
Fat: 2 g
Cholesterol: 1 mg
Sodium: 74 mg
Calcium: 27 mg
Dietary Fiber: 0 g
Sugar: 1 g

CREAMY GARLIC DRESSING

For garlic lovers – adjust amount of garlic to suit your own tastes.

$\frac{1}{2}$-1 finely minced or pressed
  garlic clove
$\frac{1}{2}$ cup nonfat plain yogurt
1 tablespoon rice vinegar
2 tablespoons olive or vegetable
  oil

1. Place all ingredients in a blender or food processor. Pulse until dressing is smooth (will be slightly thin).

2. Season to taste with salt or salt substitute and freshly ground black pepper.

- - - - - - - - - - - - - - - - - -

Yield: 6 servings (About $\frac{3}{4}$ cup)
Serving size: 2 tablespoons

Calories: 33
Protein: 1 g
Carbohydrate: 2 g
Fat: 2 g
Cholesterol: less than 1 g
Sodium: 16 mg
Calcium: 42 mg
Dietary Fiber: 0 g
Sugar: 1 g

SPICY GREEN CHILE SALAD DRESSING

Green chiles give a Southwestern flair to this full-flavored salad dressing.

$\frac{1}{2}$-$\frac{3}{4}$ cup light mayonnaise
5 tablespoons white wine or rice
  vinegar
1 (4 ounce) can diced green chiles,
  drained, amount to suit taste
1-2 teaspoons chili powder

1. Mix all ingredients to blend.

Flavor Perk: Add $\frac{1}{4}$ teaspoon ground cumin.

- - - - - - - - - - - - - - - - - - - -

Yield: 8 servings (About 1 cup)
Serving size: 2 tablespoons

Calories: 83
Protein: less than 1 g
Carbohydrate: 4 g
Fat: 8 g
Cholesterol: 8 mg
Sodium: 184 mg
Calcium: 14 mg
Dietary Fiber: less than 1 g
Sugar: 1 g

CREAMY ONION SALAD DRESSING

1 cup plain nonfat yogurt
¼ cup light or fat free mayonnaise
Onion powder to taste
½ cup skim milk

1. Mix yogurt and mayonnaise until smooth. Stir in onion powder and salt or salt substitute to taste. Stir in ½ cup skim milk or more until dressing is of desired consistency.

2. Serve immediately or cover and refrigerate.

Flavor Perk: Add 2 tablespoons green onions and tops, chopped; add 1 tablespoon chopped fresh parsley or herb of your choice.

- - - - - - - - - - - - - - - - - -

Yield: 10 servings (About 1½ cups)
Serving size: 2 tablespoons

Calories: 54
Protein: 3 g
Carbohydrate: 6 g
Fat: 2 g
Cholesterol: 3 mg
Sodium: 415 mg
Calcium: 79 mg
Dietary Fiber: 0 g
Sugar: 3 g

SKINNY GODDESS DRESSING

1 cup nonfat plain yogurt
½ cup light or fat free mayonnaise
2 teaspoons white wine vinegar
2 green onions and tops, coarsely chopped

1. Place all ingredients in blender or food processor. Pulse until smooth. Season to taste with salt or salt substitute and freshly ground black pepper.

2. Serve immediately or cover and refrigerate.

Flavor Perk: Add 2 tablespoons coarsely chopped parsley to the blender or food processor.

- - - - - - - - - - - - - - - - - -

Yield: 10 servings (About 1½ cups)
Serving size: 2 tablespoons

Calories: 56
Protein: 1 g
Carbohydrate: 4 g
Fat: 4 g
Cholesterol: 4 mg
Sodium: 106 mg
Calcium: 51 mg
Dietary Fiber: 0 g
Sugar: 2 g

EASY EVERYDAY SALAD DRESSING

½ cup nonfat plain yogurt
2 tablespoons light mayonnaise
1 tablespoon lemon juice

1. Stir ingredients together until well blended. Add ⅛ teaspoon salt or salt substitute and pinch freshly ground black pepper.

Flavor Perk: Add 2 teaspoons snipped chives or green onion tops.

Variation: Mix ingredients in blender; add ½ cucumber, peeled, sliced.

- -

Yield: 5 servings (About ⅔ cup)
Serving size: 2 tablespoons

Calories: 34
Protein: 1 g
Carbohydrate: 3 g
Fat: 2 g
Cholesterol: 2 mg
Sodium: 55 mg
Calcium: 50 mg
Dietary Fiber: 0 g
Sugar: 2 g

CURRY SALAD DRESSING

1-2 tablespoons vegetable oil
1 tablespoon apple cider or white vinegar
⅓ cup buttermilk
¼ teaspoon curry powder

1. Stir ingredients together until well blended.

- -

Yield: 4 servings (About ½ cup)
Serving size: 2 tablespoons

Calories: 39
Protein: less than 1 g
Carbohydrate: 1 g
Fat: 4 g
Cholesterol: less than 1 m
Sodium: 21 mg
Calcium: 24 mg
Dietary Fiber: 0 g
Sugar: less than 1 g

RUSSIAN DRESSING

4 tablespoons light or fat free
mayonnaise
½ cup nonfat plain yogurt
4 tablespoons salsa or ketchup

1. Stir ingredients together and season to taste with salt or salt substitute.

- - - - - - - - - - - - - - - - - -

Yield: 8 servings (About 1 cup)
Serving size: 2 tablespoons

Calories: 35
Protein: less than 1 g
Carbohydrate: 2 g
Fat: 3 g
Cholesterol: 3 mg
Sodium: 74 mg
Calcium: 32 mg
Dietary Fiber: 0 g
Sugar: 1 g

ZESTY YOGURT SALAD DRESSING

1 cup nonfat plain yogurt
¾ tablespoon mustard seeds
⅓ cup snipped fresh cilantro
leaves
⅓ cup green onion and tops, finely
chopped

1. Combine ingredients and add salt or salt substitute to taste.

Flavor Perk: Add ⅛-¼ teaspoon ground cumin.

- - - - - - - - - - - - - - - - - -

Yield: 10 servings (About 1½ cups)
Serving size: 2 tablespoons

Calories: 22
Protein: 2 g
Carbohydrate: 3 g
Fat: less than 1 g
Cholesterol: less than 1 mg
Sodium: less than 1 mg
Calcium: 66 mg
Dietary Fiber: less than 1 g
Sugar: 1 g

SOUPS

By nature, soups soothe and restore our weariness or chills and revive our spirits! What is needed to make a soup? First of all, a pot, stirring spoon, and a ladle will be needed. As to ingredients--a rummage of the refrigerator, freezer, and pantry can spark your imagination to combine unusual ingredients or seasonings.

It may be that your craving for a comforting soup will be satisfied with a delicious, simple broth. Whether you want to prepare a hearty main dish soup or a simple, lean soup, you should find recipes to your liking in this section.

CHILLED ASPARAGUS SOUP

1 (10½ ounce) can cream of asparagus soup
⅔ cup plain nonfat yogurt
½ cucumber, peeled, seeded, finely chopped
2 tablespoons finely chopped red onion

1. Stir together soup, yogurt and 1 soup can water. Add cucumber and onion.

2. Season to taste with salt/salt substitute.

3. Chill at least 4 hours and serve in chilled bowls.

- - - - - - - - - - - - - - - - - - -

Yield: 4 servings
Serving size: About 1 cup

Calories: 28
Protein: 3 g
Carbohydrate: 4 g
Fat: less than 1 g
Cholesterol: less than 1 mg
Sodium: 32 g
Calcium: 86 mg
Dietary Fiber: less than 1 g
Sugar: 2 g

FROSTY CUCUMBER SOUP

Try a bowl of this chilled soup to cool off on those hot summer days.

3 cucumbers, peeled, seeded, cut into chunks
1 (14 ounce) can reduced sodium fat free chicken broth, divided
1 (8 ounce) carton light sour cream
3 tablespoons minced fresh chives or green onion chops

1. In blender or food processor, combine cucumbers, 1 cup chicken broth and dash salt or salt substitute. Cover and process until smooth.

2. Transfer to a medium bowl; stir in remaining chicken broth and sour cream.

3. Cover and chill well before serving. Garnish each serving with chives or green onions.

Flavor Perk: Add 2 teaspoons fresh minced dill or 1 teaspoon dried dill weed when processing.

- - - - - - - - - - - - - - - - - - -

Yield: 4 servings
Serving size: About 1 cup

Calories: 105
Protein: 6 g
Carbohydrate: 9 g
Cholesterol: 18 mg
Sodium: 297 mg
Calcium: 141 mg
Dietary Fiber: 2 g
Sugar: 4 g

CHILLED SUMMER SQUASH SOUP

1 onion, finely chopped
2 pounds yellow squash, ends removed, thinly sliced
1 (14 ounce) can reduced sodium fat free chicken broth
1 (8 ounce) package reduced fat cream cheese, softened, divided

1. Place onion in a sprayed medium saucepan. Cook and stir over medium heat until onion is tender. Add squash and broth; bring to a boil.

2. Cover, reduce heat and simmer 10 minutes or until squash is tender; cool.

3. In batches, process squash soup and cream cheese in food processor or blender until well blended and smooth. Season to taste with salt/salt substitute and freshly ground black pepper.

4. Cover and chill well before serving.

- - - - - - - - - - - - - - - - - -

Yield: 6 servings
Serving size: 1 cup

Calories: 135
Protein: 6 g
Carbohydrate: 10 g
Fat: 8 g
Cholesterol: 27 mg
Sodium: 334 mg
Calcium: 35 mg
Dietary Fiber: 3 g
Sugar: 4 g

CREAM OF ASPARAGUS SOUP

1 pound fresh asparagus
1½ cups reduced sodium fat free chicken broth
2 tablespoons finely chopped or grated onion
1 cup skim milk

1. Rinse asparagus and cut off or peel coarse portion. Cook asparagus quickly in 2 cups boiling water until tender. Drain, reserving 1 cup liquid.

2. Cut off and chop asparagus tips; set aside. Place reserved liquid, chicken broth and onion in a large saucepan. Bring to a boil, and add the asparagus. Reduce heat and simmer 5 minutes.

3. In batches, puree mixture in blender or food processor. Return to the saucepan; add milk and heat through. Season to taste with salt or salt substitute and freshly ground black pepper.

4. Sprinkle each serving with chopped asparagus tips.

- - - - - - - - - - - - - - - - - -

Yield: 4 servings
Serving size: 1 cup

Calories: 55
Protein: 6 g
Carbohydrate: 9 g
Fat: less than 1 g
Cholesterol: 1 mg
Sodium: 267 mg
Calcium: 100 mg
Dietary Fiber: 2 g
Sugar: 6 g

OLD SOUTHERN BLACK-EYED PEA SOUP

2 yellow onions, finely chopped
1 turnip, peeled, diced
1 (15 ounce) can black-eyed peas, rinsed, drained
7 cups reduced sodium fat free chicken or vegetable broth

1. To a sprayed 4-5 quart soup pot, add onions and sauté 2-3 minutes or until tender. Add turnip, peas and broth. Bring to a boil; reduce heat.

2. Cover and simmer 30 minutes or until turnip is tender. Season to taste with freshly ground black pepper.

Flavor Perk: Before serving, stir in ⅓ cup fresh chopped parsley, pinch ground cumin and 6 tablespoons fresh lemon juice.

- -

Yield: 6 servings
Serving size: 1 cup

Calories: 106
Protein: 6 g
Carbohydrate: 20 g
Fat: less than 1 g
Cholesterol: 0 mg
Sodium: 741 mg
Calcium: 104 mg
Dietary Fiber: 5 g
Sugar: 5 g

RED CABBAGE "FOR WHAT AILS YOU" SOUP

A similar soup is commonly used in France as a remedy for many illnesses.

½ red cabbage, finely shredded
8 tablespoons fresh lemon juice
8 cups reduced sodium vegetable broth or homemade vegetable broth

1. Place cabbage in a deep bowl. Sprinkle with lemon juice, salt/salt substitute and freshly ground black pepper to taste. Cover and let stand 1 hour, stirring occasionally.

2. Bring broth to a boil in a 4-5 quart soup pot. Add cabbage and any liquid in the bowl to the broth. Cook about 5 minutes.

3. Serve immediately.

- -

Yield: 8 servings
Serving size: About 1 cup

Calories: 42
Protein: 1 g
Carbohydrate: 10 g
Fat: less than 1 g
Cholesterol: 0 mg
Sodium: 29 mg
Calcium: 34 mg
Dietary Fiber: 3 g
Sugar: 5 g

PUREED FRESH BROCCOLI SOUP

Purees are sauce-like foods that have been mashed and strained. Use a food processor or blender to shorten preparation time.

**1 pound broccoli
1 onion, finely chopped or 3 medium garlic cloves,
finely minced or pressed
2½ cups reduced sodium fat free chicken broth, divided
1 cup skim milk**

1. Cut broccoli florets into bite-size pieces; peel stems and cut into ¼-inch slices.

2. In a sprayed saucepan, sauté onion or garlic about 3-4 minutes or until tender. Add 2 cups broth and broccoli; bring to a boil and reduce heat. Simmer, covered, until broccoli is tender, about 10 minutes.

3. Transfer the soup to a blender or food processor and add milk; puree. Return pureed soup to the saucepan. If a thinner soup is desired, add the reserved broth or water until soup reaches desired consistency.

4. Season to taste with salt/salt substitute and freshly ground black pepper. Reheat and serve.

Flavor Perk: Add ½ teaspoon red pepper flakes to the broth before pureeing.

Variation: Substitute 1 pound cauliflower pieces for the broccoli; season with 1 teaspoon curry powder. Another variation is to substitute 1 pound peeled and sliced carrots, using ¼ teaspoon ground cumin or ginger to season.

- -

Yield: 4 servings
Serving size: About 1 cup

Calories: 73
Protein: 8 g
Carbohydrate: 12 g
Fat: less than 1 g
Cholesterol: 1 mg
Sodium: 451 mg
Calcium: 135 mg
Dietary Fiber: 4 g
Sugar: 6 g

EASY CABBAGE SOUP

2 yellow onions, thinly sliced
2 stalks celery, thinly sliced
2 (16 ounce) packages coleslaw mix (green and red cabbage, carrots) or 1 large cabbage, shredded
2 teaspoons dried herb blend or herbes de Provence

1. To a sprayed 4-5 quart soup pot, add onions and celery and sauté 3-5 minutes, stirring continuously until vegetables soften. Add 2½ quarts water; bring to a boil.

2. Add cabbage; reduce heat and simmer, covered, 2 hours. Add water as needed.

3. Add dried herbs and season to taste with salt/salt substitute and freshly ground black pepper.

4. Cover and let stand about 30 minutes. Reheat and serve.

Flavor Perk: Add 2-3 reduced sodium vegetable or chicken bouillon cubes with the water.

- - - - - - - - - - - - - - - - - -

Yield: 8 servings
Serving size: About 1 cup

Calories: 40
Protein: 2 g
Carbohydrate: 9 g
Fat: less than 1 g
Cholesterol: 0 mg
Sodium: 30 m
Calcium: 63 mg
Dietary Fiber: 3 g
Sugar: 5 g

CARROT-LEEK SOUP

1 cup uncooked brown rice or barley
3 carrots, peeled, grated
2 leeks, white parts sliced
1 bay leaf

1. To a sprayed 4-5 quart soup pot over medium-high heat, add 1 cup rice or barley. Brown lightly, stirring continuously to avoid burning.

2. Add carrots, leeks, bay leaf and 7 cups water. Bring to a boil; then reduce heat and simmer covered 45-50 minutes or until rice or barley is tender, adding more water as needed.

3. Season to taste with salt/salt substitute and white pepper.

Flavor Perk: Add ½ cup fresh chopped parsley and 1 teaspoon low sodium chicken bouillon granules.

Variation: Substitute 2 sliced onions for the leeks.

- - - - - - - - - - - - - - - - - -

Yield: 6 servings
Serving size: 1 cup

Calories: 148
Protein: 3 g
Carbohydrate: 31 g
Fat: 1 g
Cholesterol: 0 mg
Sodium: 25 mg
Calcium: 24 mg
Dietary Fiber: 3 g
Sugar: 4 g

CARROT-GINGER SOUP

This easy soup is flavorful and satisfying.

1 large yellow onion, halved, thinly sliced
3 cups grated carrots (about 3 medium carrots) or 10-12 peeled baby carrots
2-3 teaspoons freshly grated ginger
4 cups reduced sodium fat free chicken broth or unsalted homemade chicken broth

1. To a sprayed 4-5 quart soup pot, add onion and sauté over medium heat about 3-4 minutes. Stir in carrots, ginger and 2-3 tablespoons water; continue cooking 3-4 minutes.

2. Add broth and bring to a boil. Cover. Reduce heat to low and simmer about 25 minutes. Check vegetables for tenderness. If needed, continue to cook, uncovered, until vegetables are very soft.

3. Strain soup into a large bowl, reserving vegetables. Return liquid to the soup pot. Puree the vegetables in a food processor or blender. Stir puree into liquid and reheat for serving.

4. Season to taste with salt/salt substitute.

- - - - - - - - - - - - - - -
Yield: 8 servings
Serving size: About ½ cup

Calories: 32
Protein: 2 g   Sodium: 326 mg
Carbohydrate: 6 g   Calcium: 15 mg
Fat: less than 1 g   Dietary Fiber: 15 mg
Cholesterol: 0 mg   Sugar: 4 g

CREAM OF CELERY SOUP

The tender, inner stalks of celery have a better consistency and flavor for this soup.

6 stalks (about 2 cups) celery, chopped
1 small onion, finely chopped
3 cups reduced sodium fat free chicken broth
1½ cups skim milk or evaporated skim milk

1. Place the celery and onion in a large saucepan sprayed with non-stick cooking spray. Sauté 3-4 minutes over medium heat until vegetables soften.

2. Add broth and bring to a boil. Reduce heat; cover partially and simmer about 30 minutes or until celery is very tender.

3. Puree in batches in a blender or food processor. Return to saucepan; add milk and reheat slowly. Season to taste with salt or salt substitute.

4. This soup may also be served cold.

- - - - - - - - - - - - - - -
Yield: 4 servings
Serving size: About 1 cup

Calories: 63
Protein: 6 g
Carbohydrate: 10 g
Fat: less than 1 g
Cholesterol: 2 mg
Sodium: 566 mg
Calcium: 143 mg
Dietary Fiber: 2 g
Sugar: 6 g

LENTIL SOUP

1 (10 ounce) package frozen seasoning blend (onion, celery, green and red peppers and parsley), partially thawed
2 (14½ ounce) cans no salt diced tomatoes
1½ cup dried lentils, rinsed, cleaned
7 cups reduced sodium broth (chicken, beef, or vegetable)

1. In a sprayed nonstick Dutch oven, sauté seasoning blend over medium heat 6-8 minutes, stirring constantly, until water evaporates and vegetables are tender.

2. Pulse tomatoes briefly in a blender or food processor to cut into smaller pieces. Add tomatoes, lentils and broth to the Dutch oven. Bring to a boil; then reduce heat to a simmer and cook for about 1 hour until lentils are tender.

3. Season to taste with salt or salt substitute and freshly ground black pepper.

Flavor Perk: *Add 1 teaspoon herbes de Provence or ½ teaspoon each thyme and marjoram leaves, crumbled.*
Variation: *To make a creamy lentil soup, puree cooked soup in a blender or food processor; then return to the Dutch oven. Add 1½ cups skim milk and heat over low heat, stirring until hot and blended.*

- - - - - - - - - - - - - - - - - - - -

Yield: 10 servings
Serving size: About 1 cup

Calories: 70
Protein: 5 g
Carbohydrate: 12 g
Fat: less than 1 g
Cholesterol: 0 mg
Sodium: 476 mg
Calcium: 19 mg
Dietary Fiber: 4 g
Sugar: 5 g

CREAMY MUSHROOM SOUP

1 pound fresh mushrooms, finely chopped
1 large carrot, peeled, julienned (cut in matchstick pieces)
2 large onions, thinly sliced
1 cup light or fat free sour cream

1. To a sprayed 4-5 quart soup pot, add mushrooms, carrot and onions. Sauté 3-4 minutes, stirring continuously. Add 6 cups water and bring to a boil.

2. Reduce heat; cover and simmer over low heat 30-40 minutes. Season to taste with salt/salt substitute and freshly ground black pepper.

3. Stir in sour cream; heat through, but do not boil. Serve immediately.

Flavor Perk: *Substitute 4 cups fat free chicken broth for the water. Garnish with finely chopped chives or green onion tops.*

- - - - - - - - - - - - - - - - - - - -

Yield: 8 servings
Serving size: ½ cup

Calories: 70
Protein: 4 g
Carbohydrate: 7 g
Fat: 4 g
Cholesterol: 10 mg
Calcium: 69 mg
Dietary Fiber: 1 g
Sugar: 4 g

POTATO-LEEK SOUP

2 (14 ounce) cans reduced sodium
    fat free chicken broth
3-4 red potatoes, peeled, chopped
2-3 leeks, cleaned, thinly sliced
Chopped chives or green onion tops

1. Combine broth, potatoes and
   leeks in a large soup pot. Bring to
   a boil; cover and simmer until vegetables are soft, about 30 minutes.
   Cool 10-15 minutes.

2. Strain vegetables from broth. Place
   2 cups strained vegetables and 1-2
   cups broth in a food processor or
   blender, and puree. Pour pureed
   vegetables and broth back into
   soup pot or, if desired, puree all
   remaining vegetables and broth.
   Season to taste with freshly ground
   black pepper and salt/salt substitute.

3. Garnish servings with chopped
   chives or green onion tops.

- - - - - - - - - - - - - - - - - - - -

Yield: 6 servings
Serving size: ½-¾ cup

Calories: 44
Protein: 3 g
Carbohydrate: 8 g
Fat: 0 g
Cholesterol: 0 mg
Sodium: 351 mg
Calcium: 23 mg
Dietary Fiber: 2 g
Sugar: 2 g

HOT PUMPKIN SOUP

*On cold, blustery days, warm up with a
bowl of this flavorful pumpkin soup.*

1 cup coarsely chopped yellow
    onion
2 teaspoons curry powder
3 cups reduced sodium fat free
    chicken broth
2 cups canned pumpkin

1. To a sprayed 4-5 quart soup pot,
   add onion and curry powder.
   Sauté over low heat 3-4 minutes.

2. Add chicken broth, and stir in
   pumpkin. Add ¼ teaspoon salt or
   salt substitute. Bring to a boil;
   then reduce heat to low. Simmer,
   uncovered, 25-30 minutes. Cool
   slightly.

3. Puree in a food processor, and return to pot. Reheat.

*Flavor Perk: Sauté 1 finely minced garlic clove
    and ⅛ teaspoon ground cumin with
    onion and curry powder.*

- - - - - - - - - - - - - - - - - - - -

Yield: 6 servings
Serving size: About 1 cup

Calories: 48
Protein: 3 g
Carbohydrate: 10 g
Fat: less than 1 g
Cholesterol: 0 mg
Sodium: 315 mg
Calcium: 30 mg
Dietary Fiber: 3 g
Sugar: 4 g

ROASTED RED-YELLOW PEPPER SOUP

This is a fragrant, full-bodied soup that is excellent for entertaining.

**1 each fresh large, smooth red and yellow bell pepper
4 finely minced or pressed garlic cloves
2 teaspoons olive oil
5 cups reduced sodium beef or vegetable broth
or homemade vegetable broth**

1. Cut peppers into quarters and place skin side up on rack of a broiler pan. Place the peppers 4-6 inches from broiling element and broil. When peppers begin to blacken in spots, turn the peppers about every 2 minutes, using long-handled tongs.

2. As each quarter blackens and shrivels, remove and place in a resealable plastic bag and close tightly. Allow peppers to cool; then peel skin away with a sharp knife. Cut peppers into long, thin strips and set aside.

3. Add garlic and oil to a 4-5 quart soup pot; sauté garlic about 1 minute. Add peppers and continue to sauté 1-2 minutes. Add broth; bring to a boil. Reduce heat and simmer, covered, about 30 minutes.

4. Season to taste with salt/salt substitute and freshly ground black pepper. Serve hot.

Flavor Perk: Add ⅓ teaspoon saffron to soup before simmering. Pour soup over a small slice of French bread in each soup bowl for serving.

Variation: Use 1-1½ cups jarred roasted red peppers to substitute for fresh peppers.

- -

Yield: 4 servings
Serving size: 1 cup

Calories: 82
Protein: 2 g
Carbohydrate: 15 g
Fat: 3 g
Cholesterol: 0 mg
Sodium: 35 mg
Calcium: 40 mg
Dietary Fiber: 4 g
Sugar: 5 g

FRESH SPINACH SOUP

½ cup uncooked long-grain white rice
5 cups reduced sodium fat free chicken broth, divided
1 pound fresh spinach, washed, stemmed
Lemon wedges

1. Cook rice according to package directions in 1 cup broth in a small saucepan. Set aside.

2. In a 4-5 quart soup pot, add remaining 4 cups broth and bring to a boil. Reduce heat to medium and add spinach; cook until spinach wilts. Remove from heat and add cooked rice.

3. Pour soup into food processor and puree. Strain through a wire mesh strainer. Reheat soup and season to taste with salt/salt substitute.

4. Serve with lemon wedges.

- - - - - - - - - - - - - - - - -

Yield: 5 servings
Serving size: About 1 cup

Calories: 44
Protein: 6 g
Carbohydrate: 6 g
Fat: less than 1 g
Cholesterol: 0 mg
Sodium: 728 mg
Calcium: 72 mg
Dietary Fiber: 8 g
Sugar: 1 g

GOLDEN BUTTERNUT SOUP

This is a golden, rich-tasting soup.

1 large onion, halved, thinly sliced
3 cups butternut squash, peeled, cubed
3 cups zucchini, peeled, cubed
2-3 cups reduced sodium fat free chicken broth, divided

1. In a sprayed 4-5 quart soup pot, sauté onion 2-3 minutes or until tender. Add butternut and zucchini cubes; sauté about 3-4 minutes. Add 2 cups chicken broth; then bring to a boil and reduce heat.

2. Cover and simmer 30 minutes or until vegetables are tender. If liquid begins to be absorbed by the vegetables, add additional broth to keep at 2-cup level.

3. Remove from heat and pour by batches into food processor or blender. Puree all batches; return to soup pot. Season to taste with salt/salt substitute and ground white pepper.

4. Reheat and serve hot.

Flavor Perk: *Add 1-2 teaspoons dried basil leaves, crushed, to pureed soup.*

- - - - - - - - - - - - - - - - -

Yield: 6 servings
Serving size: About 1 cup

Calories: 61
Protein: 3 g
Carbohydrate: 14 g
Fat: less than 1 g
Cholesterol: 0 mg
Sodium: 213 mg
Calcium: 54 mg
Dietary Fiber: 4 g
Sugar: 6 g

WINTER HARVEST SOUP

1 finely minced garlic clove
1½ cups butternut or acorn squash
3 cups reduced sodium free
chicken broth
1 teaspoon dried thyme, crumbled
or herbes de Provence, crumbled

1. To a sprayed 4-5 quart soup pot, add garlic and sauté 1 minute. Add squash, broth and thyme. Bring to a boil; reduce heat. Cover and simmer about 15 minutes or until squash is tender.

2. Remove from heat and cool 10-15 minutes. Add the mixture to a food processor or blender and pulse to puree. If a thinner soup is desired, add 1 tablespoon water at a time until soup reaches desired consistency.

3. Reheat and serve.

- - - - - - - - - - - - - - - - - -

Yield: 4 servings
Serving size: About 1 cup

Calories: 40
Protein: 3 g
Carbohydrate: 7 g
Fat: 0 g
Cholesterol: 0 mg
Sodium: 468 mg
Calcium: 29 mg
Dietary Fiber: less than 1 g
Sugar: 2 g

QUICK 'N EASY CLAM CHOWDER

½ cup finely chopped onion
¾ cup frozen hash brown
potatoes, partially thawed
1 (6½ ounce) can minced clams,
drained, liquid reserved
1 cup skim milk

1. In a sprayed saucepan, cook onions 2-3 minutes or until translucent. Add potatoes, reserved clam liquid and ¾ cup water.

2. Bring to a boil and cook until potatoes are tender, about 5-6 minutes. Reduce heat; then stir in clams and skim milk. Heat through, but do not boil.

3. Serve immediately.

- - - - - - - - - - - - - - - - - -

Yield: 3 servings
Serving size: About ½ cup

Calories: 112
Protein: 6 g
Carbohydrate: 14 g
Fat: 4 g
Cholesterol: 9 mg
Sodium: 234 mg
Calcium: 84 mg
Dietary Fiber: less than 1 g
Sugar: 3 g

HEARTY CHICKEN SOUP

The satisfying flavors of chicken broth, tomatoes and green chilies enhance the chicken and white beans in this recipe. For fewer calories, reduce white beans to 1 (15 ounce) can.

**2 (15 ounce) cans white (cannelli or great northern) beans, drained
2 (14½ ounce) cans fat free reduced sodium chicken broth
2 (10 ounce) cans mild diced tomatoes and green chiles, undrained
2 cups cooked chicken breast, cubed**

1. Combine beans, broth and tomatoes in large pot and bring to a boil. Reduce heat, cover and simmer 30 minutes. Season to taste with freshly ground black pepper and salt or salt substitute.

2. At serving time, add chicken and simmer for about 5 minutes. Serve hot.

Flavor Perk: Sprinkle each serving with fresh chopped cilantro and serve with a lime wedge.
Variations: Substitute 2 (6 ounce) packages grilled chicken breast strips for the cooked chicken breast. Another substitute for cooked chicken is 2-3 (5 ounce) cans 98% fat free chunk breast of chicken in water, drained.

- - - - - - - - - - - - - - - - - - - -

Yield: 6 servings
Serving size: About 1½ cups

Calories: 252
Protein: 27 g
Carbohydrate: 33 g
Fat: 2 g
Cholesterol: 36 mg
Sodium: 619 mg
Calcium: 117 mg
Dietary Fiber: 8 g
Sugar: 3 g

FASTEST TORTILLA SOUP

**4 (14 ounce) cans reduced sodium fat free chicken broth
1 (10 ounce) can no salt diced tomatoes and green chiles in sauce
1-2 teaspoons chili powder
8 ounces crushed baked tortilla chips**

1. Combine broth, tomatoes and green chiles and chili power in a large saucepan or Dutch oven. Simmer 30 minutes for flavors to blend.

2. When ready to serve, stir in tortilla chips or garnish each serving with chips.

Flavor Perk: Add ½ teaspoon ground cumin with chili powder. Sprinkle each serving with snipped fresh cilantro leaves.

- - - - - - - - - - - - - - - - - - - -

Yield: 8 servings
Serving size: About 1 cup

Calories: 130
Protein: 6 g
Carbohydrate: 25 g
Fat: 2 g
Cholesterol: 0 mg
Sodium: 730 mg
Calcium: 67 mg
Dietary Fiber: 3 g
Sugar: 2 g

SOUTH OF THE BORDER TOMATO SOUP

Keep the canned ingredients on hand for preparing this spicy, easy-to-make soup.

1 (10½ ounce) can tomato soup
1 (14½ ounce) can diced tomatoes
with basil, garlic and oregano
1 (10 ounce) can chopped
tomatoes and green chilies
Fresh cilantro leaves, snipped

1. Mix canned ingredients plus 1 soup can water in a saucepan and heat to boiling, stirring often. Reduce heat.

2. Add cilantro and season to taste with salt/salt substitute. Simmer 5 minutes.

- - - - - - - - - - - - - - - - - - - -

Yield: 10 servings
Serving size: About ½ cup

Calories: 30
Protein: 1 g
Carbohydrate: 6 g
Fat: less than 1 g
Cholesterol: 0 mg
Sodium: 366 mg
Calcium: 38 mg
Dietary Fiber: less than 1 g
Sugar: 3 g

CREAMY TOMATO-BEEF BROTH

1½ cups no added salt tomato juice
1 (14 ounce) can low sodium fat
free beef broth
1 cup skim or evaporated skim milk
1 teaspoon curry powder

1. Combine tomato juice and broth in a saucepan and heat to boiling. Reduce heat to low. Add skim milk and curry powder; stir until heated through. Do not boil.

2. Season to taste with salt/salt substitute.

3. Serve immediately.

Flavor Perk: Substitute herb or spice of your choice for the curry powder.

- - - - - - - - - - - - - - - - - - - -

Yield: 8 servings
Serving size: ½ cup

Calories: 25Protein: 2 g
Carbohydrate: 3 g
Fat: less than 1 g
Cholesterol: less than 1 mg
Sodium: 33 mg
Calcium: 43 mg
Dietary Fiber: less than 1 g
Sugar: 2 g

QUICK TOMATO-BEEF SOUP

1 (10½ ounce) can low sodium
    beef broth
1½ cups tomato juice
1 teaspoon Worcestershire sauce
½-1 tablespoon fresh basil or ½
    teaspoon dried basil leaves

1. Combine all ingredients in saucepan and bring to a boil. Reduce
   heat; then cover and simmer 2-3
   minutes.

- - - - - - - - - - - - - - - - - - -

Yield: 4 servings
Serving size: About ½ cup

Calories: 28
Protein: 2 g
Carbohydrate: 4 g
Fat: less than 1 g
Cholesterol: 0 mg
Sodium: 367 mg
Calcium: 13 mg
Dietary Fiber: less than 1 g
Sugar: 3 g

CREAMY TOMATO SOUP SURPRISE

*Choose smooth or chunky peanut butter
for this unusual and delicious soup.*

2 tablespoons finely chopped
    onion
1 (14 ounce) can reduced sodium
    fat free chicken broth, divided
2 tablespoons reduced fat peanut
    butter, smooth or chunky
1 (8 ounce) can no salt tomato
    sauce

1. In a sprayed saucepan over medium heat, cook and stir onion 1-
   2 minutes until translucent. Stir in
   ½ cup broth and peanut butter
   until well blended. Add remaining broth.

2. Reduce heat and simmer 7-8 minutes. Add tomato sauce and
   freshly ground black pepper to
   taste.

Flavor Perk: Serve with lime wedges.

- - - - - - - - - - - - - - - - - - -

Yield: 6 servings
Serving size: About ½ cup

Calories: 49
Protein: 2 g
Carbohydrate: 6 g
Fat: 2 g
Cholesterol: 0 mg
Sodium: 225 mg
Calcium: 2 mg
Dietary Fiber: 1 g
Sugar: 4 g

GARLIC-TOMATO SOUP

Using fresh garlic: Select a fresh head of garlic, and discard any cloves that have dried out. To easily remove outer dry layers from a fresh garlic clove, place the clove on a cutting board. Use a wide-bladed, large knife to crush the clove. Discard the outer layers. Place the clove, halved if large, in a garlic press and squeeze juice and bits of garlic from the press. Clean the press after each clove before pressing another clove.

To mince garlic, use a large sharp knife and thoroughly chop the clove into very fine bits. Large bits of garlic are unpleasant to encounter in a prepared dish.

**10 large garlic cloves, finely minced or pressed
¼ cup olive oil
7 cups reduced sodium fat free chicken or vegetable broth, divided
1 (15 ounce) can no salt tomato sauce**

1. Add garlic and oil to a 4-5 quart soup pot. Stirring continuously, sauté garlic over low heat 5-6 minutes or until fragrant and tender. Do not allow to brown. Add 3 cups broth and tomato sauce. Stir to blend.

2. Pour into blender or food processor and process until smooth. Return to soup pot and add remaining broth. Season to taste with salt/salt substitute and freshly ground black pepper.

3. Bring to a boil; then reduce heat and simmer, covered, about 30 minutes.

4. Serve hot.

Flavor Perk: Add 1 bay leaf to simmer with the soup. Remove bay leaf before serving.

- -

**Yield: 6 servings
Serving size: About 1 cup**

Calories: 123
Protein: 5 g
Carbohydrate: 6 g
Fat: 9 g
Cholesterol: 0 mg
Sodium: 738 mg
Calcium: 30 mg
Dietary Fiber: 1 g
Sugar: 5 g

QUICK N' EASY GAZPACHO

For entertaining, serve gazpacho in very cold demitasse cups or as a first course in a fresh tomato cup with an ice cube.

2 (14½ ounce) cans diced tomatoes with green pepper, celery and onions
1 cucumber, peeled, seeded, finely chopped
½ cup red wine vinaigrette

1. For a chunky gazpacho, simply combine fresh tomatoes, cucumber, and vinaigrette.

2. For a thinner gazpacho, place ingredients in food processor or blender and pulse once or twice. Season to taste with freshly ground black pepper and salt/salt-substitute. Refrigerate and serve cold.

Variation: To prepare tomato cups for serving this soup, choose ripe, firm tomatoes. Slice off the blossom end and, holding the tomato in your hand, carefully scoop out insides.

- - - - - - - - - - - - - - - - - -

Yield: 6 servings
Serving size: About ½ cup

Calories: 87
Protein: 2 grams
Carbohydrate: 9 grams
Fat: 5 grams
Cholesterol: 0 milligrams
Sodium: 697 milligrams
Calcium: 60 milligrams
Dietary Fiber: 2 grams
Sugar: 6 grams

HEARTY TOMATO-PASTA SOUP

1 cup frozen seasoning blend (onion, celery, bell pepper and parsley), partially thawed
3 (14 ounce) cans reduced sodium fat free chicken broth
1 (10 ounce) can Italian stewed tomatoes, undrained
1½ cups cooked fettuccine or linguine pasta

1. To a sprayed 4-5 quart soup pot, add seasoning blend and sauté 3-4 minutes over medium heat or until vegetables are tender and water evaporates.

2. Add chicken broth and tomatoes. Bring to a boil; then reduce heat and simmer about 15 minutes for the flavors to blend.

3. Add cooked pasta and heat through.

Flavor Perk: Sauté 1 finely minced or pressed garlic clove with the seasoning blend; add 1-2 teaspoons Italian herb blend.

- - - - - - - - - - - - - - - - - -

Yield: 8 servings
Serving size: About 1 cup

Calories: 61
Protein: 4 g
Carbohydrate: 10 g
Fat: less than 1 g
Cholesterol: 13 mg
Sodium: 460 mg
Calcium: 13 mg
Dietary Fiber: less than 1 g
Sugar: 3 g

"HOMEMADE" CHICKEN NOODLE SOUP

1 cup uncooked cholesterol free egg noodle substitute or egg free pasta ribbons, uncooked
6 cups reduced sodium fat free chicken broth
1 stalk celery, finely chopped
½ cup cooked chicken, cut in bite-size pieces

1. Prepare pasta according to package directions; drain. Bring broth to a boil and add celery.

2. Reduce heat; cover and simmer about 5 minutes. Add noodles and chicken and cook about 2-3 minutes.

3. Season to taste with salt/salt substitute and freshly ground black pepper.

Variation: Substitute ½ cup uncooked chicken for the cooked chicken. Cook in broth mixture until chicken is firm and fork-tender.

- - - - - - - - - - - - - - - - - -

Yield: 8 servings
Serving size: ¾ cup

Calories: 131
Protein: 9 g
Carbohydrate: 22 g
Fat: less than 1 g
Cholesterol: 7 mg
Sodium: 476 mg
Calcium: 3 mg
Dietary Fiber: less than 1 g
Sugar: 2 g

VERMICELLI-VEGETABLE SOUP

1 (16 ounce) package frozen seasoning blend (celery, onion, bell pepper and parsley), thawed
2 carrots, peeled, diced
3 (10½ ounce) cans reduced sodium fat free chicken or beef broth
3 ounces uncooked vermicelli or thin spaghetti

1. In a sprayed 4-5 quart soup pot, sauté seasoning blend and carrots 3-4 minutes, adding 2-3 tablespoons water if mixture begins to stick or scorch. Add broth and bring to a boil.

2. Reduce heat and simmer, covered, about 25 minutes. Add pasta and continue cooking another 10 minutes or until pasta is barely tender. Season to taste with salt/salt substitute and freshly ground black pepper.

Flavor Perk: Sauté 1 finely minced garlic clove with seasoning blend and carrots; add ½ cup chopped fresh parsley with the pasta.

- - - - - - - - - - - - - - - - - -

Yield: 6 servings
Serving size: About 1 cup

Calories: 94
Protein: 3 g
Carbohydrate: 18 g
Fat: 0 g
Cholesterol: 0 mg
Sodium: 416 mg
Calcium: 5 mg
Dietary Fiber: 2 g
Sugar: 5 g

HERBED ONION SOUP

This is a fragrant, flavorful soup distinctive enough to serve with an elegant dinner.

4 cups thinly sliced yellow onions (about 4 large)
1 teaspoon herbes de Provence (blend of rosemary, marjoram, thyme, sage, anise seed and savory) or herb blend of your choice
5½ cups reduced sodium vegetable broth or homemade vegetable broth
Dry sherry or sherry cooking wine

1. To a sprayed 4-5 quart soup pot, add onions and herbs. Sauté over medium heat about 10 minutes, adding 1-2 tablespoons water if mixture begins to stick.

2. Add vegetable broth and bring to a boil. Reduce heat; cover and simmer 25-30 minutes. Season to taste with freshly ground black pepper.

3. When ready to serve, splash 1-2 teaspoons sherry into each serving of soup.

- - - - - - - - - - - - - - - - - -

Yield: 5 servings
Serving size: About 1 cup

Calories: 93
Protein: 3 g
Carbohydrate: 20 g
Fat: less than 1 g
Cholesterol: 0 mg
Sodium: 34 mg
Calcium: 52 mg
Dietary Fiber: 5 g
Sugar: 8 g

EASY FRENCH ONION SOUP

2 tablespoons olive oil
6 large onions, thinly sliced
6 cups reduced sodium fat free chicken, beef or vegetable broth
½ cup grated reduced fat Swiss cheese

1. Add oil and onions to a 4-5 quart soup pot. Stirring continuously, sauté onions slowly over low to medium-low heat until golden brown and caramelized. Add broth, bring to a boil and boil for 5 minutes. Reduce heat; simmer 10 minutes. Season to taste with salt/salt substitute and freshly ground black pepper.

2. Serve very hot, and sprinkle each serving with 2-3 teaspoons cheese.

3. Bake 5-10 minutes or until cheese melts and begins to bubble. Serve immediately.

- - - - - - - - - - - - - - - - - -

Yield: 5-6 servings
Serving size: 1 cup

Calories: 156
Protein: 10 g
Carbohydrate: 11 g
Fat: 9 g
Cholesterol: 13 mg
Sodium: 646 mg
Calcium: 189 mg
Dietary Fiber: 2 g
Sugar: 4 g

Kitchen Helper Recipe

STEWED OR POACHED CHICKEN AND BROTH

Chicken prepared this way may be used in many different recipes that call for cooked chicken. The chicken will stay moist and flavorful for salads, sandwiches and other dishes.

1 (2½-4 pound) whole chicken, cut in pieces
1 onion, peeled, quartered
2 carrots, peeled, cut in 2-inch pieces
2 stalks celery, cut in 2-inch pieces

1. Rinse chicken pieces. (Freeze giblets for future use or discard). Place chicken in large stock pot and add water to cover. Bring to a boil and remove foam or fat that has risen to the surface. Cover and simmer an additional 15-20 minutes, removing any accumulated foam.

2. Add onion, carrots and celery and 1 teaspoon salt or salt substitute to the pot. Continue simmering, covered, on medium low heat for 45 minutes. Remove from heat and cool until chicken can be handled.

3. Remove chicken pieces from broth. Drain and discard vegetables from the broth. Cool broth about 20 minutes; then place in refrigerator. Skin and bone chicken pieces. If chicken is not immediately used, wrap small portions tightly in plastic wrap or place in freezer plastic bags and freeze for later use.

4. When broth has chilled several hours or overnight, fat will have solidified on the surface. Remove all fat possible with a large metal spoon; and remove any remaining fat by dragging paper towels on the surface. Broth will keep 2-3 days in refrigerator. Freeze in 1-2 cup portions for later use.

Kitchen Helper

CHICKEN STOCK OR BROTH

4 pounds chicken parts (backs, wings, legs or thighs)
1 onion, coarsely chopped
1 carrot, peeled, coarsely chopped
2 stalks celery, coarsely chopped

1. Place chicken parts in a large pot and add about 16 cups water or just enough water to cover. Bring to boil; then reduce heat and simmer about 30 minutes. Skim to remove foam.

2. Add onion, carrot and celery. Simmer uncovered about 3 hours, adding water as needed to cover. Strain and cool broth, uncovered, before refrigerating. Remove fat after broth has chilled.

3. Broth will keep 2-3 days in refrigerator and also freezes well.

Flavor Perk: Add a bouquet garni of 1 small bunch parsley, 1 teaspoon dried thyme and 1 bay leaf with the vegetables. By definition, a bouquet garni is a selection of herbs tied in a cheesecloth. In this recipe, it is not necessary to tie the herbs in a bundle since the broth will be strained.

Yield: 8-10 cups
Serving size: 1 cup

TURKEY STOCK OR BROTH

1 turkey carcass and any leftover turkey meat from a 12-25 pound turkey
1 onion, quartered
1 carrot, peeled, cut in 1-inch pieces
2 stalks celery, cut in 1-inch pieces

1. Break turkey carcass into pieces and place in a large pot with small pieces of turkey meat. Add 12-16 cups water or just enough water to cover. Bring to a boil; then reduce heat and simmer about 30 minutes. Skim any foam that has risen to the surface.

2. Add onion, carrot and celery; simmer uncovered 3-4 hours. Strain and cool broth, uncovered. Place broth in refrigerator until fat solidifies. Skim the surface to remove fat.

3. Use broth immediately or freeze for later use. Broth will keep in refrigerator 2-3 days.

Flavor Perk: Add 1 small bunch parsley, 1 teaspoon dried thyme and 1 bay leaf with the vegetables.

Yield: 8-10 cups broth

Kitchen Helper

BASIC VEGETABLE BROTH

This broth is delicious for eating or for adding liquid to other soups or dishes. Vegetable broth may be made with different kinds of vegetables; however, use sparingly any strong-flavored vegetables like turnips and cabbage. To avoid bitterness, do not cook vegetable broths longer than 30 minutes.

2 stalks celery with leaves, sliced, chopped
2 onions, sliced or chopped
4 carrots, sliced or chopped
*Herb bouquet or 2 teaspoons
dried mixed herb blend of your choice

1. Place celery, onions and carrots in 4-5 quart soup pot sprayed with nonstick cooking spray. Sauté 4-5 minutes or until vegetables begin to soften, adding 2-3 tablespoons water if mixture begins to scorch or stick. Add 6 cups water and herb bouquet to the soup pot.

2. Bring to a boil; reduce heat and simmer gently for about 30 minutes. Skim any froth that rises to the surface during the cooking. Season to taste with salt or salt substitute and white or black pepper.

3. Remove herbs; strain and cool uncovered. Refrigerate or freeze in small amounts for cooking.

*To make herb bouquet or bouquet garni, tie in cheesecloth 4-5 sprigs of fresh parsley, 1 teaspoon dried thyme and 1 bay leaf.

Flavor Perk: *Sauté 2 finely minced or pressed garlic cloves with the vegetables.*

VEGETABLES

An unbelievable variety of fresh and frozen vegetables are available for purchase in today's supermarkets and specialty food stores. It goes without saying that vegetables are KEY in healthier eating and cooking.

Have you fallen into a vegetable rut, where you prepare the same 2 or 3 vegetables day after day for family dinners? There's a world of delicious vegetables to be tried, many of which may become your family's favorites. You will find an assortment of vegetable recipes using simple cooking methods in this section, which will give you and your family a chance to find some new favorite vegetables.

GRILLED VEGETABLE KABOBS

1 (8 ounce) bottle fat free
Italian salad dressing

Choose 3 of the following:
2 large green peppers,
cut in 1-inch square pieces
2 large red sweet peppers,
cut in 1-inch square pieces
1 onion, quartered,
separated into pieces
2 zucchini, cut in 1-inch pieces
2 yellow squash, cut in 1-inch pieces

1. Place vegetables in large bowl. Pour salad dressing over vegetables and mix well. Marinate 30-40 minutes. Remove vegetables from marinade; reserve marinade.

2. Thread vegetables alternately on skewers. Heat gas grill to medium heat or prepare charcoal grill for cooking. Grill kabobs using indirect heat. Place kabobs on the side of the grill, not directly over heating element or hot coals.

3. Cook 10-15 minutes, turning once and marinating with reserved marinade.

- - - - - - - - - - - - - - - - - -

Yield: 6-8 servings
Serving size: 2-3 kabobs

Calories: 44
Protein: less than 1 g
Carbohydrate: 10 g
Fat: less than 1 g
Cholesterol: 0 mg
Sodium: 272 mg
Calcium: 8 mg
Dietary Fiber: 1 g
Sugar: 3 g

ASPARAGUS VINAIGRETTE

Look for the best fresh asparagus during April and May. Count on 6-8 spears per person. The shorter the cooking time, the fresher and greener the color.

24 large fresh asparagus spears
Fat free vinaigrette dressing

1. Begin heating water to boiling in a large pot over medium-high heat. Wash asparagus and cut or break off the tough woody part at the bottom of the stalks. This preparation may be all that is needed, or, if desired, peel each stalk lightly with a vegetable peeler near the top of the stalk, and peel more deeply near the bottom of the stalk.

2. Plunge spears into the pot of boiling water; then reduce heat and boil gently for about 5 minutes. Test for tenderness by piercing the bottom of the stalks. When crisp tender, and while color is still bright green, drain well. Rinse spears gently in cold water to stop cooking.

3. Serve hot or cold with vinaigrette dressing.

- - - - - - - - - - - - - - - - - -

Yield: 4 servings
Serving size: 6 asparagus spears

Calories (without dressing): 18
Protein: 3 g   Sodium: 3 mg
Carbohydrate: 3 g   Calcium: 21 mg
Fat: less than 1 g   Dietary Fiber: 2 g
Cholesterol: 0 mg   Sugar: 3 g

STIR-FRIED ASPARAGUS

Ginger root is recognized by its light brown color and its knotty and rounded shape.

2 pounds fresh asparagus, bottoms snapped off, cut in 2-inch pieces
1 tablespoon peanut or vegetable oil
1 tablespoon peeled fresh ginger root, thinly sliced
¼ cup reduced sodium fat free chicken broth

1. Preheat a wok or large skillet over medium-high heat. Add oil (keep amount used to a minimum), asparagus and ginger. Stir-fry 2-3 minutes; then add broth. Cover the wok or skillet; then reduce heat and simmer about 5 minutes or until the asparagus is tender.

Flavor Perk: Stir-fry 2 garlic cloves, finely minced or pressed, 1 minute before adding asparagus and ginger. Sprinkle asparagus with toasted sesame seeds before serving.

- - - - - - - - - - - - - - - - - -

Yield: 4-6 servings (About 4 cups)
Serving size: ½-¾ cup asparagus

Calories: 66
Protein: 5 g
Carbohydrate: 3 g
Fat: 4 g
Cholesterol: 0 mg
Sodium: 55 mg
Calcium: 22 mg
Dietary Fiber: 2 g
Sugar: 3 g

ORANGE- ASPARAGUS SKILLET

Grated orange peel further enhances the delicious flavor of the asparagus in this recipe.

To cook asparagus in the microwave, place asparagus spears in a microwave-safe 2-quart dish. Add 2 tablespoons water. Cover and cook on full power 3 minutes; then rearrange spears. Cook an additional 3 minutes, and check to see if asparagus is crisp-tender. Rearrange and cook an additional 3 minutes, if needed. Let stand 2 minutes.

1½ tablespoons margarine
1½ tablespoons grated orange peel
Juice of ½ orange
1 pound fresh asparagus spears, bottoms snapped off, cooked

1. In a large skillet over medium heat, add margarine, orange peel and juice. Cook and stir until margarine is slightly browned. Add the cooked asparagus and toss lightly to distribute margarine-orange mixture; heat through.

2. Season to taste with salt or salt substitute and freshly ground black pepper.

- - - - - - - - - - - - - - - - - -

Yield: 4 servings
Serving size: About ½ cup asparagus

Calories: 73
Protein: 3 g
Carbohydrate: 4 g
Fat: 5 g
Cholesterol: 0 mg
Sodium: 65 mg
Calcium: 20 mg
Dietary Fiber: 1 g
Sugar: 2 g

FRESH DILLED BEETS

Note: When substituting dried herbs for fresh herbs, use 1 teaspoon dried herbs to 1 tablespoon fresh herbs.

1 (15 ounce) can whole baby beets
½ cup red wine vinegar
2 sprigs fresh dill weed or 1 teaspoon dried dill weed
1 onion, quartered

1. Combine all ingredients and refrigerate 2-3 hours. Beets will remain fresh in the refrigerator for several days.

Flavor Perk: Add sugar substitute equal to ½ teaspoon sugar.

- - - - - - - - - - - - - - - - - -

Yield: 4 servings
Serving size: About ½ cup

Calories: 51
Protein: 1 g
Carbohydrate: 10 g
Fat: less than 1 g
Cholesterol: 0 mg
Sodium: 271 mg
Calcium: 26 mg
Dietary Fiber: 2 g
Sugar: 8 g

PICKLED BEETS

This recipe is a tart and colorful additional to a meal.

1 (16 ounce) can sliced beets, drained, liquid reserved
1 small onion, sliced, separated into rings
2 tablespoons cider vinegar
3 teaspoons sugar or equivalent sugar substitute

1. In a sprayed skillet over medium heat, add beets, ½ reserved liquid, onion rings and vinegar. Cook for 3 minutes, stirring frequently.

2. Remove from heat and stir in sugar or sugar substitute. Serve hot.

Flavor Perk: Add white pepper or hot pepper sauce to taste.

- - - - - - - - - - - - - - - - - -

Yield: 4 servings
Serving size: About ½ cup

Calories: 56
Protein: 1 g
Carbohydrate: 13 g
Fat: 0 g
Cholesterol: 0 mg
Sodium: 245 mg
Calcium: 6 mg
Dietary Fiber: 2 g
Sugar: 8 g

BROCCOLI-TOMATO SAUTÉ

Broccoli belongs to the cabbage family and is available year-round, especially October to May. Broccoli is a versatile and popular vegetable. Broccoli crowns, or the florets with a short length of stalk, are now readily available. One pound will yield 2-3 servings.

1 clove garlic, minced or pressed
2 Roma (plum) tomatoes, seeded, diced
1 pound (4 cups) broccoli florets, cooked or steamed until crisp-tender
2 tablespoons fresh chopped herbs or 2 teaspoons dried herb seasoning of your choice

1. In a large skillet sprayed with non-stick cooking spray, cook garlic and tomatoes over medium heat about 1 minute, stirring frequently.

2. Add cooked broccoli; then sprinkle with herb seasoning and toss gently until heated through.

- - - - - - - - - - - - - - - - - -

Yield: 6 servings
Serving size: ½-¾ cup

Calories: 31
Protein: 3 g
Carbohydrate: 6 g
Fat: less than 1 g
Cholesterol: 0 mg
Sodium: 24 mg
Calcium: 39 mg
Dietary Fiber: less than 1 g
Sugar: 3 g

SAUTÉED BROCCOLI

1 tablespoon olive oil
2 garlic cloves, finely minced or pressed
1 (16 ounce) package frozen baby broccoli florets, cooked
Lemon wedges

1. In a large skillet over medium heat, add oil and garlic. Cook and stir 2-3 minutes; then add cooked broccoli.

2. When heated through, season to taste with salt/salt substitute and freshly ground black pepper.

3. Serve with lemon wedges.

Variation: Substitute salt free Creole seasoning for the red pepper flakes, omitting salt and pepper.

- - - - - - - - - - - - - - - - - -

Yield: 4 servings
Serving size: About ½ cup

Calories: 64
Protein: 4 g
Carbohydrate: 7 g
Fat: 4 g
Cholesterol: 0 mg
Sodium: 27 mg
Calcium: 61 mg
Dietary Fiber: 3 g
Sugar: 2 g

BRAISED BRUSSELS SPROUTS AND ONIONS

Late fall and winter months are the time to buy Brussels sprouts, named by children as "baby cabbages." Look for compact, unblemished sprouts bright green in color.

To prepare for cooking, wash in cold water, removing any wilted leaves and cutting off the stems. Pierce stem ends with a knife tip for more even cooking.

8-10 small boiling onions, trimmed
1 pound Brussels sprouts, halved, or 2 (12 ounce) packages frozen Brussels sprouts, partially thawed
1 bay leaf
¼ teaspoon dried thyme

1. In a sprayed skillet over medium heat, cook onions until lightly browned, about 10 minutes. Add 1 cup water, Brussels sprouts, bay leaf, thyme, ¼ teaspoon salt or salt substitute and ⅛ teaspoon freshly ground black pepper.

2. Reduce heat; then cover and simmer until Brussels sprouts are tender, about 10-15 minutes. Remove bay leaf before serving.

- - - - - - - - - - - - - - - - - -

Yield: 4 servings
Serving size: About ½ cup sprouts

Calories: 61
Protein: 4 g
Carbohydrate: 14 g
Fat: less than 1 g
Cholesterol: 0 mg
Sodium: 36 mg
Calcium: 88 mg
Dietary Fiber: 5 g
Sugar: 4 g

QUICK CRUNCHY CABBAGE

1 teaspoon low sodium instant beef bouillon granules
6 cups packaged shredded cabbage with carrots (coleslaw mix)
4 green onions and tops, chopped
½ cup sliced water chestnuts, rinsed

1. Place ¼ cup water and bouillon granules in a large saucepan or Dutch oven. Heat until granules dissolve. Add cabbage, green onions, water chestnuts, salt/salt substitute and freshly ground pepper to taste.

2. Cook, covered, over medium heat about 5 minutes or until cabbage is crisp-tender. Drain excess liquid, if necessary.

Flavor Perk: Toss cooked cabbage with 1 teaspoon Dijon-style mustard; sprinkle with paprika.

- - - - - - - - - - - - - - - - - -

Yield: 4-6 servings
Serving size: ½ cup

Calories: 39
Protein: 2 g
Carbohydrate: 8 g
Fat: less than 1 g
Cholesterol: 0 mg
Sodium: 25 mg
Calcium: 64 mg
Dietary Fiber: 3 g
Sugar: 4 g

CREAMY CABBAGE BAKE

6 cups packaged shredded cabbage and carrots (coleslaw mix)
1 (10½ ounce) can reduced fat cream of mushroom or cream of chicken soup
⅔ cup skim milk
1 (8 ounce) package reduced fat shredded cheddar cheese

1. Preheat oven to 325°. Place cabbage in a baking dish sprayed with nonstick cooking spray. Cover and bake 15 minutes or until crisp-tender. Drain liquid from dish.

2. Blend soup and skim milk and pour over cabbage. Bake, covered, 15-20 minutes or until soup mixture bubbles.

3. Remove from oven; then sprinkle with cheese and bake, uncovered, another 5 minutes.

- - - - - - - - - - - - - - - - - - -

Yield: 8 servings
Serving size: About ½ cup

Calories: 112
Protein: 10 g
Carbohydrate: 8 g
Fat: 5 g
Cholesterol: 19 mg
Sodium: 339 mg
Calcium: 281 mg
Dietary Fiber: 1 g
Sugar: 3 g

RED CABBAGE AND APPLES

1 onion, chopped
2 pounds red cabbage, shredded or chopped
2 Granny Smith apples, peeled, cored, thinly sliced
2 tablespoons red wine vinegar

1. In a large skillet sprayed with non-stick cooking spray, sauté the onion until clear and tender. Stir in cabbage, apples and vinegar.

2. Cover and cook over low heat for 10 minutes. Add ½ cup water and salt or salt substitute to taste. Serve hot.

Flavor Perk: Stir in sugar substitute to taste and pinch of cayenne pepper.

- - - - - - - - - - - - - - - - - - -

Yield: 8 servings
Serving size: ½ cup

Calories: 56
Protein: 2 g
Carbohydrate: 13 g
Fat: less than 1 g
Cholesterol: 0 mg
Sodium: 13 mg
Calcium: 63 mg
Dietary Fiber: 3 g
Sugar: 11 g

BRAISED CARROTS

Carrots, rich in vitamin A, are a staple vegetable. They are available year-round in many different forms. When choosing fresh carrots, look for fairly small, firm and smooth carrots that are free of dry, shriveled or blemished areas.

Prepackaged, cleaned baby carrots are certainly convenient for quick, healthy snacks or to carry along for lunches. Even prepackaged grated carrots are now available in produce sections. Carrots are good served with just about everything, and are pleasing to most people.

The sweetness of carrots used in a soup or stew may overpower the flavors of other vegetables, so use sparingly and add to suit your own taste.

1 pound carrots
½ cup reduced sodium fat free chicken broth
Sugar substitute to equal 1 teaspoon sugar
1 teaspoon dried tarragon

1. Peel carrots, quarter lengthwise, and cut into even sticks. Place in a large skillet and add chicken broth, sugar substitute and ½ teaspoon salt/salt substitute. Bring to a boil; then reduce heat, cover and simmer 15-20 minutes or until the carrots are tender and most of liquid has been absorbed.

2. Add tarragon and continue cooking for 2-3 more minutes. Season to taste with freshly ground black pepper.

- -

Yield: 4 servings
Serving size: ½ cup carrots

Calories: 53
Protein: 1 g
Carbohydrate: 11 g
Fat: less than 1 g
Cholesterol: 0 mg
Sodium: 136 mg
Calcium: 3 mg
Dietary Fiber: 3 g
Sugar: 8 g

DIJON-GLAZED CARROTS

This tangy mustard glaze is appealing and delightful on tender-crisp sweet carrots.

2 pounds carrots, peeled, cut diagonally into ¼ inch slices
3 tablespoons Dijon-style mustard
3 tablespoons liquid butter substitute
2 tablespoons brown sugar or honey

1. Boil or steam carrots 5-10 minutes until tender-crisp. Drain well, and stir in mustard, butter substitute and sugar.

2. Cook 1-2 minutes over medium heat, stirring constantly until carrots are glazed.

- - - - - - - - - - - - - - - - - - - -

Yield: 6 servings
Serving size: About ½ cup

Calories: 148
Protein: 2 g
Carbohydrate: 18 g
Fat: 7 g
Cholesterol: less than 1 mg
Sodium: 227 mg
Calcium: 43 mg
Dietary Fiber: 5 g
Sugar: 13 g

PARSLIED CARROTS

1 (16 ounce) package carrots, peeled, thinly sliced or 1 (16 ounce) package frozen crinkle-cut carrots
1 tablespoon margarine
½ teaspoon fresh lemon juice
1 tablespoon chopped fresh parsley

1. Steam or cook fresh carrots in boiling water until crisp-tender, or follow package directions to cook frozen carrots until crisp-tender. Drain and set aside.

2. In a large skillet over medium heat, melt margarine and add lemon juice. Add cooked carrots, salt or salt substitute and freshly ground black pepper to taste. Heat through; then remove from heat.

3. Sprinkle with parsley to serve.

- - - - - - - - - - - - - - - - - - - -

Yield: 4 servings
Serving size: ½ cup

Calories: 77
Protein: 1 g
Carbohydrate: 11 g
Fat: 3 g
Cholesterol: 0 mg
Sodium: 92 mg
Calcium: 2 mg
Dietary Fiber: 3 g
Sugar: 7 g

SAUTÉED CAULIFLOWER

1 small head cauliflower, cut into
small florets
1 tablespoon olive oil
2 garlic cloves, finely minced or
pressed
Lemon wedges

1. In an electric steamer, steam florets 5 minutes. To cook in microwave oven, place florets in a microwave-safe dish, and add 1 tablespoon water. Cover and cook on full power 3-5 minutes or until crisp-tender. Let stand, covered, 2 minutes.

2. To a large skillet over medium heat, add oil and garlic; sauté 2-3 minutes. Add the cooked cauliflower and red pepper flakes. Increase heat to high, and sauté about 6 minutes or until cauliflower browns in places.

3. Remove from heat and season to taste with salt or salt substitute. Serve with lemon wedges.

- - - - - - - - - - - - - - - - - -

Yield: 4 servings
Serving size: About ½ cup

Calories: 41
Protein: 1 g
Carbohydrate: 3 g
Fat: 3 g
Cholesterol: 0 mg
Sodium: 15 mg
Calcium: 14 mg
Dietary Fiber: 1 g
Sugar: 1 g

SPICY SAUTÉED CHARD

1½ pounds (2 medium bunches)
red or green chard
1 tablespoon oil
2 garlic cloves, finely minced or
pressed
¼ teaspoon hot pepper sauce

1. Remove stems from the chard, and cut stems into ½-inch pieces. Rinse the leaves and coarsely chop, leaving water clinging to the chopped leaves.

2. To a large skillet over medium heat, add oil and garlic. Sauté 2-3 minutes. Add the chard stems and salt or salt substitute to taste. Cook and stir about 2 minutes or until the stems are nearly tender.

3. Add the chard leaves and cook, partially covered, about 3-5 minutes or until leaves and stems are tender. Season to taste with hot pepper sauce.

Flavor Perk: Sprinkle sautéed chard with 1-2 tablespoon fresh lemon juice.

- - - - - - - - - - - - - - - - - -

Yield: 4-6 servings
Serving size: About ½ cup

Calories: 52
Protein: 3 g
Carbohydrate: 5 g
Fat: 3 g
Cholesterol: 0 mg
Sodium: 276 mg
Calcium: 70 mg
Dietary Fiber: 2 g
Sugar: 2 g

BAKED FRESH CHILES WITH CHEESE

6 roasted and peeled fresh Anaheim or poblano chiles
6 ounces shredded reduced fat cheddar or Monterey jack cheese (or a combination of both)
4 green onions and tops, chopped
Salsa

1. Preheat oven to 350°. Make a slit in the side of each roasted pepper. Remove seeds and membrane; rinse. Pat dry and place on a sprayed baking sheet.

2. Mix cheese and green onions and mold into 6 logs. Gently stuff cheese logs into the peppers, and close slit.

3. Bake 10-15 minutes or until heated through. Serve immediately with salsa.

- - - - - - - - - - - - - - - - - - -

Yield: 6 servings
Serving size: 1 chile

Calories: 137
Protein: 13 g
Carbohydrate: 11 g
Fat: 7 g
Cholesterol: 20 mg
Sodium: 234 mg
Calcium: 300 mg
Dietary Fiber: less than 1 g
Sugar: less than 1 g

EGGPLANT-SQUASH-BELL PEPPER GRILL

1 large eggplant
1 pound small zucchini or yellow crookneck squash
2 green, red or yellow bell peppers, seeded, quartered
Fat free vinaigrette salad dressing or fat free marinade

1. Preheat gas grill to medium, or prepare hot coals on a barbecue grill. Cut the eggplant into ½-inch slices. Cut the squash in half lengthwise.

2. Add the eggplant, squash and bell peppers to a vegetable grilling basket, or place directly on the grill about 4 inches from heat or coals. Brush vegetables with salad dressing or marinade and season to taste with salt or salt substitute and freshly ground black pepper.

3. Grill vegetables about 7-10 minutes until tender and lightly browned, turning 2-3 times with spatula and brushing frequently with marinade or salad dressing.

Flavor Perk: Add 1 teaspoon dried basil to salad dressing or marinade.

- - - - - - - - - - - - - - - - - - -

Yield: 6 servings
Serving size: About ¾ cup

Calories: 45
Protein: 2 g
Carbohydrate: 10 g
Fat: less than 1 g
Cholesterol: 0 mg
Sodium: 6 mg
Calcium: 21 mg
Dietary Fiber: 4 g
Sugar: 6 g

EGGPLANT PARMIGIANA

Eggplant is known as aubergine in France and England. Several varieties and sizes exist. The large, tapered, deep-purple eggplant is the one most readily available in supermarkets, especially July through October.

To store, place unwashed eggplant in a plastic bag and refrigerate up to 5 days.

**2 small (about 1 pound each) eggplants, unpeeled
1 teaspoon dried basil leaves or dried Italian-style herb blend
2 cups prepared reduced fat spaghetti sauce, divided
2 cups shredded reduced fat mozzarella cheese, divided**

1. Preheat oven to 350°. Slice off eggplant ends; cut remaining eggplant into ½-inch slices. Arrange eggplant in a single layer on a microwave-safe plate lined with paper towels. Sprinkle with basil and season to taste with salt or salt substitute and freshly ground black pepper.

2. Microwave on full power, uncovered, about 6 minutes or until tender. Let stand for 2 minutes; then drain. In a sprayed 9 x 13-inch baking dish, place one layer of eggplant slices. Spoon 1 cup spaghetti sauce over eggplant; top with 1 cup cheese. Repeat with remaining eggplant slices, sauce and cheese.

3. Bake, uncovered, 25 minutes or until sauce bubbles and cheese is lightly browned.

- -

Yield: 6 servings
Serving size: 1½ cups

Calories: 259
Protein: 24 g
Carbohydrate: 19 g
Fat: 8 g
Cholesterol: 27 mg
Sodium: 798 mg
Calcium: 704 mg
Dietary Fiber: 5 g
Sugar: 10 g

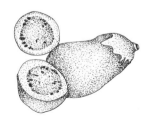

GREEN BEAN CASSEROLE

No cook should be without a recipe for the all-time favorite green bean casserole. This recipe has trimmed calories and replaced French-fried onion rings with a small amount of toasted nuts.

1 (10½ ounce) can reduced fat cream of mushroom or cream of chicken soup
½ cup skim milk
2 (16 ounce) packages frozen French-style cut green beans, cooked, drained
⅓ cup toasted almonds or pine nuts

1. Heat oven to 350°. Mix soup, milk and freshly ground black pepper to taste in a 2-quart baking dish sprayed with nonstick cooking spray. Stir in beans and sprinkle with nuts.

2. Bake, uncovered, 25-30 minutes or until hot in center.

- - - - - - - - - - - - - - - - - -

Yield: 6 servings
Serving size: About ¾ cup

Calories: 128
Protein: 5 g
Carbohydrate: 14 g
Fat: 5 g
Cholesterol: 5 mg
Sodium: 228 mg
Calcium: 124 mg
Dietary Fiber: 5 g
Sugar: 6 g

FRESH GREEN BEANS AND TOMATOES

1 onion, finely chopped
1 garlic clove, finely minced or pressed
1 pound fresh green beans, trimmed
1 (14.5 ounce) can diced tomatoes with herbs

1. In a large skillet or Dutch oven sprayed with nonstick cooking spray, sauté onion and garlic over medium heat until onion is tender and clear, about 4 minutes. Do not scorch. (Add 2-3 tablespoons water, if needed, to cook onion until tender.)

2. Add green beans and tomatoes. Reduce heat; cover and simmer about 20 minutes or until beans are crisp-tender.

3. Season to taste with salt or salt substitute and freshly ground black pepper.

- - - - - - - - - - - - - - - - - -

Yield: 4 servings
Serving size: About 1 cup

Calories: 47
Protein: 2 g
Carbohydrate: 11 g
Fat: less than 1 g
Cholesterol: 0 mg
Sodium: 8 mg
Calcium: 49 mg
Dietary Fiber: 4 g
Sugar: 4 g

GREEN BEAN-MUSHROOM SAUTÉ

Green beans were once known as "string beans." Fortunately, today's green beans are stringless, requiring just the ends to be broken or cut off.

Green beans are available year-round, especially in spring and summer. Look for crisp, firm beans with good, fresh color (avoid beans with excessive brown spots). One pound will yield 3-4 servings. Green beans are a favorite vegetable and good with just about everything!

2 teaspoons olive oil
8 ounces fresh sliced mushrooms
1 tablespoon minced onion
1 pound fresh green beans, trimmed, boiled*

1. In a large skillet over medium heat, add oil, mushrooms and onion. Cook 3-5 minutes or until mushrooms are tender. Add the cooked green beans to the skillet. Season to taste with salt/salt substitute and freshly ground black pepper.

2. Toss mixture and heat through.

Variation: Substitute ¼ cup slivered almonds or ¼ cup pine nuts for the mushrooms and onions. Add 1 tablespoon fresh lemon juice with salt and pepper.

- -

Yield: 3-4 servings
Serving size: About ¾ cup

Calories: 82
Protein: 5 g
Carbohydrate: 11 g
Fat: 4 g
Cholesterol: 0 mg
Sodium: 10 mg
Calcium: 48 mg
Dietary Fiber: 5 g
Sugar: 5 g

*To Boil Green Beans:

In a large pot, bring 12 cups water to a boil. Add 1 pound trimmed fresh green beans; then stir and bring quickly back to a boil. Thin green beans will be cooked crisp-tender in 2-4 minutes; larger beans will need 4-8 minutes. Remove and immediately drain in a colander.

GREEN BEANS AND ZUCCHINI

1 large zucchini
1½ pounds green beans, ends trimmed
Fresh Basil Salad Dressing (p. 165)
2 small garlic cloves, minced

1. Cut off zucchini ends; then cut remaining zucchini crosswise in 2-inch slices. With a small knife or vegetable peeler, cut out centers of zucchini slices to form oblong rings.

2. Steam green beans until crisp-tender; then rinse in cold water to stop cooking. Steam zucchini rings until crisp-tender; then rinse in cold water to stop cooking.

3. Push 6-8 green beans into each zucchini ring. Arrange bundles in a shallow dish and pour dressing over.

- - - - - - - - - - - - - - - - - - -

Yield: 8 servings
Serving size: 1 zucchini ring

Calories: 31
Protein: 2 g
Carbohydrate: 7 g
Fat: less than 1 g
Cholesterol: 0 mg
Sodium: 6 mg
Calcium: 37 mg
Dietary Fiber: 3 g
Sugar: 3 g

FRESH BASIL SALAD DRESSING

1 tablespoon Dijon-style mustard
¼ cup red or white wine vinegar
1 tablespoon fresh basil leaves or 2 teaspoons dried basil, crumbled
½ cup olive or vegetable oil

1. In a blender or food processor, combine mustard, vinegar, ¼ cup water, ½ teaspoon freshly ground black pepper and fresh or dried basil leaves. Pulse to blend. With blender or food processor running, slowly pour in oil and pulse until all ingredients are well blended.

2. Cover and refrigerate up to 3 days. Shake well before using.

- - - - - - - - - - - - - - - - - - -

Yield: 12 servings (About ¾ cup)
Serving size: About 1 tablespoon

Calories: 83
Protein: 0 g
Carbohydrate: 0 g
Fat: 9 g
Cholesterol: 0 mg
Sodium: 29 mg
Calcium: less than 1 g
Dietary Fiber: 0 g
Sugar: 0 g

SAUTÉED MUSHROOMS

1-2 tablespoons margarine or vegetable oil
2 (8 ounce) packages sliced mushrooms
2 garlic cloves, finely minced or pressed
¼ cup chopped fresh parsley

1. Heat margarine or oil in a large skillet over medium-high to high heat. Add sliced mushrooms and cook, stirring constantly, about 5-7 minutes or until mushrooms begin to brown.

2. Add garlic and parsley, and cook another minute. Season to taste with salt/salt substitute and freshly ground black pepper.

- - - - - - - - - - - - - - - - - -

Yield: 4-5 servings
Serving size: ¼-½ cup

Calories: 54
Protein: 3 g
Carbohydrate: 3 g
Fat: 4 g
Cholesterol: 0 mg
Sodium: 36 mg
Calcium: 11 mg
Dietary Fiber: less than 1 g
Sugar: 2 g

PIZZA PORTOBELLO

4 large or 8 small Portobello mushrooms, stemmed
1-1½ cups prepared chunky spaghetti sauce
¾-1 cup freshly grated Parmesan or Romano cheese
Dried basil or oregano

1. Preheat oven to 350°. Place the mushroom caps, stem side up, on a baking sheet sprayed with non-stick cooking spray. Onto each mushroom cap, spoon 1-2 tablespoons spaghetti sauce, 1 tablespoon cheese and a sprinkling of basil or oregano.

2. Bake for 5 minutes; then broil until cheese melts.

- - - - - - - - - - - - - - - - - -

Yield: 4 servings
Serving size: 1 large or 2 small mushrooms

Calories: 113
Protein: 9 g
Carbohydrate: 9 g
Fat: 6 g
Cholesterol: 12 mg
Sodium: 528 mg
Calcium: 231 mg
Dietary Fiber: 1 g
Sugar: 6 g

FRESH MUSHROOM SAUTÉ

To clean mushrooms, wipe with a damp cloth or rinse briefly under cold running water and pat dry. Trim stem base and slice lengthwise, through the stem, or use a hard-cooked egg slicer to slice mushrooms evenly.

1 tablespoon margarine
2 cloves garlic, finely minced or pressed
1 pound (6 cups) mushrooms, sliced
Chopped fresh parsley for garnish

1. In a large skillet over low heat, add margarine and garlic and cook 1-2 minutes, stirring constantly. Increase heat to medium and add sliced mushrooms and freshly ground black pepper to taste.

2. Cook 4-6 minutes, stirring constantly until mushrooms are lightly browned. Sprinkle with parsley.

- - - - - - - - - - - - - - - - - - - -

Yield: 4 servings
Serving size: About ½ cup mushrooms

Calories: 59
Protein: 4 g
Carbohydrate: 4 g
Fat: 5 g
Cholesterol: 0 mg
Sodium: 38 mg
Calcium: 7 mg
Dietary Fiber: less than 1 g
Sugar: 2 g

SOUTHERN OKRA AND TOMATOES

2 pounds fresh okra, sliced or 2 (16 ounce) packages sliced frozen okra, thawed, drained
1½ tablespoons vegetable or olive oil
No salt Creole seasoning or salt free seasoning blend of your choice
2 (16 ounce) cans no salt diced tomatoes

1. In a sprayed skillet over medium high heat, preheat oil. Add okra and cook, stirring constantly to prevent okra from sticking, until okra is crisp-tender and no longer slimy.

2. Add tomatoes and seasoning; reduce heat to medium. Cook uncovered, stirring frequently, about 30 minutes.

Flavor Perk: Garnish with fresh chopped parsley.

- - - - - - - - - - - - - - - - - - - -

Yield: 4 servings
Serving size: About 1 cup

Calories: 165
Protein: 6 g
Carbohydrate: 23 g
Fat: 5 g
Cholesterol: 0 mg
Sodium: 108 mg
Calcium: 223 mg
Dietary Fiber: 11 g
Sugar: 7 g

CHEESY ONION BAKE

For this recipe, choose white, yellow or the sweeter Vidalia onion. Rather than buying a bag of onions, be choosy and select onions from an open bin. Look for firm, dry onions with a brittle outer skin. Avoid onions with dark or soft spots or with sprouting green shoots.

Stored in a cool, dry, dark place, unpeeled onions will keep well for up to 2 months.

2 large onions, sliced, separated into rings
1 cup reduced fat Swiss cheese, shredded, divided
1 (10½ ounce) can reduced fat cream of chicken soup
1 teaspoon soy sauce

1. Preheat oven to 350°. In a nonstick skillet sprayed with nonstick cooking spray, sauté onions until clear and tender, adding 1-2 tablespoons water if needed for moisture. Arrange onions in a sprayed baking dish and sprinkle ¾ cup cheese on top.

2. Blend soup, soy sauce, ⅓ cup water and freshly ground black pepper to taste. Pour over cheese and onions and lightly mix. Sprinkle remaining cheese on top.

3. Bake uncovered for 20-30 minutes or until heated through.

Variation: Substitute ⅓ cup skim milk for the ⅓ cup water.

- - - - - - - - - - - - - - - - - - -

Yield: 8 servings
Serving size: About ½ cup

Calories: 125	Sodium: 185 mg
Protein: 9 g	Calcium: 256 mg
Carbohydrate: 7 g	Dietary Fiber: less
Fat: 7 g	than 1 g
Cholesterol: 23 mg	Sugar: 1 g

CREAMED ONIONS

This is a traditional Thanksgiving dish that serves well as a side dish anytime.

To remove strong onion smell from hands, sprinkle with salt and rinse with cold water. Repeat if needed.

1 pound pearl onions
1½ tablespoons margarine
1½ tablespoons flour
1⅓ cups skim milk

1. Preheat oven to 350°. Place onions in a large saucepan and cover with water. Bring water to boiling; boil for 1 minute. Remove onions; then peel and return to the saucepan. Reduce heat and simmer about 10 minutes or until onions are tender; drain. Place onions in a shallow baking dish.

2. Melt margarine in a small saucepan over medium heat. Add flour and cook, stirring constantly, about 2-3 minutes. Add skim milk to the flour mixture; then cook about 3 minutes, stirring constantly until thickened.

3. Season to taste with salt or salt substitute and freshly ground black pepper. Pour sauce over the onions. Place in oven and bake about 15 minutes or until sauce bubbles.

- - - - - - - - - - - - - - - - - - -

Yield: 6 servings
Serving size: About ½ cup

Calories: 111	
Protein: 5 g	Sodium: 142 mg
Carbohydrate: 14 g	Calcium: 68 mg
Fat: 3 g	Dietary Fiber: 3 g
Cholesterol: 1 mg	Sugar: 8 g

NEW RED POTATOES WITH ROSEMARY

2 pounds very small new red potatoes (approximately 30 potatoes)
2 tablespoons olive oil
1 tablespoon fresh rosemary leaves or 1 teaspoon dried rosemary leaves

1. Cook the new potatoes in boiling water for about 12-15 minutes until fork tender. Drain and let cool slightly.

2. Slice potatoes in half and place in a large bowl. Toss lightly with oil, rosemary and salt or salt substitute to taste.

- - - - - - - - - - - - - - - - -

Yield: 5 servings
Serving size: About ½ cup

Calories: 100
Protein: 3 g
Carbohydrate: 11 g
Fat: 5 g
Cholesterol: 0 mg
Sodium: 9 mg
Calcium: 12 mg
Dietary Fiber: 5 g
Sugar: 2 g

STIR-FRIED SNOW PEAS

1 teaspoon peanut oil
2 teaspoons peeled fresh ginger, minced
1 pound package frozen snow peas, thawed, drained
3 teaspoons chopped fresh basil or ½ teaspoon dried basil leaves

1. Heat oil in a wok or large skillet over medium-high to high heat; add ginger. Stir-fry for 30 seconds; then add snow peas and stir vigorously.

2. Add basil and ½ teaspoon salt or salt substitute. Continue cooking snow peas 1-2 more minutes. Serve immediately.

- - - - - - - - - - - - - - - - -

Yield: 4 servings
Serving size: About ½ cup

Calories: 58
Protein: 3 g
Carbohydrate: 8 g
Fat: 1 g
Cholesterol: 0 mg
Sodium: 5 mg
Calcium: 57 mg
Dietary Fiber: 4 g
Sugar: 0 g

CREAMED SPINACH

Spinach is the king of the dark green leafy vegetables, well known for its high vitamin and mineral content. It is one of the most versatile veggies, too, and is used in numerous recipes throughout this book. Stock fresh and frozen spinach for ready cooking.

2 pounds fresh spinach, stemmed
1 tablespoon margarine
1 tablespoon flour
1½ cups skim milk

1. Rinse spinach and place in a large saucepan or pot over medium heat. Do not add water. Cook, covered, 4-5 minutes or until spinach wilts. Transfer to a colander; then rinse with cold water and press out liquid. Chop spinach finely and set aside.

2. In a saucepan, melt margarine over medium heat. Stir in flour and cook until mixture bubbles. Continue cooking and stirring at least one minute. Whisk in skim milk and cook, stirring, until sauce thickens.

3. Season sauce to taste with salt or salt substitute and freshly ground black pepper. Pour sauce over spinach and serve hot.

- -

Yield: 4-6 servings
Serving size: About ½ cup

Calories: 70
Protein: 8 g
Carbohydrate: 5 g
Fat: 3 g
Cholesterol: 1 mg
Sodium: 280 mg
Calcium: 233 mg
Dietary Fiber: 16 g
Sugar: 3 g

SAUTÉED SPINACH

2 garlic cloves, halved
2 pounds fresh spinach
1 tablespoon lemon juice

1. Spray a large saucepan or Dutch oven with nonstick cooking spray and preheat over medium-high heat. Add garlic and sauté about 1 minute or until garlic begins to brown.

2. Stir in spinach, cooking just until spinach begins to wilt; discard garlic. Add lemon juice and ⅛ teaspoon salt or salt substitute; continue cooking about 2 minutes.

- -

Yield: 4-6 servings
Serving size: About ½ cup

Calories: 20
Protein: 5 g
Carbohydrate: less than 1 g
Fat: less than 1 g
Cholesterol: 0 mg
Sodium: 216 mg
Calcium: 144 mg
Dietary Fiber: 16 g
Sugar: 0 g

SPINACH AND PINE NUTS

2 pounds fresh spinach, stemmed
1 tablespoon olive oil
¼ cup pine nuts
2 garlic cloves, finely minced or
   pressed

1. Wash spinach, but do not dry. Coarsely chop spinach and place in a large saucepan. Season to taste with salt or salt substitute. Cover and cook over medium heat about 5 minutes or just until spinach wilts. Drain and set aside.

2. Heat oil in a large skillet over medium heat. Add pine nuts and cook about 2 minutes. Add garlic and cook 1 minute. Add spinach and freshly ground black pepper to taste and cook, stirring frequently, about 5 minutes.

3. Serve immediately.

- - - - - - - - - - - - - - - - -

Yield: 4-6 servings
Serving size: About ½ cup

Calories: 82
Protein: 7 g
Carbohydrate: 2 g
Fat: 7 g
Cholesterol: 0 mg
Sodium: 216 mg
Calcium: 146 mg
Dietary Fiber: 16 g
Sugar: 0 g

SQUASH-CABBAGE SAUTÉ

1 cup chopped green or red bell
   pepper
2 cups sliced zucchini or yellow
   crookneck squash
2 cups packaged shredded cabbage
   and carrots (coleslaw mix)
1 tablespoon cider vinegar

1. Preheat a large sprayed skillet or Dutch oven over medium heat. Add green pepper, squash and cabbage; reduce heat. Cook vegetables over low heat, tossing occasionally, for 5-10 minutes or until squash is crisp-tender.

2. Stir in vinegar, salt or salt substitute and freshly ground black pepper to taste. Serve immediately.

Flavor Perk: Add ¼ teaspoon each dried oregano leaves and dried thyme to skillet with the vinegar.

- - - - - - - - - - - - - - - - -

Yield: 4-6 servings
Serving size: About ½ cup

Calories: 27
Protein: 1 g
Carbohydrate: 6 g
Fat: less than 1 g
Cholesterol: 0 mg
Sodium: 9 mg
Calcium: 28 mg
Dietary Fiber: 2 g
Sugar: 3 g

SPINACH-RICOTTA STUFFED SQUASH

4 yellow crookneck squash or zucchini
1 (10 ounce) package frozen chopped spinach, thawed
¼ cup egg substitute
1 cup ricotta cheese

1. Cut ends off squash; then cut squash in half lengthwise. With a teaspoon, scoop out seeds and part of pulp, leaving shells ½-inch thick. Steam squash shells in an electric steamer or steamer basket over boiling water about 5 minutes until crisp-tender. Rinse quickly with cold water. Drain well and set aside.

2. Preheat oven to 350°. Drain and squeeze spinach to remove liquid. Combine spinach, egg substitute and ricotta cheese. Season to taste with salt or salt substitute and freshly ground black pepper.

3. Mound 2-3 tablespoons spinach mixture inside squash shells. Arrange stuffed squash in a shallow baking dish. Bake, uncovered, about 20 minutes or until filling is heated through.

Flavor Perk: Add 1 teaspoon Italian-herb seasoning and 2 tablespoons grated Parmesan cheese to the spinach mixture. Spray stuffed squash shells with nonstick cooking spray before placing in oven to keep shells moist during cooking.

- -

Yield: 8 servings
Serving size: 1 squash shell with filling

Calories: 65
Protein: 6 g
Carbohydrate: 5 g
Fat: 3 g
Cholesterol: 10 mg
Sodium: 101 mg
Calcium: 124 mg
Dietary Fiber: 2 g
Sugar: less than 1 g

SPINACH STUFFED TOMATOES

2 firm, ripe tomatoes, halved crosswise
1 (16 ounce) package frozen chopped spinach, thawed, drained or 2 (10 ounce) packages fresh washed spinach, coarsely chopped
1 tablespoon coarsely chopped onion
½ cup skim milk, divided

1. Gently squeeze the seeds out of the tomatoes. Remove stem ends and about 1 tablespoon pulp from the center of each tomato. Pierce the skin of the tomatoes in several places to keep them from splitting during cooking.

2. Season tomatoes to taste with freshly ground black pepper and salt or salt substitute. Place tomatoes on a baking sheet under the broiler for about 4-5 minutes. Remove and keep warm on the baking sheet.

3. Preheat oven to 375°. Place spinach, onion and ¼ cup skim milk in food processor or blender. Pulse once or twice until mixture is finely chopped. Transfer to a medium skillet or saucepan; add remaining ¼ cup skim milk and simmer 5 minutes. Season to taste with freshly ground black pepper and salt or salt substitute.

4. Spoon spinach mixture onto tomato halves. Place in oven for 5-6 minutes or until heated through.

Flavor Perk: Sprinkle 1 teaspoon grated Parmesan cheese over each spinach-topped tomato before baking.

- -

Yield: 4 servings
Serving size: 1 tomato half

Calories: 52
Protein: 4 g
Carbohydrate: 7 g
Fat: less than 1 g
Cholesterol: less than 1 mg
Sodium: 179 mg
Calcium: 123 mg
Dietary Fiber: 3 g
Sugar: 4 g

BRAISED SUMMER SQUASH

1 tablespoon olive oil
1½ pounds yellow crookneck
  squash, sliced or diced
3 tablespoons fresh chopped
  parsley
1 teaspoon grated lemon peel

1. Place olive oil in a large skillet and heat over medium-high to high heat. Add squash and sauté about 7-10 minutes or until squash is golden and tender.

2. Remove to a serving dish; toss with parsley and lemon peel. Serve immediately.

- - - - - - - - - - - - - - - - - -

Yield: 4 servings
Serving size: ¾ cup

Calories: 63
Protein: 2 g
Carbohydrate: 7 g
Fat: 4 g
Cholesterol: 0 mg
Sodium: 5 mg
Calcium: 40 mg
Dietary Fiber: 3 g
Sugar: 0 g

GRILLED SQUASH-MUSHROOM KABOBS

2 zucchini, cut in 1-inch pieces
2 crookneck yellow squash, cut in
  1-inch pieces
12 large mushroom caps
¾ cup fat free marinade or fat free
  vinaigrette salad dressing

1. Preheat gas grill to medium heat or ready hot coals on a barbecue grill. In a large mixing bowl, place zucchini, squash, mushroom caps and marinade or salad dressing; toss lightly. Marinate 30-40 minutes.

2. Remove vegetables from marinade, reserving marinade. Thread vegetables on long metal skewers. Cook on the grill by indirect heat, placing vegetables to the side, not directly over hot coals or heating element.

3. Grill 10-15 minutes or until lightly browned in spots, turning once and basting with marinade.

Flavor Perk: Add ½ teaspoon dried thyme to marinade.

- - - - - - - - - - - - - - - - - -

Yield: 4 servings
Serving size: 2-3 kabobs

Calories: 122
Protein: 4 g
Carbohydrate: 24 g
Fat: 1 g
Cholesterol: 0 mg
Sodium: 386 mg
Calcium: 83 mg
Dietary Fiber: 4 g
Sugar: 3 g

PASTA & RICE

In the search for palatable dishes to replace the high fat foods on the traditional dinner table, Americans have come to recognize the nutritional advantages of grains and grain products to replace foods high in fat and cholesterol. Today, a wide variety of different types of pasta and rice is readily available in supermarkets and are used extensively in main dish preparation.

For greatest nutritional value, choose less refined brown rice rather than refined white rice for your cooking. The same holds true for pasta—look for whole wheat products and healthier cholesterol-free noodles and ribbons when preparing pasta dishes.

ANGEL HAIR PASTA AND WHITE BEANS

4 ounces dried angel hair or
vermicelli pasta, uncooked
2 tablespoons lemon juice and 1
tablespoon finely grated peel
½ cup reduced sodium fat free
chicken broth
8 ounces cooked, drained white
(canellini or navy) beans

1. Prepare pasta according to package
directions; drain. Place cooked
pasta in large mixing bowl.
Sprinkle pasta with lemon juice
and grated lemon peel; lightly toss.

2. Heat broth in a large skillet over
medium heat. Add beans and heat
through. Add beans and broth to
pasta, and season to taste with salt
or salt substitute and freshly
ground black pepper. Gently toss
to mix.

3. Serve immediately.

*Flavor Perk: Before serving, add 2 tablespoons
fresh chopped basil leaves or 1
teaspoon dried basil leaves, tossing
lightly.*

- - - - - - - - - - - - - - - - - - -

Yield: 4 servings
Serving size: ¾-1 cup

Calories: 204
Protein: 9 g
Carbohydrate: 40 g
Fat: less than 1 g
Cholesterol: 0 mg
Sodium: 79 mg
Calcium: 48 mg
Dietary Fiber: 5 g
Sugar: 3 g

BROWN RICE AND CARROT PILAF

*Onion and carrot lend sweetness to the
nutty flavor of brown rice.*

1 large onion, finely chopped
1 cup coarsely shredded carrots
1 cup long-grain brown rice
2½ cups reduced sodium fat free
chicken broth

1. Place onion and carrots in a 2-
quart saucepan sprayed with nonstick cooking spray. Sauté until
onion is soft, about 5 minutes.
Add rice and continue to cook,
stirring, until rice begins to brown
slightly.

2. Add broth and bring to a boil;
cover. Reduce heat and simmer
until rice is tender and liquid is
absorbed, about 45 minutes.

3. Season to taste with salt or salt
substitute and freshly ground
black pepper.

*Flavor Perk: Stir in ½ cup fresh chopped parsley
before serving.*

*Variation: Add 2 cups fresh or canned bean
sprouts before serving.*

- - - - - - - - - - - - - - - - - - -

Yield: 6 servings
Serving size: ½-¾ cup

Calories: 136
Protein: 4 g
Carbohydrate: 28 g
Fat: less than 1 g
Cholesterol: 0 mg
Sodium: 268 mg
Calcium: 16 mg
Dietary Fiber: 2 g
Sugar: 2 g

BROWN RICE AND LENTILS

Sometimes overlooked, lentils are versatile, nutritious and inexpensive. In this recipe, lentils combine with brown rice for a hearty main dish.

1 cup lentils, rinsed, sorted
3 cups reduced sodium fat free chicken broth
½ cup brown rice, uncooked
2 cups sliced onions

1. Place lentils and 5 cups water in a large pot or Dutch oven. Bring to boiling; then cover and reduce heat. Simmer about 20 minutes. Drain, and return lentils to pot. Add broth and brown rice.

2. In a sprayed skillet, cook onions for about 15 minutes, stirring frequently until soft and clear. Add onions to pot, reserving ⅓ cup. Bring lentil mixture to a boil; then cover and reduce heat. Simmer about 45-50 minutes or until rice is tender. Transfer the mixture to a serving dish. Spread the reserved ⅓ cup onions on top and serve.

Flavor Perk: Add 1 teaspoon cumin to the mixture before simmering. Serve with lime or lemon wedges.

- - - - - - - - - - - - - - - - - - -

Yield: 10-12 servings
Serving size: ½ cup

Calories: 84
Protein: 6 g
Carbohydrate: 15 g
Fat: less than 1 g
Cholesterol: 0 mg
Sodium: 172 mg
Calcium: 15 mg
Dietary Fiber: 6 g
Sugar: 2 g

RED BEANS AND BROWN RICE

½ cup chopped onion
1 cup chopped green or red bell pepper
3 cups cooked brown rice
1 (15 ounce) can dark kidney beans, drained, rinsed

In a Dutch oven or large saucepan sprayed with nonstick cooking spray, sauté onion and bell pepper about 5-6 minutes until onion is tender and pepper is crisp-tender. Add rice and beans and stir gently over low heat until heated through. (Add 2 tablespoons water at a time if mixture sticks to pan while heating.) Season to taste with freshly ground black pepper.

Microwave directions: After onion and bell pepper are sautéed, transfer to a large microwave-safe bowl or dish. Stir in rice and beans; then cover and heat on high 1 minute. Stir. Continue heating 30 seconds at a time, stirring until heated through.

Flavor Perk: Add ¼ cup chopped parsley, lite Cajun or Creole seasoning or hot pepper sauce to taste.

Variation: Substitute pinto or black beans for the kidney beans.

- - - - - - - - - - - - - - - - - - -

Yield: 8-10 servings
Serving size: 1 cup

Calories: 120
Protein: 4 g
Carbohydrate: 24 g
Fat: less than 1 g
Cholesterol: 0 mg
Sodium: 165 mg
Calcium: 21 mg
Dietary Fiber: 5 g
Sugar: 2 g

BROWN RICE PATTIES

Nutritionally, brown rice is considered superior to white rice, since the whitening process strips the high fiber and nutrient content found in the rice's bran layer. Brown rice has a nutty flavor and slightly firm texture that combines well with other foods.

Despite a longer cooking time and shorter shelf life than white rice, health-conscious cooks generally choose brown over white rice. If preparation time is short, instant brown rice is also available.

½ cup chopped onion
1½ cups cooked brown rice
½ cup egg substitute
1 teaspoon Italian herb blend or dried basil leaves

1. Sauté onion in a sprayed skillet over medium heat until clear and tender. Remove onion and place in a mixing bowl. Add brown rice, egg substitute and herbs. If desired, season to taste with salt or salt substitute and freshly ground pepper.

2. Form 6 patties, using ½ cup mixture for each patty. Add patties to the skillet and flatten each with a spatula to about 3 inches in diameter. Cook patties over medium heat about 10 minutes or until lightly browned. Turn patties over and cook an additional 5 minutes.

3. Serve hot.

Flavor Perk: Add ½ cup toasted pine nuts or sunflower seeds to the rice mixture.

- -

Yield: 4 servings
Serving size: 1 patty

Calories: 104
Protein: 5 g
Carbohydrate: 19 g
Fat: less than 1 g
Cholesterol: 0 mg
Sodium: 54 mg
Calcium: 21 mg
Dietary Fiber: 2 g
Sugar: less than 1 g

CURRIED COUSCOUS

Couscous is often used in place of rice, so it is sometimes mistaken as a grain. However, couscous is the tiniest of pastas and is a staple of North African cooking.

½ teaspoon curry powder
¼ teaspoon ground allspice
2 cups reduced sodium fat free chicken broth
1 (10 ounce) box couscous mix

1. Add curry and allspice to a sprayed saucepan over medium heat. Cook spices, stirring constantly, for about 1 minute. Add broth and bring to boiling; then stir in couscous.

2. Cover; remove from heat and let stand 5 minutes. Uncover and toss lightly with fork.

3. Serve immediately.

- - - - - - - - - - - - - - - - - -

Yield: 4 servings
Serving size: About ½ cup

Calories: 240
Protein: 10 g
Carbohydrate: 48 g
Fat: less than 1 g
Cholesterol: 0 mg
Sodium: 418 mg
Calcium: 15 mg
Dietary Fiber: 3 g
Sugar: less than 1 g

FAVORITE CHEESE GRITS

1 cup uncooked white hominy grits
1½ cups reduced fat Velveeta, cubed
2 green onions with tops, sliced
½ cup egg substitute

1. Preheat oven to 350°. Prepare grits according to package directions.

2. Stir cheese into cooked grits and blend until cheese melts. Add green onions and egg substitute; then season to taste with salt or salt substitute and freshly ground black pepper.

3. Pour grits into a 9 x 13-inch baking dish sprayed with nonstick cooking spray. Bake, uncovered, 25-30 minutes or until lightly browned and bubbling.

Flavor Perk: Add liquid hot pepper sauce to taste.

Variation: Substitute Mexican-flavored Velveeta for the regular Velveeta.

- - - - - - - - - - - - - - - - - -

Yield: 8 servings
Serving size: ½-¾ cup

Calories: 163
Protein: 11 g
Carbohydrate: 20 g
Fat: 5 g
Cholesterol: 23 mg
Sodium: 701 mg
Calcium: 8 mg
Dietary Fiber: less than 1 g
Sugar: 3 g

MAC N' CHEESE

6 ounces uncooked elbow macaroni
6 ounces light Velveeta, cubed
1 cup skim or evaporated skim milk
1 tablespoon melted stick margarine

1. Prepare macaroni according to package directions; drain. Preheat oven to 450°.

2. Combine cooked macaroni, cheese, milk and margarine. Season to taste with freshly ground black pepper. Spoon macaroni mixture into a sprayed 2-quart baking dish.

3. Bake 15-18 minutes until lightly browned and bubbly. Let stand 5 minutes before serving.

- - - - - - - - - - - - - - - - - - -

Yield: 4-6 servings
Serving size: ½ cup

Calories: 236
Protein: 12 g
Carbohydrate: 31 g
Fat: 6 g
Cholesterol: 19 mg
Sodium: 593 mg
Calcium: 67 mg
Dietary Fiber: less than 1 g
Sugar: 6 g

FETTUCCINE PRIMAVERA

8 ounces fettuccine or linguine, uncooked
¼ cup finely chopped onion
1 (16 ounce) package frozen bite-size vegetable blend (carrots, broccoli, zucchini and mushrooms), thawed, drained
1 cup Alfredo Sauce (p. 181)

1. Prepare pasta according to package directions; drain. In a sprayed large skillet over medium heat, sauté onion until tender. Add vegetables and cook, stirring frequently, until vegetables are crisp-tender.

2. Add Alfredo Sauce and cooked fettuccine and heat through. Serve immediately.

Flavor Perk: Sprinkle with 1 tablespoon grated Parmesan cheese.

Variation: Substitute 4 cups fresh vegetables for the frozen vegetables.

- - - - - - - - - - - - - - - - - - -

Yield: 4 servings
Serving size: 1 cup

Calories (without sauce): 255
Protein: 9 g
Carbohydrate: 50 g
Fat: less than 1 g
Cholesterol: 0 mg
Sodium: 43 mg
Calcium: 39 mg
Dietary Fiber: 4 g
Sugar: 5 g

ALFREDO SAUCE

Toss this sauce with freshly cooked fettuccine pasta as a side or main dish. To trim calories and fat, this recipe replaces heavy cream with skim milk and reduces the amounts of margarine and Parmesan cheese. Try it on cooked vegetables for a creamy side dish.

¼ cup margarine
¼ cup skim or evaporated skim milk
½ cup grated or shredded Parmesan cheese

1. Heat margarine and milk in a skillet over medium heat, stirring constantly until margarine melts. Reduce heat to low and simmer, stirring frequently, about 6 minutes or until slightly thickened.

2. Remove from heat, stir in cheese, freshly ground black pepper and salt or salt substitute to taste.

- - - - - - - - - - - - - - - - - - - -

Yield: 4 servings (About 2 cups)
Serving size: ¼ cup

Calories: 158
Protein: 5 g
Carbohydrate: 2 g
Fat: 14 g
Cholesterol: 9 mg
Sodium: 335 mg
Calcium: 179 mg
Dietary Fiber: 0 g
Sugar: 1 g

LEMONY LINGUINE

8 ounces dried linguine, uncooked
½ cup fresh lemon juice and 2 teaspoons finely grated lemon peel
2 teaspoons olive or vegetable oil
1-2 finely minced or pressed garlic cloves

1. Prepare linguine according to package directions; drain. Place warm cooked linguine in a large bowl; then sprinkle with lemon juice and peel and toss.

2. Heat oil in a small skillet over medium heat. Add garlic and sauté 2-3 minutes. Pour the garlic-oil mixture over the linguine and toss again. Serve immediately.

Flavor Perk: Sprinkle with Parmesan cheese and fresh parsley.

- - - - - - - - - - - - - - - - - - - -

Yield: 4 servings
Serving size: 1 cup

Calories: 240
Protein: 7 g
Carbohydrate: 45 g
Fat: 3 g
Cholesterol: 0 mg
Sodium: 2 mg
Calcium: 15 mg
Dietary Fiber: 2 g
Sugar: 3 g

NOODLES PARMESAN

8 ounces cholesterol free egg noodle substitute or egg free pasta ribbons, uncooked
¼ cup reduced fat margarine
¼ cup reduced fat grated Parmesan-style topping
Skim milk

1. Prepare noodles according to package directions; drain. Preheat oven to 325°.

2. In a mixing bowl, combine noodles, margarine and cheese. Season to taste with salt or salt substitute and freshly ground black pepper. If a thinner mixture is desired, add 1 tablespoon milk at a time until mixture reaches desired consistency.

3. Spoon noodle mixture into a sprayed baking dish, and bake 15-20 minutes or until heated through.

4. Serve immediately.

Flavor Perk: Add 2 tablespoons fresh chopped parsley or 2 teaspoons dried parsley flakes.

- - - - - - - - - - - - - - - - - - -

Yield: 4 servings
Serving size: ½-¾ cup

Calories: 286
Protein: 9 g
Carbohydrate: 47 g
Fat: 7 g
Cholesterol: 0 mg
Sodium: 184 mg
Calcium: 5 mg
Dietary Fiber: 1 g
Sugar: 3 g

ORZO AND SUN-DRIED TOMATOES

4 tablespoons sun-dried tomatoes, no oil
¾ cup frozen seasoning blend (onion, celery, bell pepper and parsley), partially thawed
2 tablespoons red wine vinegar
2 cups cooked orzo (rice-shaped pasta)

1. Combine tomatoes with 4 tablespoons hot water; cover and let stand 15 minutes. Drain well. Chop tomatoes and set aside.

2. In a sprayed skillet over medium heat, cook and stir seasoning blend until vegetables are tender, about 2-3 minutes. Add chopped tomatoes and vinegar and heat about 1 minute.

3. Remove from heat; add orzo and toss lightly. Season to taste with salt or salt substitute and freshly ground black pepper.

4. Serve immediately.

Flavor Perk: Use 2 teaspoons olive oil to sauté seasoning blend.
Variation: Substitute ¼ cup chopped onion, ¼ cup chopped celery and ¼ cup bell pepper for the frozen seasoning blend; sauté in 2 teaspoons olive oil before adding tomatoes.

- - - - - - - - - - - - - - - - - - -

Yield: 4 servings
Serving size: ½ cup

Calories: 330
Protein: 11 g
Carbohydrate: 67 g
Fat: 1 g   Calcium: 19 g
Cholesterol: 0 mg   Dietary Fiber: 3 g
Sodium: 83 mg   Sugar: 4 g

PENNE PASTA STIR-FRY

12 ounces dry penne pasta or similar size pasta of choice, uncooked
2 finely minced or pressed garlic cloves
2 carrots, peeled, thinly sliced
8 ounces snow peas, ends clipped

1. Prepare pasta according to package directions; drain. In a sprayed non-stick wok pan or a large skillet over medium-high heat; add garlic. Stir constantly until garlic is fragrant and lightly brown, about 1 minute.

2. Remove garlic and set aside. Add carrots and stir fry 1-2 minutes or until crisp-tender, adding 1 tablespoon water at a time if needed.

3. Add snow peas and stir-fry 1 minute. Stir in pasta and garlic; then season to taste with salt or salt substitute and freshly ground black pepper.

4. Heat through and serve immediately.

Flavor Perk: Add 2-3 tablespoons light soy sauce with the pasta and garlic.
Variation: Stir in Simple Stir-Fry Sauce (p. 183) with pasta and garlic.

- - - - - - - - - - - - - - - - - - - -

Yield: 4 servings
Serving size: About 1 cup

Calories: 355
Protein: 13 g
Carbohydrate: 72 g
Fat: 2 g
Cholesterol: 0 mg
Sodium: 16 mg
Calcium: 50 mg
Dietary Fiber: 4 g
Sugar: 7 g

SIMPLE STIR-FRY SAUCE

2 teaspoons cornstarch
3 tablespoons reduced sodium soy sauce
3 tablespoons rice or white wine vinegar
1 cup chicken broth or 1 teaspoon chicken broth granules (plus 1 cup water)

1. Stir cornstarch and soy sauce together in small saucepan. Add vinegar and broth. Stirring constantly, heat to boiling and cook 1 minute or until sauce clears and thickens.

- - - - - - - - - - - - - - - - - - - -

Yield: 10 servings
Serving size: About 2 tablespoons

Calories: 10
Protein: less than 1 g
Carbohydrate: 1 g
Fat: 0 g
Cholesterol: 0 mg
Sodium: 214 mg
Calcium: 1 mg
Dietary Fiber: 0 g
Sugar: less than 1 g

PASTA PIZZA PLEASE

8 ounces uncooked rigatoni (spiral) or wagon wheel pasta
½ cup egg substitute
1 cup pizza sauce
1½ cups reduced fat mozzarella cheese, shredded

1. Prepare pasta according to package directions; drain. Preheat oven to 400°.

2. Stir together cooked pasta, egg substitute and freshly ground black pepper to taste. Spread in a prepared 9 x 9-inch baking dish; bake 10 minutes.

3. Remove from oven and spread sauce over pasta. Sprinkle cheese on top and return to oven to bake an additional 10 minutes.

4. Cut in squares to serve.

Flavor Perk: Add hot red pepper flakes and reduced fat Parmesan cheese.

- - - - - - - - - - - - - - - - - -

Yield: 4 servings
Serving size: 2 (3-inch) squares

Calories: 227
Protein: 14 g
Carbohydrate: 32 g
Fat: 5 g
Cholesterol: 11 mg
Sodium: 212 mg
Calcium: 214 mg
Dietary Fiber: 2 g
Sugar: 3 g

POBLANO CHILE PASTA BAKE

7 ounces dried small shells, macaroni or wagon wheel pasta, uncooked
1 (10½ ounce) can cream of chile poblano (Mexican pepper) soup
¼ cup skim milk
¼ cup reduced fat Monterey jack or cheddar cheese, shredded

1. Prepare pasta according to package directions; drain. Preheat oven to 350°.

2. In a saucepan over medium heat, stir soup and milk together; heat just to boiling. Stir in cooked pasta and season to taste with salt or salt substitute and freshly ground black pepper.

3. Pour mixture in a sprayed 2-quart baking dish. Sprinkle with cheese. Bake, uncovered, 15-20 minutes or until sauce bubbles and cheese melts.

Flavor Perk: Garnish with fresh cilantro leaves.

Variation: Substitute fiesta nacho cheese soup for cream of chile poblano soup.

- - - - - - - - - - - - - - - - - -

Yield: 4 servings
Serving size: About 1 cup

Calories: 303
Protein: 12 g
Carbohydrate: 44 g
Fat: 8 g
Cholesterol: 12 mg
Sodium: 663 mg
Calcium: 140 mg
Dietary Fiber: 2 g
Sugar: 3 g

POPPY SEED-NOODLE BAKE

8 ounces cholesterol free egg
noodle substitute or egg free wide
pasta ribbons, uncooked
1 cup reduced fat sour cream
1 tablespoon poppy seeds
¼ teaspoon paprika

1. Prepare noodles according to package directions; drain. Preheat oven to 300°.

2. Combine noodles, sour cream and poppy seeds. Season to taste with salt or salt substitute and freshly ground black pepper. Spread in a shallow baking dish sprayed with nonstick cooking spray.

3. Sprinkle with paprika and bake about 15-20 minutes or until heated through. Serve immediately.

- - - - - - - - - - - - - - - - - - -

Yield: 4-5 servings
Serving size: About 1 cup

Calories: 268
Protein: 11 g
Carbohydrate: 41 g
Fat: 6 g
Cholesterol: 18 mg
Sodium: 36 mg
Calcium: 36 mg
Dietary Fiber: 1 g
Sugar: 6 g

QUICK N' EASY NOODLES

8 ounces cholesterol free egg
noodle substitute or egg free pasta
ribbons, uncooked
¼ cup melted light margarine
2 tablespoons poppy seeds
Skim milk

1. Cook noodles according to package directions; drain. In a mixing bowl, stir together noodles, margarine and poppy seeds. If a thinner mixture is desired, add 1 tablespoon milk at a time until mixture reaches desired consistency.

2. Spoon noodle mixture into a microwave-safe dish; cover and place in microwave oven. Microwave on full power 2-3 minutes and check to see if heated through. If needed, continue heating.

3. Serve immediately.

- - - - - - - - - - - - - - - - - - -

Yield: 4-5 servings
Serving size: ½ cup

Calories: 248
Protein: 8 g
Carbohydrate: 40 g
Fat: 6 g
Cholesterol: less than 1 g
Sodium: 65 mg
Calcium: 58 mg
Dietary Fiber: 1 g
Sugar: 3 g

RICE-ONION BAKE

1 cup white long grain rice, uncooked
½ cup prepared liquid butter substitute
1 (10½ ounce) can French onion soup
1 (8 ounce) can sliced water chestnuts, rinsed, drained

1. Preheat oven to 350°. In a large bowl, combine all ingredients and 1¼ cups water. Pour into a sprayed 2-quart baking dish.

2. Bake, covered, for 1 hour.

Flavor Perk: Add ½ cup diced pimiento to mixture.

- - - - - - - - - - - - - - - - - -

Yield: 8 servings
Serving size: About ½ cup

Calories: 241
Protein: 2 g
Carbohydrate: 23 g
Fat: 15 g
Cholesterol: 2 mg
Sodium: 308 mg
Calcium: 15 mg
Dietary Fiber: 1 g
Sugar: 2 g

RISOTTO

Arborio, a short-grained Italian or risotto rice, has a higher starch content than regular short-grain rice. As the rice cooks, the starch is released, giving the rice a creamy texture.

½ cup chopped onion
1½ cups uncooked Arborio or other short-grain white rice
2 cups reduced sodium fat free chicken broth, warmed
¼ cup reduced fat grated Parmesan topping

1. In a Dutch oven sprayed with non-stick cooking spray, sauté onion over medium heat until tender. Add uncooked rice and cook over medium heat, stirring constantly, about 5 minutes.

2. Combine warmed chicken broth and 1 cup warm water. Pour ½ cup broth mixture over rice and cook uncovered, stirring occasionally, until liquid is absorbed. Repeat with remaining broth mixture, ½ cup at a time, until rice is tender and creamy.

3. Season to taste with freshly ground black pepper and sprinkle with cheese. Serve immediately.

Variation: Risotto with Peas – Just before serving risotto, stir in 10 ounces frozen green peas, cooked, drained.

- - - - - - - - - - - - - - - - - -

Yield: 6 servings
Serving size: ½-¾ cup

Calories: 190
Protein: 5 g   Sodium: 282 mg
Carbohydrate: 40 g   Calcium: 3 mg
Fat: 1 g   Dietary Fiber: 1 g
Cholesterol: 0 mg   Sugar: less than 1 g

ROTINI-BROCCOLI BAKE

4½ ounces dry rotini (spiral) or penne pasta, uncooked
2 cups cooked broccoli florets
6 ounces reduced fat Velveeta, cubed
1 cup evaporated skim milk

1. Prepare pasta according to package directions; drain. Preheat oven to 450°.

2. Place cooked pasta in a large saucepan; add broccoli and cheese and stir until well blended. Spoon mixture into a prepared 6-cup baking dish. Pour milk evenly over the top.

3. Bake 12-15 minutes, until lightly browned and bubbly.

Flavor Perk: Add salt free seasoning blend of your choice to the pasta mixture before baking.

- - - - - - - - - - - - - - - - -

Yield: 6 servings
Serving size: 1 cup

Calories: 179
Protein: 12 g
Carbohydrate: 25 g
Fat: 4 g
Cholesterol: 17 mg
Sodium: 506 mg
Calcium: 138 mg
Dietary Fiber: less than 1 g
Sugar: 3 g

SIMPLE RICE PILAF

½ cup chopped white, yellow or green onion
½ cup thinly sliced mushrooms
1 cup uncooked long grain white rice
2 cups reduced sodium fat free chicken broth

1. In a large sprayed saucepan over medium heat, sauté onion and mushrooms about 3 minutes, stirring frequently. Add rice and cook 5 minutes, stirring frequently. Add broth; then stir and heat to boiling.

2. Reduce heat to low; then cover and simmer 15 minutes. Do not lift cover or stir.

3. Remove from heat and let stand, covered, 5 minutes before serving.

Flavor Perk: Add ½ cup fresh chopped parsley or 1 tablespoon dried parsley.

Variation: Substitute brown rice for the long-grain rice; cook 50 minutes. Another variation is to substitute ¼ cup each raisins, coarsely chopped dried apricots and dried cranberries for the onion and mushrooms.

- - - - - - - - - - - - - - - - -

Yield: 4-5 servings
Serving size: ½-¾ cup

Calories: 166
Protein: 5 g
Carbohydrate: 35 g
Fat: less than 1 g
Cholesterol: 0 mg
Sodium: 279 mg
Calcium: 15 mg
Dietary Fiber: less than 1 g
Sugar: 1 g

CREAMY, CHEESY NOODLE BAKE

This noodle dish takes advantage of the no-cholesterol "yolkless" egg noodles now available.

6 ounces cholesterol free egg noodle substitute or egg free pasta ribbons, uncooked
1 cup reduced fat cottage cheese
1 cup reduced fat sour cream
¼ cup reduced fat grated Parmesan topping

1. Cook noodles according to package directions; drain. Preheat oven to 350°. Combine cooked noodles, cottage cheese and sour cream. Season to taste with salt or salt substitute and freshly ground black pepper.

2. Place noodles in a 2-quart baking dish sprayed with nonstick cooking spray. Sprinkle with cheese. Bake 20 minutes or until heated through.

Flavor Perk: Add 1 teaspoon freeze-dried chives or 1 tablespoon finely chopped green onion tops.

- - - - - - - - - - - - - - - - - -

Yield: 5 servings
Serving size: About ¾ cup

Calories: 251
Protein: 15 g
Carbohydrate: 29 g
Cholesterol: 27 mg
Sodium: 271 mg
Calcium: 157 mg
Dietary Fiber: less than 1 g
Sugar: 3 g

SPAGHETTI BAKE

4 ounces dried spaghetti or thin spaghetti, uncooked
1 cup part skim ricotta cheese, stirred
1 (14 ounce) jar reduced fat spaghetti sauce
½ cup reduced fat mozzarella cheese, shredded

1. Prepare spaghetti according to package directions; drain. Preheat oven to 375°.

2. Place cooked spaghetti in a 9-inch square baking dish or a 9-inch pie plate. Press spaghetti gently on bottom and 1 inch up on sides of dish.

3. Spoon and gently spread ricotta cheese over spaghetti. Spoon and spread spaghetti sauce over ricotta cheese. Sprinkle with mozzarella cheese.

4. Bake 35-45 minutes. Let stand 5 minutes before serving.

5. Serve with shredded or grated reduced fat Parmesan cheese.

Flavor Perk: Pour ½ cup egg substitute over spaghetti in dish; add 1 tablespoon fresh chopped basil or parsley to ricotta cheese.

- - - - - - - - - - - - - - - - - -

Yield: 4 servings
Serving size: 1 cup

Calories: 260
Protein: 16 g
Carbohydrate: 32 g
Fat: 7 g
Cholesterol: 25 mg
Sodium: 450 mg
Calcium: 298 mg
Dietary Fiber: 2 g
Sugar: 9 g

SPINACH-CHEESE RAVIOLI

2 (14½ ounce) cans diced tomatoes with basil, garlic and oregano
2 (9 ounce) packages refrigerated cheese ravioli
4 cups fresh spinach, coarsely chopped
2 tablespoons reduced fat grated Parmesan-style topping

1. Place tomatoes in a large saucepan and bring to boiling. Add ravioli; reduce heat and cover. Cook about 5 minutes, stirring frequently. Uncover and cook an additional 5 minutes or until ravioli is tender.

2. Stir in spinach, salt or salt substitute and freshly ground black pepper to taste. Cook 2 minutes; then remove from heat and let stand, covered, about 5 minutes.

3. Sprinkle with Parmesan topping before serving.

- - - - - - - - - - - - - - - - - -

Yield: 8 servings
Serving size: About 1 cup

Calories: 175
Protein: 9 g
Carbohydrate: 25 g
Fat: 4 g
Cholesterol: 22 mg
Sodium: 761 mg
Calcium: 223 mg
Dietary Fiber: 3 g
Sugar: 7 g

THAI FRIED RICE WITH VEGETABLES

1 cup jasmine rice, uncooked
1 tablespoon finely minced or pressed garlic
12 ounces fresh or frozen mixed bite-size or sliced vegetables
3 tablespoons oyster or fish sauce

1. Cook rice according to package directions. In a sprayed nonstick wok pan or a large skillet over medium-high heat, stir-fry garlic about 1 minute.

2. Add vegetables and stir-fry until crisp-tender, about 1-2 minutes. Stir in sauce and mix; then add rice and heat through.

3. Serve immediately.

- - - - - - - - - - - - - - - - - -

Yield: 3-4 servings
Serving size: 1 cup

Calories: 244
Protein: 5 g
Carbohydrate: 54 g
Fat: less than 1 g
Cholesterol: 0 mg
Sodium: 625 mg
Calcium: 48 mg
Dietary Fiber: 3 g
Sugar: 6 g

THAI CHICKEN AND NOODLE STIR-FRY

1 (7 ounce) package thin rice
noodles, uncooked
4 ounces slivered chicken tenders
1 tablespoon fish sauce
2 tablespoons reduced sodium soy
sauce

1. Prepare noodles according to package directions; drain. In a sprayed nonstick wok or a large skillet over medium-high heat, add chicken. Stir-fry 1 minute.

2. Add drained noodles, fish sauce and soy sauce and stir-fry 3-5 minutes.

3. Serve immediately.

Flavor Perk: Add 1 tablespoon sugar substitute with soy sauce.

Variation: Substitute 4 ounces sliced or bite-size fresh or frozen vegetables for the chicken.

- - - - - - - - - - - - - - - - - - - -

Yield: 4 servings
Serving size: 1 cup

Calories: 230
Protein: 10 grams
Carbohydrate: 44 grams
Fat: 2 grams
Cholesterol: 24 milligrams
Sodium: 734 milligrams
Calcium: 13 milligrams
Dietary Fiber: less than 1 gram
Sugar: 1 gram

TWO-CHEESE POLENTA

1 cup yellow cornmeal
4 cups water, divided
$\frac{2}{3}$ cup reduced fat grated
Parmesan-style topping, divided
$\frac{1}{3}$ cup reduced fat Swiss cheese,
shredded

1. Heat oven to 350°. Mix cornmeal and $\frac{3}{4}$ cup water in medium saucepan. Stir in 3-$\frac{1}{4}$ cups boiling water. Cook, stirring constantly, until mixture boils and thickens.

2. Reduce heat; cover and simmer about 10 minutes, stirring frequently. When mixture is very thick, remove from heat and stir until smooth.

3. In a sprayed 1$\frac{1}{2}$-quart baking dish, layer a third of polenta and sprinkle with $\frac{1}{3}$ cup Parmesan cheese. Repeat. Spoon on remaining polenta; then sprinkle with Swiss cheese.

4. Bake, uncovered, 15-20 minutes or until lightly browned.

- - - - - - - - - - - - - - - - - - - -

Yield: 6 servings
Serving size: $\frac{1}{2}$-$\frac{3}{4}$ cup

Calories: 166
Protein: 6 g
Carbohydrate: 21 g
Fat: 6 g
Cholesterol: 9 mg
Sodium: 221 mg
Calcium: 111 mg
Dietary Fiber: 1 g
Sugar: 0 g

VEGETABLES ALFREDO

8 ounces dried rotini (spiral) or shells pasta
1 (16 ounce) package frozen vegetable blend (carrots, broccoli, zucchini and cauliflower), partially thawed
1½ cups Alfredo Sauce (p.181) or 1 (10 ounce) jar light Alfredo sauce
2 tablespoons coarsely chopped fresh tarragon or 1½ teaspoons dried tarragon leaves, crumbled

1. Prepare pasta according to package directions; remove and drain. Spray the same pot with nonstick cooking spray; add vegetables. Cook vegetables about 2-3 minutes over medium heat, stirring constantly until crisp-tender.

2. Add cooked pasta and keep warm. Heat Alfredo Sauce and tarragon in a saucepan over medium heat about 1 minute or until heated through. Place pasta and vegetables in a warmed serving dish.

3. Pour Alfredo Sauce over pasta and vegetables. Serve immediately.

Flavor Perk: Add ¼ teaspoon crushed red pepper flakes to sauce.

- - - - - - - - - - - - - - - - - -

Yield: 4-6 servings
Serving size: 1 cup

Calories (without sauce): 197
Protein: 7 g
Carbohydrate: 40 g
Fat: less than 1 g
Cholesterol: 0 mg
Sodium: 24 mg
Calcium: 30 mg
Dietary Fiber: 3 g
Sugar: 4 g

VERMICELLI AND PESTO

16 ounces dried vermicelli (thin spaghetti), uncooked
¾ cup freshly-made pesto or prepared refrigerated pesto
½ cup freshly-grated Parmesan cheese
3 tablespoons part-skim ricotta cheese

1. Prepare the pasta according to package directions; drain. In a small bowl, mix the pesto, Parmesan cheese and ricotta cheese until blended.

2. When ready to serve, stir 2-3 tablespoons hot water into the mixture. Pour the pesto sauce over the vermicelli, toss lightly and serve hot.

Flavor Perk: Garnish with toasted pine nuts.

Variation: Substitute spaghetti or fettuccine for the vermicelli.

- - - - - - - - - - - - - - - - - -

Yield: 6 servings
Serving size: ¾-1 cup

Calories: 344
Protein: 10 g
Carbohydrate: 59 g
Fat: 4 g
Cholesterol: 8 g
Sodium: 259 mg
Calcium: 138 mg
Dietary Fiber: 3 g
Sugar: 1 g

VEGETABLE-STUFFED MANICOTTI

7-8 dried manicotti shells, uncooked
1½ cups frozen bite-size vegetable blend
(broccoli, carrots, mushrooms, zucchini)
1 tablespoon chopped fresh basil or ¼ teaspoon dried basil
1½ cups shredded reduced fat Monterey jack or Swiss cheese, divided

1. Prepare pasta according to package directions; drain. Preheat oven to 350°. In a sprayed skillet over medium heat, place frozen vegetables, basil and ¼ cup water. Bring to a boil; then reduce heat to medium low.

2. Stirring frequently, cook vegetables until crisp-tender, about 4-5 minutes. Drain water from vegetables and stir 1 cup cheese into vegetables. Season to taste with salt or salt substitute and freshly ground black pepper.

3. With a small spoon, fill shells with vegetable-cheese mixture. Sprinkle tops with remaining cheese. Place shells in a single layer in a sprayed rectangular baking pan and cover with foil.

4. Bake 15 minutes or until cheese melts and dish is heated through.

Flavor Perk: Spoon heated marinara sauce over each serving and garnish with grated Parmesan cheese.

Variation: Add ½ cup low fat ricotta cheese to the vegetable-cheese mixture before stuffing shells.

- -

Yield: 6-8 servings
Serving size: 1 shell

Calories: 317
Protein: 23 g
Carbohydrate: 22 g
Fat: 15 g
Cholesterol: 48 mg
Sodium: 92 mg
Calcium: 608 mg
Dietary Fiber: 1 g
Sugar: 2 g

EGGS & CHEESE

You may ask why egg recipes are included in a cookbook promoting healthy eating. Simply put, eggs have unique qualities and offer great versatility in preparing many different dishes—from tender cakes and fluffy meringues to moist meat balls and fish croquettes.

In the last 15 to 20 years, far fewer eggs have been consumed by Americans, mainly due to concerns over the cholesterol found in the yolk of eggs. Nutritionally speaking, eggs have a place in well-balanced, healthy diets, although nutritionists agree that eggs should be eaten in moderation.

Should you be concerned about lowering cholesterol in your food intake, consider using a cholesterol-free egg product in your cooking. These cholesterol-free products are a satisfactory substitute for whole eggs, and you will find these products used in recipes in this section and throughout the book.

Whether used as a garnish or as a main ingredient, cheeses are greatly favored in cooking for their flavor and texture. As a general rule for healthy eating, high fat cheeses should be consumed in moderation. Check out the dairy products available in your supermarket to find and try fat free and lower fat cheeses.

CHEESY FRESH BASIL OMELET

1 cup egg substitute
2 teaspoons light stick margarine
2 tablespoons feta or goat cheese, coarsely crumbled
1 tablespoon fresh chopped basil leaves or 1 teaspoon dried basil leaves

1. Place egg substitute in bowl. Add 1 tablespoon water, salt or salt substitute and freshly ground black pepper to taste. Stir to blend.

2. Melt margarine in a nonstick omelet pan or skillet on medium heat. Pour in egg mixture and cook, gently lifting cooked portion to allow uncooked egg to flow underneath. Continue cooking until there is no more liquid, but top is still moist and creamy.

3. Immediately sprinkle cheese and basil on top; slide omelet to a serving plate and fold over. Cut into fourths and serve immediately.

- - - - - - - - - - - - - - - - - -

Yield: 4 Servings

Calories: 59
Protein: 7 g
Carbohydrate: 1 g
Fat: 3 g
Cholesterol: 4 mg
Sodium: 174 mg
Calcium: 45 mg
Dietary Fiber: 0 g
Sugar: less than 1 g

MUSHROOM-CHEESE OMELET

½ cup egg substitute
2 tablespoons skim milk
½ cup mushrooms, finely chopped
¼ cup shredded reduced fat cheddar cheese

1. In a small bowl, beat eggs and skim milk.

2. Preheat a nonstick skillet over medium heat and add egg mixture. Season to taste with salt or salt substitute and freshly ground black pepper. When egg mixture is partially set, sprinkle mushrooms and cheese on top.

3. Reduce heat to low and cook until bottom of omelet is lightly browned. Using a spatula, fold the omelet in half and serve.

4. Serve with sliced tomatoes.

- - - - - - - - - - - - - - - - - -

Yield: 1 serving

Calories: 224
Protein: 31 g
Carbohydrate: 7 g
Fat: 10 g
Cholesterol: 31 mg
Sodium: 558 mg
Calcium: 479 mg
Dietary Fiber: less than 1 g
Sugar: 3 g

HUEVOS RANCHEROS
(RANCH-STYLE EGGS)

This is a popular brunch dish in Southwestern cooking.

**1 cup egg substitute
4 (6 inch) whole wheat or flour tortillas
1 cup canned red chile enchilada sauce, warmed
1 cup shredded reduced fat cheddar or part-skim mozzarella cheese**

1. In a preheated sprayed skillet over medium heat, pour egg substitute. Season to taste with salt or salt substitute and freshly ground black pepper. Stirring constantly, cook just until egg substitute is set, but still moist. Remove from skillet and keep warm.

2. Heat enchilada sauce in small saucepan over low heat. Place tortillas in a microwave-safe tortilla warmer and heat 15-30 seconds.

3. Preheat oven broiler. For one serving, place 1 warmed tortilla on broiler-safe plate. Top with ¼ cup scrambled egg substitute, ¼ cup enchilada sauce and ¼ cup shredded cheese. Place plate under broiler just until cheese melts, about 1-2 minutes. Serve immediately.

Flavor Perk: Garnish with fresh cilantro leaves and serve with salsa.

Variation: Substitute canned green chile enchilada sauce for the red chile enchilada sauce.

- -

Yield: 4 servings

Calories: 284
Protein: 26 g
Carbohydrate: 25 g
Fat: 11 g
Cholesterol: 30 mg
Sodium: 848 mg
Calcium: 453 mg
Dietary Fiber: 13 g
Sugar: less than 1 g

MEXI-EGGS

Tomato, green chiles and onion add zesty flavors to this egg dish.

1 Roma (plum) tomato, diced
2 tablespoons onion, diced
2 teaspoons canned diced green chilies
½ cup egg substitute

1. In a sprayed skillet over low heat, combine tomato, onion and green chilies. Cook and stir 2-3 minutes.

2. Add egg substitute and cook, stirring, 1-2 minutes or until eggs are set.

3. Serve with warmed 6-inch whole wheat flour tortillas.

- - - - - - - - - - - - - - - - - - -

Yield: 2 servings

Calories: 48
Protein: 7 g
Carbohydrate: 5 g
Fat: less than 1 g
Cholesterol: 0 mg
Sodium: 124 mg
Calcium: 32 mg
Dietary Fiber: 1 g
Sugar: 2 g

SPEEDY GONZALES CHEESE ENCHILADAS

12 (6 inch) whole wheat tortillas
1 (8 ounce) package shredded reduced fat cheddar cheese or part-skim mozzarella cheese, divided
½ cup chopped onion, divided
2 (10 ounce) cans green or red enchilada sauce

1. Cover stack of tortillas on both sides with slightly damp paper towels. Microwave on full power for 45 seconds.

2. Place ⅓ cup cheese and a sprinkling of onions on each tortilla; roll up. Place tortillas seam side down in a 9 x 9-inch baking dish.

3. Pour enchilada sauce over tortillas. Sprinkle with remaining cheese and onions.

4. Cover and microwave on 50% power for 5-6 minutes.

5. Serve with fresh salsa and reduced fat sour cream.

- - - - - - - - - - - - - - - - - - -

Yield: 6 servings
Serving size: 2 enchiladas

Calories: 270
Protein: 14 g
Carbohydrate: 31 g
Fat: 9 g
Cholesterol: 27 mg
Sodium: 782 mg
Calcium: 318 mg
Dietary Fiber: 19 g
Sugar: 1 g

MUSHROOM EMPANADAS

Variations of empanadas or turnovers are found throughout the world, with different fillings reflecting local cuisines. Both sweet and meat-type fillings are used in this versatile pastry-like dish.

**½ cup reduced fat cream of mushroom soup
2 teaspoons Dijon-style mustard
4 reduced fat refrigerated biscuits
1 cup mushrooms, chopped**

1. Preheat oven to 350°. Combine soup and mustard and set aside. Using a rolling pin, roll each biscuit between 2 sheets of wax paper, forming a circle 6 inches in diameter.

2. Place biscuit circles on a sprayed baking sheet. Spread ¼ mustard mixture on each biscuit circle and top with ¼ cup mushrooms.

3. Moisten edges of biscuit circle with water and fold over, turnover style. Press edges with tines of a fork to seal. Bake 10-15 minutes or until lightly browned.

4. Serve immediately.

Flavor Perk: *Add ½ teaspoon parsley flakes or dried herb of your choice.*

- -

Yield: 4 servings

Calories: 86
Protein: 3 g
Carbohydrate: 14 g
Fat: 2 g
Cholesterol: 3 mg
Sodium: 422 mg
Calcium: 34 mg
Dietary Fiber: less than 1 g
Sugar: less than 1 g

EGGS BENEDICT

In this recipe, the classic Eggs Benedict has been modified to reduce calories, sodium and cholesterol. One serving of Eggs Benedict traditionally consists of ½ buttered and toasted English muffin, a large slice of ham or Canadian bacon and a poached egg, topped with high calorie, high fat Hollandaise Sauce. Our healthier version uses cholesterol free fat free egg substitute for the poached egg, a tomato slice for the ham and a reduced sodium and fat Hollandaise sauce.

3 whole grain English muffins, split, freshly toasted
1 large tomato, cut into ¼-inch slices
1½ cups scrambled egg substitute
¾ cup Hollandaise Sauce (p. 198), warmed

1. Top each muffin half with a tomato slice and ¼ cup scrambled egg substitute. Spoon 2 tablespoons Hollandaise sauce over each muffin half.

2. Serve immediately.

Flavor Perk: Garnish with fresh chopped parsley.

Variation: Substitute 1¼ cups cheese sauce for Hollandaise sauce; sprinkle with paprika.

- - - - - - - - - - - - - - - - - -

Yield: 6 servings
Serving size: ½ muffin

Calories (with sauce): 154
Protein: 11 g
Carbohydrate: 16 g
Fat: 5 g
Cholesterol: 15 g
Sodium: 380 mg
Calcium: 133 mg
Dietary Fiber: 2 g
Sugar: 3 g

HOLLANDAISE SAUCE

This famous sauce was named for the country of Holland. Traditional Hollandaise sauce can be tricky to make and is loaded with fat and calories. The modified version here has no tricks and is made with fewer calories.

6 ounces reduced fat cream cheese
⅓ cup light sour cream
3-4 tablespoons skim milk
2 teaspoons fresh lemon juice

1. Place all ingredients in a saucepan over medium-low heat. Stirring constantly, heat mixture until smooth and heated through. Do not boil.

2. Serve immediately.

- - - - - - - - - - - - - - - - - -

Yield: 6 servings (About 1½ cups)
Serving size: ¼ cup

Calories: 94
Protein: 3 g
Carbohydrate: 2 g
Fat: 8 g
Cholesterol: 27 mg
Sodium: 121 mg
Calcium: 44 mg
Dietary Fiber: 0 g
Sugar: less than 1 g

BAKED CHILES RELLENOS

Chiles rellenos or "stuffed peppers" is one of the best-known dishes served by Mexican restaurants in America. Originally, chiles were stuffed with cheese. Today, a wide range of fillings are used, including meat, poultry, seafood, vegetables and cheeses.

This chiles rellenos recipe has been adapted to baking, in contrast to preparation based on frying.

4 large smooth-skinned poblano or Anaheim peppers, roasted, peeled
⅔ cup fat free ricotta cheese
1 cup shredded part-skim mozzarella cheese, divided
½ cup finely chopped green onions and tops

1. Preheat oven to 350°. To prepare peppers, carefully slit open lengthwise. Remove and discard seeds and membrane. Rinse peppers and pat dry.

2. In a small bowl, combine ricotta cheese, ⅔ cup mozzarella cheese and green onion. Shape into 4 logs. Place 1 log into each prepared pepper; fold sides of pepper to enclose filling.

3. Place stuffed peppers, seam-side down, on a sprayed baking sheet. Spray peppers lightly with nonstick cooking spray. Sprinkle remaining mozzarella cheese on top. Bake 7-10 minutes or until cheese melts. Serve immediately.

4. Serve with fresh salsa and reduced fat sour cream.

Variation: Substitute canned whole green chilies for fresh roasted peppers. Remove seeds and membrane; then rinse, dry and stuff.

- -

Yield: 4 servings
Serving size: 1 pepper

Calories: 192
Protein: 20 g
Carbohydrate: 7 g
Fat: 9 g
Cholesterol: 36 mg
Sodium: 346 mg
Calcium: 557 mg
Dietary Fiber: less than 1 g
Sugar: 2 g

SOUTHERN CHEESE GRITS

In many homes in the southern United States, grits are served daily. This is a reduced-calorie version of one of the most popular grits dishes.

1 cup uncooked quick white hominy grits
1½ cups light Velveeta, cubed
2 green onions and tops, chopped
½ cup egg substitute

1. Heat oven to 350°. Heat 4 cups water to boiling in large saucepan or Dutch oven. Gradually add grits, stirring constantly. Reduce heat and simmer uncovered about 5 minutes, stirring frequently until thickened. Stir in cheese and onions.

2. Remove from heat and cool about 15 minutes. Gradually stir egg substitute into grits mixture. Season to taste with freshly ground black pepper. Pour grits mixture into a sprayed 1½-quart baking dish.

3. Bake, uncovered, 35-40 minutes or until set. Let stand 10 minutes before serving.

Flavor Perk: Sprinkle paprika on top before baking.
Variation: Substitute ¼ cup chopped green chiles for the green onions.

- - - - - - - - - - - - - - - - - - -

Yield: 8 servings
Serving size: About ⅓ cup

Calories: 163
Protein: 11 g
Carbohydrate: 20 g
Fat: 5 g
Cholesterol: 23 mg
Sodium: 701 mg
Calcium: 8 mg
Dietary Fiber: less than 1 g
Sugar: 3 g

FRENCH TOAST STICKS

¼ cup egg substitute
2 tablespoons evaporated skim milk
Sugar substitute equal to 2 teaspoons sugar
3 slices reduced calorie whole wheat bread, cut into 3 strips each

1. Combine egg substitute, skim milk and sugar substitute in a shallow bowl; mix thoroughly. Coat each bread strip with the mixture.

2. Heat a sprayed skillet over medium heat; add bread strips. Cook, turning once, about 2-3 minutes or until golden brown. Spray skillet with nonstick cooking spray, as needed.

Flavor Perk: Add ½ teaspoon vanilla, and a dash each of ground cinnamon and ground nutmeg to the milk mixture.

- - - - - - - - - - - - - - - - - - -

Yield: 3-4 servings
Serving size: 2-3 sticks

Calories: 56
Protein: 4 g
Carbohydrate: 10 g
Fat: less than 1 g
Cholesterol: less than 1 mg
Sodium: 140 mg
Calcium: 54 mg
Dietary Fiber: 2 g
Sugar: less than 1 g

ENGLISH MUFFIN CROWNS

¼ cup sugar substitute or brown sugar replacement
½-1 teaspoon ground cinnamon
2 English muffins, split, lightly toasted
1⅓ cups fat free or reduced fat cottage cheese, drained

1. Preheat oven broiler. In a small bowl, mix sugar substitute and cinnamon. Spread ⅓ cup cottage cheese onto each English muffin half, covering top of muffin. Sprinkle with cinnamon-sugar mixture.

2. Place muffins on baking sheet 4-5 inches under broiler element for 4-5 minutes until cottage cheese is hot.

3. Serve immediately.

- - - - - - - - - - - - - - - - - - -

Yield: 4 servings
Serving size: 1 English muffin half

Calories: 123
Protein: 11 g
Carbohydrate: 17 g
Fat: less than 1 g
Cholesterol: 0 mg
Sodium: 380 mg
Calcium: 134 mg
Dietary Fiber: less than 1 g
Sugar: 2 g

FRESH TOMATO TOAST WEDGES

Freshly prepared, this dish with ripe and tasty tomatoes is excellent served for a light lunch.

1 slice reduced calorie wheat bread, toasted
½ tomato, thinly sliced
⅓ cup low fat small curd cottage cheese
½ teaspoon dried basil

1. Place toast on serving plate and arrange tomato slices on top.

2. Add cottage cheese and sprinkle with basil. Cut diagonally and serve immediately.

Variation: Add 2 teaspoons finely chopped green onion with tops to cottage cheese.

- - - - - - - - - - - - - - - - - - -

Yield: 1 serving

Calories: 127
Protein: 13 g
Carbohydrate: 16 g
Fat: 2 g
Cholesterol: 6 mg
Sodium: 426 mg
Calcium: 84 mg
Dietary Fiber: 4 g
Sugar: 5 g

CREAMY SPINACH PIE

Who needs a pastry crust? This full-flavored combination of spinach and cheese baked in a creamy mushroom sauce is delightfully satisfying.

¹/₂ cup reduced fat cream of mushroom soup
¹/₂ cup egg substitute
1 (10 ounce) package frozen chopped spinach, cooked, well-drained
¹/₂ cup shredded reduced fat cheddar cheese

1. Preheat oven to 350°. In a mixing bowl, combine soup, egg substitute, cooked spinach and cheese. Mix thoroughly. Season to taste with salt or salt substitute and freshly ground black pepper.

2. Pour mixture into a sprayed 9-inch pie plate. Bake 40-45 minutes. Pie is done when a toothpick or table knife is inserted in the center and comes out clean.

Flavor Perk: Add red pepper flakes to taste to the spinach mixture.

- - - - - - - - - - - - - - - - - - -

Yield: 6 servings
Serving size: About ¹/₃ cup

Calories: 80
Protein: 9 g
Carbohydrate: 4 g
Fat: 3 g
Cholesterol: 12 mg
Sodium: 292 mg
Calcium: 191 mg
Dietary Fiber: 1 g
Sugar: 1 g

FRESH ZUCCHINI FRITTATA

A frittata has the basic characteristics of an omelet and is popular in vegetarian cooking. In Italy, vegetable frittatas are popular year-round as a main course. Frittatas are prepared with available vegetables in season, from cauliflower to zucchini.

1 cup frozen seasoning blend (onion, celery, bell pepper and parsley), thawed, drained
1 zucchini, coarsely chopped or grated
1¹/₂ cups egg substitute
1 cup shredded part-skim mozzarella cheese or ¹/₄ cup Parmesan cheese, grated

1. Preheat oven to 350°. Preheat a nonstick skillet over medium heat; spray with nonstick cooking spray and add seasoning blend and zucchini. Stirring frequently, cook vegetables until soft, about 5 minutes.

2. Remove from heat. Stir in egg substitute, cheese, salt or salt substitute and freshly ground black pepper to taste. Pour into a sprayed 9-inch pie plate or oven-proof skillet. Bake 25-30 minutes or until puffed and lightly browned.

3. To serve, cut into 6 wedges and serve hot or at room temperature.

Flavor Perk: Add ¹/₂ teaspoon Italian herb blend or dried basil leaves.

- - - - - - - - - - - - - - - - - - -

Yield: 6 servings
Serving size: 1 wedge

Calories: 87
Protein: 11 g
Carbohydrate: 4 g
Fat: 3 g

Cholesterol: 11 mg
Sodium: 192 mg
Calcium: 144 mg
Dietary Fiber: less than 1 g
Sugar: 2 g

BEEF & PORK

Meat, namely beef and pork, is considered the most common source of protein for Americans, although consumers today seek out lower fat and lower cholesterol foods. Fortunately, the meat industry offers to consumers beef and pork products that are considerably lower in fat than those sold some 20 years ago.

When visiting meat sections of supermarkets, consumers are confronted with weighed and labeled cartons of a wide variety of prepackaged meats. As a general rule for healthy cooking and eating of meat, consumers should choose leaner cuts and trim all visible fat before cooking the meat. The recipes found in this section emphasize not only the selection of leaner cuts of meats, but the use of cooking methods which use less fat.

JUST THE BEEF FAJITAS

3 tablespoons fresh lime juice
3 finely minced or pressed garlic cloves
1½ teaspoons ground cumin
12 ounces flank steak, trimmed of visible fat, thinly sliced on diagonal

1. Combine lime juice, garlic and cumin in resealable plastic bag. Add steak strips; then seal and refrigerate at least 20 minutes, turning occasionally. Drain and discard marinade.

2. Preheat a sprayed nonstick skillet over medium-high heat. Add the steak and cook 3-4 minutes until lightly browned but still pink in center. Season to taste with salt or salt substitute and freshly ground black pepper.

3. Serve with sautéed onion and bell pepper, salsa and light sour cream.

- - - - - - - - - - - - - - - - - -

Yield: 2 servings
Serving size: About ¾ cup

Calories: 314
Protein: 37
Carbohydrate: 4 g
Fat: 15 g
Cholesterol: 72 mg
Sodium: 108 mg
Calcium: 33 mg
Dietary Fiber: less than 1 g
Sugar: less than 1 g

FLAT SOMBREROS

10 white or yellow corn tortillas
1 pound lean ground beef
2 cups red enchilada sauce, hot or mild
1½ cups shredded reduced fat cheddar or Monterey jack cheese, divided

Microwave Oven:
Place tortillas in a resealable plastic bag and heat 1 minute on full power. Brown meat in sprayed skillet over medium heat. Remove from skillet and drain. Return meat to skillet. Add enchilada sauce and cheese and heat through. Place each heated tortilla on a microwave-safe plate. Add 2-3 tablespoons meat mixture and a sprinkling of cheese. Heat each enchilada 45 seconds-1 minute on full power. Serve immediately.

Conventional Oven:
Preheat oven to 375˚. Wrap tortillas in foil and heat 7-10 minutes. Brown meat in a sprayed skillet over medium heat. Remove meat from skillet and drain. Return meat to skillet. Add enchilada sauce and cheese and heat through. Place heated tortillas on sprayed baking sheet. Spoon 2-3 tablespoons meat mixture on each tortilla. Sprinkle with cheese. Bake 5-6 minutes or just until heated through. Serve immediately.

- - - - - - - - - - - - - - - - - -

Yield: 10 servings
Serving size: 1 enchilada

Calories: 328	Calcium: 300 mg
Protein: 24 g	Dietary Fiber: 5 g
Carbohydrate: 21 g	Sugar: less than 1 g
Fat: 16 g	
Cholesterol: 66 mg	
Sodium: 549 mg	

EASY BEEF ENCHILADAS

1 pound extra lean ground beef, ground turkey or a combination
2 (10 ounce) cans red enchilada sauce, mild or hot, divided
1½ cups shredded reduced fat cheddar or Monterey jack cheese, divided
12 corn tortillas

1. Preheat oven to 375°. Brown ground beef in skillet over medium heat. Drain and rinse (if desired) ground beef. Return meat to skillet and stir in ¾ cup enchilada sauce and 1 cup cheese. Set aside.

2. Preheat griddle or another nonstick skillet over medium-high heat. Using nonstick cooking spray, coat tortillas on both sides and place 1-2 on griddle at a time, turning once, until both sides are soft and pliable. Spoon 1-2 tablespoons of meat-cheese mixture on each tortilla.

4. Roll each tortilla around the filling and place seam side down in a sprayed baking dish. Pour enchilada sauce from the skillet over the tortillas, and sprinkle ½ cup cheese on top. Bake, uncovered, 15-20 minutes or until cheese melts and sauce bubbles.

Flavor Perk: Add ½ cup chopped onion to ground beef while browning. Garnish with coarsely chopped fresh cilantro and serve with salsa.

- -

Yield: 12 servings
Serving size: 1-2 enchiladas

Calories: 287
Protein: 21 g
Carbohydrate: 20 g
Fat: 14 g
Cholesterol: 55 mg
Sodium: 479 mg
Calcium: 258 mg
Dietary Fiber: 4 g
Sugar: less than 1 g

BEEF-STUFFED CABBAGE ROLLS

1 (3 pound) head green cabbage
1 pound extra lean ground beef
¼ cup finely chopped onion
½ cup egg substitute

1. Trim outer leaves of cabbage and remove core. In a large saucepan or pot, cover cabbage with boiling water and let stand 5 minutes or until leaves are limp. Remove cabbage from water and separate leaves, carefully reserving 6-8 largest leaves for the rolls.

2. Combine meat thoroughly with onion, egg substitute, salt or salt substitute and freshly ground black pepper to taste. Place 2 tablespoons meat mixture on each leaf and fold up "envelope" fashion. Fasten with toothpick.

3. Place rolls, flaps down, in Dutch oven or heavy saucepan. Add ½ cup water and cover rolls with remaining cabbage leaves. Simmer, covered, for 1 hour.

4. Serve with Easy Tomato Sauce (p. 207) or sauce of your choice.

Flavor Perk: Add ½ teaspoon garlic powder and ¼ cup toasted pine nuts to meat mixture.

Variation: Substitute ground turkey for a portion of the ground beef.

- -

Yield: 6-8 servings
Serving size: 1 cabbage roll

Calories: 237
Protein: 24 g
Carbohydrate: 11 g
Fat: 11 g
Cholesterol: 69 mg
Sodium: 105 mg
Calcium: 104 mg
Dietary Fiber: 5 g
Sugar: 7 g

EASY TOMATO SAUCE

1 (10 ounce) package frozen seasoning blend (celery, onion, bell pepper and parsley), partially thawed
1 (14½ ounce) can no salt diced tomatoes, undrained
1 teaspoon dried basil leaves

1. In a sprayed skillet over medium heat, sauté seasoning blend until clear and tender, and most of water evaporates. Add tomatoes, basil, salt or salt substitute and freshly ground black pepper to taste; heat to boiling.

2. Mash large chunks of tomato. Reduce heat and simmer 30 minutes or until slightly thickened.

3. Refrigerate or freeze for later use.

- - - - - - - - - - - - - - - - - -

Yield: 8 servings
Serving size: About ⅓ cup

Calories: 21
Protein: less than 1 g
Carbohydrate: 5 g
Fat: 0 g
Cholesterol: 0 mg
Sodium: 32 mg
Calcium: 8 mg
Dietary Fiber: 1 g
Sugar: 3 g

BEEF-SNOW PEA STIR-FRY

To make the most of this quick cooking method, have the snow peas ready to cook immediately after the steak.

1 pound flank or sirloin steak
Stir-fry Marinade (p. 208)
1 tablespoon peanut oil
20 snow peas, ends and strings removed

1. Trim steak of fat and slice thinly across the grain. Cut in strips 1½ inches in length. Place in marinade and stir to coat. Marinate 15 minutes.

2. Heat oil in uncovered wok or large skillet, using high heat (400° for electric wok or skillet). Add meat and stir-fry 2 minutes. Add ½ teaspoon salt or salt substitute and snow peas to the wok; stir-fry 1 minute.

3. Serve immediately.

- - - - - - - - - - - - - - - - - -

Yield: 6 servings
Serving size: About ½ cup

Calories: 156
Protein: 18 g
Carbohydrate: 3 g
Fat: 7 g
Cholesterol: 30 mg
Sodium: 377 mg
Calcium: 12 mg
Dietary Fiber: less than 1 g
Sugar: 2 g

STIR-FRY MARINADE

¼ cup light soy sauce
1 tablespoon cornstarch
1 tablespoon dry sherry or sherry
cooking wine
Sugar substitute to equal 1
teaspoon sugar

1. Stir ingredients together until well blended.

- - - - - - - - - - - - - - - - -

Yield: 2 servings

Calories: 56
Protein: 3 g
Carbohydrate: 9 g
Fat: 0 g
Cholesterol: 0 mg
Sodium: 1010 mg
Calcium: 12 mg
Dietary Fiber: 0 g
Sugar: 5 g

EASY ORANGE STIR-FRY SAUCE

½ cup orange juice plus 1
teaspoon grated orange peel
1 tablespoon cornstarch
1 tablespoon light (reduced
sodium) soy sauce
Sugar substitute to equal 1
teaspoon sugar
1 teaspoon instant beef bouillon
granules

1. Stir ingredients together in a small bowl.

- - - - - - - - - - - - - - - - -

Yield: 2 servings

Calories: 55
Protein: 1 g
Carbohydrate: 12 g
Fat: less than 1 g
Cholesterol: 0 mg
Sodium: 658 mg
Calcium: 15 mg
Dietary Fiber: less than 1 g
Sugar: 1 g

BEEF-SPINACH STIR-FRY

Pre-packaged spinach and frozen seasoning blend speed the preparation of this stir-fried steak dish.

1 pound beef round steak or flank steak, well trimmed of fat and membrane
1 (16 ounce) package frozen seasoning blend (onions, celery, bell pepper and parsley)
2 (10 ounce) bags fresh washed spinach, coarsely shredded
Easy Orange Stir-Fry Sauce (p. 208)

1. Partially freeze beef for easier slicing. Blot or pat beef dry before slicing. Thinly slice beef across the grain into bite-size strips. Set aside.

2. In a nonstick wok or large skillet lightly sprayed with nonstick cooking spray, sauté seasoning blend over medium-high heat for 2-3 minutes. Remove seasoning blend and juices, and set aside. Add beef to the wok and cook, stirring, 2-3 minutes.

3. Push beef away from center of wok. Add Easy Orange Stir Fry Sauce to center of wok and cook until bubbly. Return seasoning blend to wok and add spinach. Stir to coat ingredients with sauce. Cover and cook 1 minute or until heated through. Serve immediately.

Flavor Perk: Add 1 finely minced garlic clove to the wok with the seasoning blend; add ½ cup canned sliced water chestnuts, rinsed and drained, with the spinach.

Variation: Substitute 4 green onions and tops, sliced diagonally into 1 inch pieces, for the frozen seasoning blend.

- -

Yield: 6 servings
Serving size: About ¾ cup beef and sauce

Calories (with sauce): 217
Protein: 27 g
Carbohydrate: 12 g
Fat: 6 g
Cholesterol: 59 mg
Sodium: 509 mg
Calcium: 103 mg
Dietary Fiber: 2 g
Sugar: 5 g

STEAK-BOK CHOY STIR-FRY

Bok choy, a cabbage-like green vegetable, is generally available year-round. Choose heads with bright white stalks and shiny dark leaves. A medium head, about 1½ pounds, will be enough for this 6-serving recipe.

To clean bok choy, plunge into a large bowl of cold water; lift out and drain. Cut leaves from stems; then slice stems crosswise and coarsely shred leaves.

1 pound round steak, trimmed, patted dry
3 tablespoons light (reduced sodium) soy sauce
1 head bok choy (Chinese cabbage), cleaned, stems sliced, leaves shredded
2 teaspoons cornstarch mixed with 2 teaspoons cold water

1. Slice steak thinly across the grain into 1½ inch long strips. Preheat a sprayed nonstick wok or large skillet (400° for electric wok or skillet). Add strips in batches, if needed, to brown quickly, about 1 minute per batch. Take care not to scorch the strips.

2. With all meat strips in the wok, add soy sauce and bok choy; stir-fry 1 minute. Stir cornstarch mixture and add to wok. Stir-fry until sauce thickens. Serve immediately.

- - - - - - - - - - - - - - - -

Yield: 6 servings
Serving size: 1 cup

Calories: 174
Protein: 27 g
Carbohydrate: 5 g
Fat: 5 g

Cholesterol: 60 mg
Sodium: 382 mg
Calcium: 152 mg
Dietary Fiber: 1 g
Sugar: 1 g

LONDON BROIL

The supermarket meat department may occasionally offer a cut of meat labeled "London Broil," which is flank steak. If this cut is unavailable, ask a butcher to cut one. Flank steak is a very lean cut of meat and is most tender cooked to rare, with pink still in the middle. Slice the cooked steak thinly on the bias, across the grain, for serving.

1½ pound flank steak, trimmed of fat and connective tissue
1 clove garlic, minced or 2 teaspoons Dijon-style mustard

1. Preheat the oven broiler. Score the steak on both sides by drawing a sharp knife in a ½-inch lattice pattern, about ¼-inch deep. Rub with garlic or mustard. Spray both sides with nonstick cooking spray.

2. Broil 3-5 inches below broiling element, 4-5 minutes each side for medium and 3-4 minutes for rare. Remove, and season to taste with salt or salt substitute and freshly ground black pepper. Slice the steak thinly, across the grain diagonally.

Variation: Instead of garlic or mustard, choose a reduced fat marinade. Marinate the trimmed flank steak 4-5 hours in the refrigerator. Drain on paper towels and broil as directed.

- - - - - - - - - - - - - - - -

Yield: 5 servings
Serving size: About 4 ounces steak

Calories: 312
Protein: 43 g
Carbohydrate: less than 1 g
Fat: 14 g
Cholesterol: 75 mg
Sodium: 90 mg

Calcium: 8 mg
Dietary Fiber: 0 g
Sugar: 0 g

SWISS STEAK

1½ tablespoons flour
1½ pounds lean round steak, trimmed
1 onion, thinly sliced
1½ cups canned no salt diced tomatoes, undrained or stewed tomatoes
with Cajun, Mexican or Italian seasonings, undrained

1. Preheat oven to 325°. Combine flour, salt or salt substitute and freshly ground black pepper to taste. Sprinkle half the flour mixture on one side of the steak; pound steak with a meat-tenderizing mallet or the rim of a saucer. Repeat the process on the other side of the steak.

2. Preheat a sprayed Dutch oven over medium heat; add steak. Brown both sides of meat, being careful not to scorch flour. Add 1-2 tablespoons water or 1 teaspoon oil to aid in browning, if needed.

3. Remove steak. Reduce heat and add onion. Add up to ¼ cup water to onion in Dutch oven; cover and cook 4-5 minutes or until onion is clear and tender.

4. Remove from heat and return steak to Dutch oven. Add tomatoes. Cover and bake about 2 hours or until steak is tender.

Flavor Perk: Add 1 finely minced or pressed garlic clove to the Dutch oven with the onion; add 1 teaspoon Worcestershire sauce with the tomatoes.

Variation: Use range-top cooking to replace baking. After all ingredients are in the Dutch oven, bring to a boil; then reduce heat and simmer about 2 hours.

- -

Yield: 6 servings
Serving size: 3 ounces steak (about the size of a deck of cards)

Calories: 254
Protein: 36 g
Carbohydrate: 6 g
Fat: 9 g
Cholesterol: 88 mg
Sodium: 83 mg
Calcium: 20 mg
Dietary Fiber: 1 g
Sugar: 3 g

COMPANY BEEF ROAST

To stay on the healthy side, be conscious
of the 3-ounce serving size of this roasted beef sirloin.

1 (3½ pound) lean boneless beef sirloin roast
1 tablespoon olive oil
Instant-read meat thermometer

1. Preheat oven to 450°. Trim any visible fat from the roast and pat dry. Tie the roast with string every 1½ inches to keep the roast from separating during cooking. Rub olive oil on the roast, and season to taste with salt or salt substitute and freshly ground black pepper.

2. Place roast on rack in roasting pan. Rather than a broiler-type pan, use a roasting pan nearly the size of the roast and 2-5 inches high on sides. Place the roasting pan on the center rack or in the center of the oven. Roast for 10 minutes at 450°; then reduce heat to 250°.

3. Insert an instant-read thermometer in several places on the roast. Medium rare reads 125-130° on thermometer, and medium reads 135-145°. Note that the roast will heat an additional 5 degrees when removed from oven. Cover the roast loosely with foil, and let stand 15-20 minutes before serving.

Variation: Cook the roast at 250° 20-30 minutes per pound.

- -

Yield: 8 servings
Serving size: 3 ounces (about the size of a deck of cards)

Calories: 383
Protein: 55 g
Carbohydrate: 0 g
Fat: 16 g
Cholesterol: 131 mg
Sodium: 127 mg
Calcium: 10 mg
Dietary Fiber: 0 g
Sugar: 0 g

SLOW COOKER BEEF ROAST

Crock-pot cooking is a wonderful convenience for busy cooks.

1 (3 pound) boneless beef tip roast
1 teaspoon mixed dried herbs
2 finely minced or pressed garlic cloves
1 cup fat free reduced sodium beef broth or red wine vinegar

1. This recipe calls for a 4-5 quart slow cooker.

2. Preheat a large sprayed nonstick skillet over medium-high heat. Add roast and sear on all sides, about 10-15 minutes. Sprinkle roast with herbs and season to taste with salt or salt substitute and freshly ground black pepper.

3. Place garlic in crock pot; then add browned roast. Pour broth or vinegar into the side of the pot, taking care not to wash meat seasonings into the pot. Cover crock pot and cook on low setting 6-8 hours or until beef is fork tender but not dry.

- - - - - - - - - - - - - - - - - - -

Yield: 10-12 servings
Serving size: ½-inch slice

Calories: 294
Protein: 38 g
Carbohydrate: 7 g
Fat: 11 g
Cholesterol: 110 mg
Sodium: 124 mg
Calcium: 11 mg
Dietary Fiber: 0 g
Sugar: 7 g

SPICY MEATLOAF

1 (7 ounce) package herb-seasoned stuffing mix and seasoning packet
¼ cup egg substitute
¼ cup salsa or hot and spicy ketchup
1½ pounds lean ground beef or combination of beef and turkey

1. Preheat oven to 350°. In large bowl, combine stuffing mix, seasoning, egg substitute, salsa and ⅓ cup water; mix well.

2. Add ground beef to the stuffing mixture.

3. Pack into a sprayed 9 x 5-inch loaf pan; then turn out onto a broiler pan rack or a rimmed baking pan. Dip fingers in water, and mold mixture lightly with hands, if needed, to hold mixture together.

4. Cover meatloaf loosely with foil to keep it moist; place pan in oven. Bake 45 minutes; then remove foil and bake an additional 15 minutes. Note: An instant-read thermometer should read 160° internal temperature to insure that the meatloaf is completely cooked.

5. Let meatloaf stand 15-20 minutes before serving.

Variation: Substitute ½ cup no salt tomato sauce for salsa.

- - - - - - - - - - - - - - - - - -

Yield: 6-8 servings
Serving size: ½ inch slice

Calories: 336
Protein: 29 g
Carbohydrate: 19 g
Fat: 14 g
Cholesterol: 91 mg
Sodium: 431 mg
Calcium: 34 mg
Dietary Fiber: 2 g
Sugar: 1 g

JUST-THE-BEEF POT ROAST

Serve this full-flavored pot roast with oven-roasted vegetables.

1 (2½-3 pound) boneless beef chuck pot roast
¾ cup beef or chicken broth, beer, red or white wine; or ¾ cup water
plus 1 teaspoon instant beef broth
1 tablespoon Worcestershire sauce
1 teaspoon crushed dried basil leaves or mixed dried herbs

1. Trim fat and membrane from the roast and pat dry with paper towels. Season to taste with salt or salt substitute and freshly ground black pepper. Preheat a sprayed Dutch oven over medium high heat and add the roast to brown all sides. Reduce heat if meat or drippings begin to burn, or add 1 teaspoon vegetable oil.

2. Stir together beef broth, Worcestershire sauce and basil. Pour mixture over roast and bring to a boil. Reduce heat and simmer about 2-2½ hours or until roast is fork tender in thickest part.

3. Serve with cooked or roasted vegetables of your choice.

- -

Yield: 8 servings
Serving size: About 3-4 ounces beef & broth

Calories: 336
Protein: 34 g
Carbohydrate: less than 1 g
Fat: 21 g
Cholesterol: 113 mg
Sodium: 136 mg
Calcium: 16 mg
Dietary Fiber: less than 1 g
Sugar: 0 g

Conventional Oven directions: Prepare the roast the same way until ready to simmer. Instead, preheat oven to 325° and cook in a covered Dutch oven for 2-2½ hours.

Slow Cooker directions: Place ingredients in 4-5 quart slow cooker. Cover and cook on low setting 10-12 hours or on high setting 5-6 hours. Note: Browning the roast before placing in the slow cooker is recommended for best flavor.

STEWED BEEF

A note about herbs: Before adding dried herbs to a dish, rub the herbs between your hands to crumble or crush, or use a mortar and pestle to release the full flavor of the herbs. Discard old bottles of dried herbs that may have lost their potency. Store new bottles of dried herbs in the freezer.

**3-4 tablespoons flour
1 teaspoon mixed dried herbs, divided
2 pounds lean boneless stewing beef, cut in 2-inch cubes
2-3 cups beer, beef or chicken broth, dry red or white wine**

1. Mix flour, herbs, salt or salt substitute and freshly ground pepper to taste. Blot and pat dry the meat thoroughly, trimming any membrane or fat, and place on wax paper. Using a flour sifter or wire mesh strainer, evenly coat cubes with flour mixture.

2. Preheat a sprayed heavy saucepan or Dutch oven over medium-high heat. Place 1 meat cube in the pan; if the cube sizzles, the pan is ready to add meat.

3. Brown the meat in batches, about 2-3 minutes per batch. Be careful not to crowd the pan or scorch the meat or browned flour crust in the bottom of the pan. Note: If all batches of meat are not browning adequately, add 1 teaspoon vegetable oil.

4. When all meat is browned, remove from heat and sprinkle meat with herbs. Add enough broth, beer or wine to cover the meat. Bring to a boil; reduce heat to low. Cover and simmer 1½-2 hours or until meat is fork-tender. Liquid will be thin.

Flavor Perk: Add 2 bay leaves with the dried herbs. Add 2-3 carrots, peeled, cut into 1- inch chunks, with the liquid. Garnish with parsley.

Variation: If a thicker "gravy" is desired, combine 2-3 teaspoons cornstarch with an equal amount of water. Bring stew liquid to a boil and stir in the cornstarch mixture. Cook and stir until gravy thickens.

- -

**Yield: 8 servings
Serving size:** ½-¾ cup

**Calories: 259
Protein: 37 g
Carbohydrate: 4 g
Fat: 7 g
Cholesterol: 93 mg
Sodium: 118 mg
Calcium: 14 mg
Dietary Fiber: less than 1 g
Sugar: less than 1 g**

BASIC MEATLOAF

Meatloaf, one of those "comfort" foods that reminds of home and times gone by, now appears again on many dining tables. It is a versatile dish, so more than one kind of meat can be used. Remember, however, that pork and sausage are generally fattier than beef. Include leaner meats, such as ground turkey, as part of the beef mixture. Meatloaf is easy to prepare and is satisfying hot, cold or as leftovers.

To ensure a fully cooked product, meatloaf should read 160° internal temperature on an instant-read thermometer.

1½ pounds lean ground beef, ground turkey or a combination
½ cup egg substitute
1 cup skim milk
1 cup coarsely-crumbed whole wheat bread

1. Preheat oven to 350°. Combine beef or turkey, egg substitute, milk and crumbs in a mixing bowl and mix well. Season to taste with salt or salt substitute and freshly ground black pepper.

2. Pack into a 9 x 5-inch loaf pan coated with nonstick cooking spray; then turn out the loaf onto a sprayed broiler pan rack or a sprayed baking pan with rim. Mold mixture lightly with your hands, if needed, to hold mixture together. Cover meatloaf with foil to keep moist; place in oven and bake 45 minutes.

3. Remove foil and bake an additional 15 minutes to brown top of meatloaf. Let stand 15-20 minutes before serving.

Flavor Perk: Pour 2 tablespoons chili sauce or hot and spicy ketchup over the meatloaf when half-baked to create a light crust.

Variation: For faster cooking, pack meatloaf into individual muffin tins. Bake 20-30 minutes.

- -

Yield: 8 servings
Serving size: ½-inch slice

Calories: 241
Protein: 18 g
Carbohydrate: 5 g
Fat: 16 g
Cholesterol: 62 mg
Sodium: 133 mg
Calcium: 54 mg
Dietary Fiber: less than 1 g
Sugar: 2 g

BEEF-SALSA MEATBALLS

Salsa is such an all-time favorite, we find many uses for it in cooking.

1 pound extra lean ground beef or turkey
¼ cup egg substitute
¼-½ cup salsa
½ cup fresh whole wheat bread crumbs

1. Mix beef, egg substitute, salsa and bread crumbs. Season to taste with salt or salt substitute and freshly ground black pepper. Form into 1½-inch meatballs.

2. Preheat a sprayed skillet on medium heat. Brown meatballs in batches, being careful not to crowd the skillet. Stir frequently to brown meatballs on all sides. Drain on paper towels.

Variation: Substitute no salt tomato sauce for the salsa.

- - - - - - - - - - - - - - - - - - -

Yield: 5-6 servings
Serving size: 3-4 meatballs

Calories: 276
Protein: 28 g
Carbohydrate: 6 g
Fat: 15 g
Cholesterol: 84 mg
Sodium: 195 mg
Calcium: 19 mg
Dietary Fiber: less than 1 g
Sugar: less than 1 g

HEARTY BEEF NOODLES

1 pound boneless beef round steak
3 cups low sodium beef broth
1 teaspoon dried marjoram leaves
6 ounces cholesterol free egg noodle substitute

1. Trim fat and membrane from meat and cut in ¾-inch cubes. Season to taste with salt or salt substitute and freshly ground black pepper. Place in a sprayed Dutch oven and brown beef cubes over medium heat. Add broth and marjoram and bring to a boil. Reduce heat and simmer 1½ hours or until beef is tender.

2. Cook noodles according to package directions. Add noodles to the beef-broth mixture; heat thoroughly and serve.

Flavor Perk: After browning meat, brown ½ cup chopped onion and 1 finely minced or pressed garlic clove, and add with the broth.
Variation: If a thicker "gravy" is desired, combine 2-3 teaspoons cornstarch with an equal amount of water. Bring stew liquid to a boil and stir in the cornstarch mixture. Cook and stir until gravy thickens.

- - - - - - - - - - - - - - - - - - -

Yield: 8 servings
Serving Size: ¾ cup

Calories: 170
Protein: 17 g
Carbohydrate: 16 g
Fat: 4 g
Cholesterol: 27 mg
Sodium: 56 mg
Calcium: 8 mg
Dietary Fiber: less than 1 g
Sugar: 1 g

BEEF STROGANOFF

Beef in a cream-based sauce, or Beef Stroganoff, originated in Russia in the 18th century. Today there are many variations of this hearty and popular dish.

1 (1½ pound) lean beef tenderloin, top loin or sirloin tip,
trimmed of fat
1 teaspoon onion powder
1 (10¾ ounce) can reduced fat cream of mushroom soup
3 tablespoons light sour cream

1. Slice beef into very thin slices and sprinkle onion powder on slices. Season to taste with salt or salt substitute and freshly ground black pepper.

2. Heat a large skillet coated with nonstick cooking spray over medium-high heat, and add beef in batches to avoid overcrowding the skillet. Keeping heat medium-high to high, quickly brown or sear the strips. Remove the strips and keep warm.

3. Reduce heat to medium; then add the soup and bring to a boil. Remove from heat and stir in sour cream. Season the sauce to taste with freshly ground black pepper, not salt. Spoon the sauce over the beef and serve immediately.

4. Serve with cooked rice or cholesterol free egg noodle substitute.

Flavor Perk: Add 1 teaspoon Dijon-style mustard or Worcestershire sauce to the sauce; sprinkle each serving lightly with caraway seed and fresh chopped parsley.

- -

Yield: 6 servings
Serving size: ½-¾ cup beef and sauce

Calories: 318
Protein: 31 g
Carbohydrate: 5 g
Fat: 18 g
Cholesterol: 103 mg
Sodium: 276 mg
Calcium: 59 mg
Dietary Fiber: 0 g
Sugar: less than 1 g

BROILED BEEF PATTIES WITH MUSHROOM SAUCE

Mushroom sauce dresses up simple broiled beef patties.

1 pound extra lean ground beef
2 tablespoons finely chopped onion
2 teaspoons Dijon-style mustard
Hearty Mushroom Sauce (p. 219)

1. Combine beef, onion and mustard. Season to taste with salt or salt substitute and freshly ground black pepper. Form into 5-6 patties.

2. Preheat oven broiler. Place patties on broiler pan sprayed with non-stick cooking spray. Broil 3-5 inches from heating element, 4-5 minutes on each side or until cooked to desired doneness. Serve immediately with Hearty Mushroom Sauce (p. 219).

- - - - - - - - - - - - - - - - -

Yield: 5-6 servings
Serving size: 3 ounces or 1 patty

Calories: 300
Protein: 27 g
Carbohydrate: 7 g
Fat: 18 g
Cholesterol: 78 mg
Sodium: 153 mg
Calcium: 101 mg
Dietary Fiber: less than 1 g
Sugar: 4 g

HEARTY MUSHROOM SAUCE

1 tablespoon stick margarine
1 (8 ounce) carton sliced fresh mushrooms
1 tablespoon flour
1½ cups skim milk

1. In a saucepan over medium heat, melt margarine. Add mushrooms and cook until mushrooms are tender. Stir in flour and salt or salt substitute and freshly ground black pepper to taste.

2. After mixture is blended with no lumps, add milk. Cook and stir until sauce comes to a boil and thickens. Continue cooking and stirring 1 minute to completely cook flour.

Variation: Substitute ⅔ cup skim milk for the 1½ cups skim milk. After sauce is completely cooked, add ½ cup light sour cream and heat through but do not boil.

- - - - - - - - - - - - - - - - -

Yield: 5 servings (1½ cups)
Serving size: ¼ cup

Calories: 64
Protein: 4 g
Carbohydrate: 6 g
Fat: 3 g
Cholesterol: 1 mg
Sodium: 67 mg
Calcium: 93 mg
Dietary Fiber: less than 1 g
Sugar: 4 g

BEEF-ZUCCHINI PATTIES WITH ONION GRAVY

Zucchini, a remarkably versatile vegetable, reduces the calorie density in these beef patties.

¾ **pound extra lean ground beef or ground turkey**
1 zucchini, grated
¼ **cup egg substitute**
Sauteed Onion Gravy (p. 220), prepared, warm

1. Combine beef, zucchini and egg substitute and season to taste with salt or salt substitute and freshly ground black pepper. Form into 6 patties. Preheat oven broiler.

2. Place patties on broiler pan rack sprayed with nonstick cooking spray. Broil 3-5 inches from heating element 4-5 minutes on each side or until cooked to desired doneness. Serve at once with Onion Gravy.

- - - - - - - - - - - - - - - - - - -

Yield: 5-6 servings
Serving size: 1 patty

Calories: 156
Protein: 14 g
Carbohydrate: 1 g
Fat: 10 g
Cholesterol: 45 mg
Sodium: 59 mg
Calcium: 15 mg
Dietary Fiber: less than 1 g
Sugar: less than 1 g

SAUTEED ONION GRAVY

2 onions, halved, sliced
1-1½ tablespoons margarine
1-1½ tablespoons flour
1 cup reduced sodium beef broth

1. In a skillet over medium heat, sauté onions in margarine 3-4 minutes or until clear and soft. Do not brown. Reduce heat to low; then stir in flour and cook about 1 minute or until flour bubbles.

2. Increase heat to medium and add broth gradually, continuing to stir and cook until sauce boils and thickens. Season to taste with salt or salt substitute and freshly ground black pepper.

- - - - - - - - - - - - - - - - - - -

Yield: 8 servings
Serving size: About ¼ cup

Calories: 31
Protein: 1 g
Carbohydrate: 3 g
Fat: 2 g
Cholesterol: 0 mg
Sodium: 26 mg
Calcium: 7 mg
Dietary Fiber: less than 1 g
Sugar: less than 1 g

EASY, EASY BROILED PORK CHOPS

4 "butterflied" boneless pork chops
Nonstick cooking spray
Salt free Creole seasoning

1. Preheat oven to broil or heat a charcoal or gas grill. Trim any visible fat from pork chops. Spray with nonstick cooking spray and sprinkle with Creole seasoning.

2. Broil 3-5 minutes on each side until brown, but still juicy.

- - - - - - - - - - - - - - - - - -

Yield: 4 servings
Serving size: 1 pork chop

Calories: 153
Protein: 21 g
Carbohydrate: 0 g
Fat: 7 g
Cholesterol: 58 mg
Sodium: 46 mg
Calcium: 22 mg
Dietary Fiber: 0 g
Sugar: 0 g

OVEN-ROASTED PORK TENDERLOIN

Pork tenderloin is delicious and lean. This is an easy recipe for entertaining.

3-4 pound pork tenderloin, fat trimmed
½ teaspoon dried thyme
Meat thermometer

1. Preheat oven to 350°. Place the tenderloin on a rack in a shallow open pan. Rub lightly with thyme and salt or salt substitute and freshly ground black pepper to taste. Tie every 2 inches with cotton string to hold roast together.

2. Roast tenderloin 1½-2 hours or until a meat thermometer registers 160°. Remove, and let stand 15 minutes before slicing.

- - - - - - - - - - - - - - - - - -

Yield: 10-12 servings
Serving size: 1 (3 ounce) slice (about the size of a deck of cards)

Calories: 273
Protein: 38 g
Carbohydrate: 0 g
Fat: 12 g
Cholesterol: 114 mg
Sodium: 74 mg
Calcium: 21 mg
Dietary Fiber: 0 g
Sugar: 0 g

PORK STEW WITH GREEN CHILES

The wonderful flavor of green chiles gives tender pork a Southwestern flair. This recipe is even better with fresh roasted Anaheim or New Mexico green chiles.

2 pounds boneless pork, cubed
1 cup finely chopped onion
2 garlic cloves, minced
3 cups canned diced tomatoes and chiles

1. In a sprayed Dutch oven over medium heat, brown pork on all sides. Remove and set aside.

2. Add onions and garlic to the Dutch oven and cook over low heat until onion is soft. Add pork, tomatoes, freshly ground pepper and enough water to cover pork cubes.

3. Cover and simmer 1½ hours or until pork is very tender.

4. Serve warm with whole wheat tortillas.

Flavor Perk: Add ¼ teaspoon cumin.
Variations: Substitute 1 (4 ounce) can chopped green chiles and 2 cans no salt diced tomatoes for the canned tomatoes and chiles. If you prefer fresh chiles, you will need 15-20 fresh green chiles, roasted, peeled and chopped.

- - - - - - - - - - - - - - - - - - - -

Yield: 4-6 servings
Serving size: ¾ cup

Calories: 290
Protein: 40 grams
Carbohydrate: 5 grams
Fat: 11 grams
Cholesterol: 99 milligrams
Sodium: 183 milligrams
Calcium: 35 milligrams
Dietary Fiber: 1 gram
Sugar: 2 grams

HERBED PORK CHOP SKILLET

4 boneless pork chops
1 small onion, chopped
½ cup orange juice
1 teaspoon dried rosemary, crumbled or ½ teaspoon dried sage leaves, crumbled

1. Trim any visible fat from pork chops. Season to taste with salt or salt substitute and freshly ground black pepper.

2. In a sprayed skillet over medium heat, brown pork chops on both sides. Add onion to skillet and sauté until tender and clear.

3. Stir rosemary or sage into orange juice, and pour over pork chops and onion. Bring to boiling; then reduce heat and cover. Simmer about 15-20 minutes or until pork is tender.

4. Remove pork chops and keep warm. If desired, the orange juice mixture can be reduced to concentrate flavors by boiling gently until about ¼ cup remains. Pour orange juice mixture over pork chops and serve immediately.

Variation: Substitute 1 (8 ounce) can pineapple tidbits or chunks, undrained, for the orange juice; replace herb with 1½ teaspoons curry powder.

- - - - - - - - - - - - - - - - - - - -

Yield: 4 servings
Serving size: 1 pork chop

Calories: 177	Sodium: 31 mg
Protein: 21 g	Calcium: 16 mg
Carbohydrate: 6 g	Dietary Fiber: less
Fat: 7 g	than 1 g
Cholesterol: 51 mg	Sugar: 4 g

STIR-FRY PORK AND PEA PODS

1 pound lean boneless pork
1 (6 ounce) package frozen pea pods or sugar snap peas, thawed
Pork Stir-fry Sauce (p.223)

1. Prepare Pork Stir-fry Sauce. Trim pork of any fat and thinly slice into 1-2 inch pieces on the cross grain. Spray a nonstick wok with non-stick cooking spray and preheat on medium-high heat.

2. Add ½ the pork pieces; cook and stir 2-3 minutes or until juices run clear. Set aside and keep warm. Add remaining pork pieces and cook and stir 2-3 minutes. Add all cooked pork to the wok, pushing other ingredients away from the center of the wok.

3. Stir the sauce and pour into the center of the wok. Cook and stir until sauce bubbles and thickens. Stir pork and pea pods to evenly coat with the sauce. Serve immediately.

4. Serve with hot cooked brown rice.

- - - - - - - - - - - - - - - - - - - -

Yield: 4 servings
Serving size: ¾-1 cup

Calories (without sauce): 271
Protein: 32 grams
Carbohydrate: 4 grams
Fat: 13 grams
Cholesterol: 79 milligrams
Sodium: 63 milligrams
Calcium: 21 milligrams
Dietary Fiber: 1 gram
Sugar: less than 1 gram

PORK STIR-FRY SAUCE

2 teaspoons cornstarch
3 tablespoons light (reduced sodium) soy sauce
½ cup orange juice and 2 teaspoons finely grated orange peel
1 teaspoon grated fresh ginger or ½ teaspoon ground ginger

1. Stir cornstarch and soy sauce together in small saucepan. Add orange juice, orange peel, ginger and ¼ cup water. Stirring constantly, heat to boiling and cook 1 minute or until sauce clears and thickens.

- - - - - - - - - - - - - - - - - - - -

Yield: 4 servings

Calories: 31
Protein: 1 g
Carbohydrate: 6 g
Fat: 0 g
Cholesterol: 0 mg
Sodium: 379 mg
Calcium: 8 mg
Dietary Fiber: less than 1 g
Sugar: 5 g

SWEDISH MEATBALLS

½ cup fine dry bread crumbs or 1 cup fine whole wheat bread crumbs
1½ cups skim milk
1 pound very lean ground pork
¼ cup egg substitute

1. Soak bread crumbs in skim milk in a mixing bowl for 15 minutes. Mix in pork and egg substitute and season to taste with salt or salt substitute and freshly ground black pepper.

2. Dip fingers in cold water and shape 2 tablespoons mixture into balls. Heat a sprayed nonstick skillet over medium heat. Add meatballs in batches to avoid crowding skillet. Cook, stirring frequently, until meatballs are browned on all sides.

3. Serve with Meatball Gravy (p. 224); garnish with fresh chopped parsley.

- - - - - - - - - - - - - - - - - - -

Yield: About 5 servings
Serving size: 3 meatballs

Calories: 344
Protein: 28 g
Carbohydrate: 12 g
Fat: 20 g
Cholesterol: 88 mg
Sodium: 218 mg
Calcium: 139 mg
Dietary Fiber: less than 1 g
Sugar: 4 g

MEATBALL GRAVY

¼ cup finely chopped onion
1 tablespoon flour
⅛ teaspoon allspice
1 cup reduced sodium fat free chicken broth

1. Coat a saucepan with nonstick cooking spray and place over medium heat. Add onion and sauté over medium heat until onion is until clear and soft. Stir in flour and cook until well blended and flour bubbles, adding 1 tablespoon water or 1 teaspoon oil if needed to blend flour and onion.

2. Add allspice, salt or salt substitute to taste, and broth. Bring to a boil, stirring constantly, and cook for 1 minute to completely cook the flour.

- - - - - - - - - - - - - - - - - - -

Yield: 4 servings
Serving size: About ¼ cup

Calories: 18
Protein: 2 g
Carbohydrate: 3 g
Fat: 0 g
Cholesterol: 0 g
Sodium: 310 mg
Calcium: 2 mg
Dietary Fiber: less than 1 g
Sugar: less than 1 g

CHICKEN & TURKEY

When is a chicken breast really 'done'?

Directions to cook a chicken breast "until tender" may be more confusing than helpful to some cooks. "Until tender" is a rather vague and generalized explanation, when a more specific one may be in order.

A chicken breast cooked to the stage of "tender" should be easily cut or chewed and "done" beyond the stage of pink juices or meat. Doneness can be checked by piercing the thick part of the chicken breast to check for clear juices. Return chicken to the oven, skillet or grill if the juices are pink.

Checking the internal temperature of chicken breasts with a meat thermometer is considered by experts as the most reliable method for determining doneness. Should you want to purchase a meat thermometer, inexpensive digital thermometers are available that are accurate and easy to use.

To be assured of wholesomeness and quality, reliable sources recommend that boneless or bone-in chicken breasts reach an internal temperature of 170°F. Internal temperatures vary for doneness with other parts of chicken. Whereas chicken wings should be cooked to an internal temperature of 170°F, legs, thighs or drumsticks should be cooked to an internal temperature of 180°F, and whole chicken to 180°F as measured in the thigh.

APRICOT-CHICKEN BAKE

Boneless skinless chicken breasts are split chicken breasts with all skin and bone removed. Low in fat and quickly cooked, boneless skinless chicken breasts are more popular in the United States than any other type of poultry or meat. Chicken breast "tenders" sold in supermarkets are simply boneless skinless chicken breasts cut into strips. Since both boneless skinless chicken breasts and chicken tenders are relatively expensive, you may choose less expensive whole chicken breasts to bone, skin and cut into smaller portions.

1 cup light sugar free apricot preserves
1 (8 ounce) bottle fat free catalina dressing
1 (1.6 ounce) packet dry onion soup mix
6-8 boneless skinless chicken breasts with skin

1. Preheat oven to 325°. In a mixing bowl, combine preserves, salad dressing and soup mix. Place chicken breasts in a large sprayed baking dish and pour apricot mixture over chicken.

2. Bake, uncovered, for 1 hour. Check chicken for doneness by cutting a small slit in thickest part of chicken breast. If juices are still pink, continue cooking until done. Do not overcook or chicken will toughen and be dry.

- -

Yield: 6-8 servings
Serving size: 1 chicken breast (about 3 ounces meat)

Calories: 265
Protein: 24 g
Carbohydrate: 24 g
Fat: 10 g
Cholesterol: 72 mg
Sodium: 766 mg
Calcium: 12 mg
Dietary Fiber: 1 g
Sugar: 8 g

BAKED CHICKEN BREASTS WITH LEMON

A busy kitchen needs to have handy at least one kitchen timer to help the cook stay organized and on-track. Today's busy lifestyles afford so little time for food preparation; nobody wants to discard a recipe and start over due to overcooking! It is also a good idea to check the accuracy of the oven temperature from time to time with a reliable oven thermometer. Timers and thermometers are great tools for quality, healthful cooking.

4 boneless skinless chicken breasts
Juice of 1 lemon
1 tablespoon minced parsley

1. Preheat oven to 400°. Coat chicken breasts on both sides with nonstick cooking spray. Season to taste with salt or salt substitute and freshly ground black pepper.

2. Place chicken in a shallow baking pan and bake, uncovered, for 20 minutes. Check the doneness of the chicken by cutting a slit in the thickest part of the breast. If the chicken is still pink, continue cooking 5-10 minutes longer; then check again. Overcooking will dry and toughen the chicken.

3. Remove chicken and place on serving dish. Sprinkle with lemon juice and parsley.

Flavor Perk: Sprinkle ½ teaspoon dried herbs or seasoning blend over chicken before baking.

- -

Yield: 4 servings
Serving size: 1 chicken breast

Calories: 178
Protein: 34 g
Carbohydrate: 3 g
Fat: 4 g
Cholesterol: 85 mg
Sodium: 411 mg
Calcium: 3 mg
Dietary Fiber: less than 1 g
Sugar: less than 1 g

BAKED CHICKEN
IN LIGHT MUSHROOM SAUCE

4 boneless skinless chicken breasts
1 (8 ounce) package sliced fresh mushrooms
1¼ cup reduced sodium fat free chicken broth, divided
1 tablespoon cornstarch

1. Preheat oven to 400°. Season chicken breasts to taste with salt or salt substitute and freshly ground black pepper. Place chicken breasts in a sprayed shallow baking dish and bake, uncovered, about 20 minutes. Check for doneness and tenderness by making a small cut in the thickest part of the breast. If chicken is still pink, bake an additional 5-10 minutes and check again for doneness. Do not overcook or chicken will toughen and be dry.

2. Remove chicken from oven and keep warm. Meanwhile, prepare the mushrooms and sauce. In a sprayed skillet over medium heat, sauté mushrooms 3-5 minutes. Remove mushrooms and keep warm.

3. In a small bowl, mix ¼ cup chicken broth and cornstarch until well blended; set aside. Add remaining broth to the skillet and bring to a boil. Add cornstarch mixture and stir constantly until sauce is clear and thickened. Return mushrooms to skillet. Season sauce to taste with salt or salt substitute and freshly ground black pepper. Pour mushroom sauce over chicken and serve.

Flavor Perk: Sprinkle ½ teaspoon crushed dried thyme, oregano leaves or rosemary over chicken breasts before baking. Garnish with sprigs of fresh parsley.

- -

Yield: 4 servings
Serving size: 1 chicken breast

Calories: 198
Protein: 37
Carbohydrate: 4 g
Fat: 5 g
Cholesterol: 85 mg
Sodium: 606 mg
Calcium: 2 mg
Dietary Fiber: less than 1 g
Sugar: 1 g

CHICKEN DIJON BAKE

Dijon mustard adds a pleasantly sharp and unique flavor. Originating from Dijon, France, this mustard gives many recipes a needed piquancy, or tartness.

2 tablespoons Dijon-style mustard
1½ tablespoons vegetable oil
½ teaspoon salt free seasoning blend
4 boneless skinless chicken breasts

1. Mix mustard, oil and seasoning in a resealable plastic bag. Add chicken breasts; seal and refrigerate 15 minutes. Preheat oven to 375°.

2. Remove chicken from bag and place in a sprayed shallow baking pan. Bake, uncovered, for 20 minutes; then check for doneness. Cut a small slit in thickest part of chicken breast to check for doneness. If chicken is still pink, continue cooking, checking frequently. (Do not overbake or chicken will toughen.)

Flavor Perk: Add 1 teaspoon garlic powder to mustard mixture.

- -

Yield: 4 servings
Serving size: 1 chicken breast

Calories: 223
Protein: 34 g
Carbohydrate: 0 g
Fat: 9 g
Cholesterol: 85 mg
Sodium: 583 mg
Calcium: 4 mg
Dietary Fiber: 0 g
Sugar: 0 g

FANCY CHICKEN BAKE

Sour cream, soy sauce and onion combine flavors for a delicious, easily prepared chicken dish.

5-6 boneless skinless chicken breasts
½ cup light sour cream
¼ cup light (reduced sodium) soy sauce
1 (10½ ounce) can French onion soup

1. Preheat oven to 350°. Place chicken in a 9 x 13-inch baking dish coated with nonstick cooking spray.

2. In saucepan, combine sour cream, soy sauce and soup; heat just enough to mix well. Pour over chicken breasts.

3. Bake, covered, for 45 minutes. Check chicken for doneness by cutting a slit in the thickest part of a chicken breast. If juice is clear and chicken is firm and not pink, chicken is done. If still pink, cook an additional 5-10 minutes until done.

Flavor Perk: Garnish with fresh parsley sprigs.

- - - - - - - - - - - - - - - - - - - -

Yield: 5-6 servings
Serving size: 1 chicken breast

Calories: 207
Protein: 33 g
Carbohydrate: 4 g
Fat: 6 g
Cholesterol: 86 mg
Sodium: 822 mg
Calcium: 27 mg
Dietary Fiber: less than 1 g
Sugar: 2 g

CHILES RELLENO-CHICKEN BAKE

This recipe combines the favorite flavors of chicken, cheese and green chiles.

4 boneless skinless chicken breasts
4 whole canned green chiles, drained, liquid reserved
4 (½ inch x 3 inch) strips reduced fat Monterey jack or cheddar cheese
4 green onions and tops, sliced or chopped

1. Preheat oven to 375°. With a meat mallet or the edge of a saucer, lightly pound each chicken breast to flatten into a rectangle. Place flattened chicken breasts on wax or parchment paper and season to taste with salt or salt substitute and freshly ground black pepper.

2. Split and open green chiles. Place 1 chile on each flattened chicken breast; lay cheese strip on one edge of chile. Sprinkle with 1 tablespoon green onion. Fold ends and sides of chile to encase cheese strip and onions. Roll chicken breast around stuffed chile. Tie with cotton string if chicken breast does not stay rolled. Brush or spoon reserved green chile liquid on the chicken breasts

3. Place chicken on baking sheet and bake 20 minutes, basting with any remaining liquid from chiles. Check each chicken breast for doneness (firmness and clear juices.) If not done, continue baking another 5-10 minutes.

4. Serve immediately.

Flavor Perk: Garnish with grated Monterey jack cheese and chopped fresh cilantro; serve with salsa.

Variation: Place chicken breasts in shallow baking pan and spoon 10 ounces red or green chile enchilada sauce over chicken before baking. Baste frequently with sauce.

- -

Yield: 4 servings
Serving size: 1 chicken breast

Calories: 257
Protein: 41 g
Carbohydrate: 2 g
Fat: 10 g
Cholesterol: 105 mg
Sodium: 689 mg
Calcium: 219 mg
Dietary Fiber: less than 1 g
Sugar: less than 1 g

CREAMY CHICKEN BAKE

6-8 boneless skinless chicken breasts
1 (10½) ounce can reduced fat cream of mushroom soup
¾ cup white wine or white cooking wine
1 (8 ounce) carton light or fat free sour cream

1. Preheat oven at 350°. Place chicken breasts in a large shallow baking pan. Season to taste with salt or salt substitute and freshly ground black pepper. Bake, uncovered, for 30 minutes.

2. In saucepan over low heat, combine soup, wine and sour cream. When well blended, remove from heat. Remove chicken from oven and pour sour cream mixture over chicken.

3. Return to oven to cook an additional 20 minutes, basting and checking for doneness every 10 minutes.

Flavor Perk: Garnish with fresh parsley or cilantro sprigs.

- - - - - - - - - - - - - - - - - - - -

Yield: 6-8 servings
Serving size: 1 chicken breast

Calories: 270
Protein: 36 g
Carbohydrate: 6 g
Fat: 9 g
Cholesterol: 101 mg
Sodium: 770 mg
Calcium: 50 mg
Dietary Fiber: 0 g
Sugar: less than 1 g

LEMON-GARLIC BAKED CHICKEN

3 tablespoons lemon juice
1 finely minced or pressed garlic clove
2 tablespoons vegetable or olive oil
4 boneless skinless chicken breasts, rinsed, patted dry

1. Preheat oven to 350°. In a small bowl, combine lemon juice, garlic and oil. Season chicken to taste with salt or salt substitute and freshly ground black pepper. Place chicken in a shallow baking pan and pour lemon mixture over the chicken.

2. Cover and bake about 40 minutes or until chicken is tender, basting occasionally. Uncover and bake an additional 10 minutes to allow the chicken to brown lightly.

Flavor Perk: Garnish with lemon slice twists and chopped parsley.

Variation: Substitute 8 skinless chicken thighs for the chicken breasts; increase cooking time if needed.

- - - - - - - - - - - - - - - - - - - -

Yield: 4 servings
Serving size: 1 chicken breast

Calories: 234
Protein: 34 g
Carbohydrate: 1 g
Fat: 11 g
Cholesterol: 85 mg
Sodium: 410 mg
Calcium: 7 mg
Dietary Fiber: 0 g
Sugar: less than 1 g

LEMON-SESAME CHICKEN

What could be simpler than basting baked chicken with lemon juice and toasted sesame seeds?

4 boneless skinless chicken breasts, rinsed, patted dry
¼ cup toasted sesame seeds*, divided
Juice of 1 lemon, divided

1. Preheat oven to 375°. Spray chicken breasts on both sides with nonstick cooking spray. Place in shallow baking pan; sprinkle with half of sesame seeds and lemon juice.

2. Bake 30 minutes or until lightly browned. Turn chicken breasts and sprinkle with remaining sesame seeds and lemon juice. Bake an additional 10-15 minutes, basting occasionally, until chicken is tender.

- - - - - - - - - - - - - - - - - -

Yield: 4 servings
Serving size: 1 chicken breast

Calories: 228
Protein: 36 g
Carbohydrate: 5 g
Fat: 8 g
Cholesterol: 85 mg
Sodium: 411 mg
Calcium: 91 mg
Dietary Fiber: 1 g
Sugar: less than 1 g

To toast sesame seeds: Place seeds in a dry skillet over medium heat. Stir constantly until seeds are lightly browned and fragrant. Remove seeds immediately.

PINEAPPLE-ORANGE CHICKEN

Orange juice and crushed pineapple lend a tropical flavor to this baked chicken.

4 boneless skinless chicken breasts
¾ cup orange juice
½ cup raisins
1 (8 ounce) can crushed pineapple in juice

1. Preheat oven to 350°. Season chicken breasts with salt or salt substitute and freshly ground black pepper. In a skillet coated with nonstick cooking spray, lightly brown chicken breasts.

2. Place browned chicken breasts in a shallow baking pan. Mix orange juice, raisins and crushed pineapple. Spoon mixture over chicken breasts. Bake, uncovered, about 30 minutes or until thickest part of chicken breasts is tender.

Flavor Perk: Add ¼ teaspoon ground cinnamon to pineapple mixture.

- - - - - - - - - - - - - - - - - -

Yield: 4 servings
Serving size: 1 chicken breast

Calories: 285
Protein: 35 g
Carbohydrate: 29 g
Fat: 4 g
Cholesterol: 85 mg
Sodium: 418 mg
Calcium: 15 mg
Dietary Fiber: 1 g
Sugar: 25 g

QUICK CHICKEN PARMESAN

⅔ cup fine dry bread crumbs
⅓ cup reduced fat grated Parmesan topping
¼ cup fat free Italian salad dressing
4 boneless skinless chicken breasts

1. Preheat oven to 350°. Combine bread crumbs and cheese; place on a plate. Pour salad dressing in a shallow dish. Dip chicken in salad dressing; then coat with crumb mixture. Place chicken in a shallow baking pan coated with nonstick cooking spray.

2. Bake, uncovered, about 50 minutes.

Flavor Perk: Add ½ teaspoon garlic powder to breadcrumb mixture.

- - - - - - - - - - - - - - - - - -

Yield: 4 servings
Serving size: 1 chicken breast

Calories: 290
Protein: 37 g
Carbohydrate: 19 g
Fat: 6 g
Cholesterol: 85 mg
Sodium: 927 mg
Calcium: 40 mg
Dietary Fiber: less than 1 g
Sugar: 2 g

SKILLET CHICKEN-SAUERKRAUT TWIST

Sauerkraut, traditionally served with sausages and pork, provides a unique flavor to this chicken dish. To reduce sodium content, rinse and drain the sauerkraut.

6 boneless skinless chicken breasts
½ (32 ounce) jar refrigerated (deli-case) sauerkraut, drained
¼ cup toasted pine nuts
or ½ teaspoon caraway seeds
Light or fat free sour cream for garnish

1. In a large skillet sprayed with nonstick cooking spray, season chicken with freshly ground black pepper to taste. Cook over medium heat about 15 minutes until chicken is brown on both sides.

2. Spoon sauerkraut over chicken. Cover and cook over low heat until chicken is done, about 30 minutes.

3. Toast pine nuts in a dry skillet on medium heat, stirring constantly until golden brown. Sprinkle chicken and sauerkraut with toasted pine nuts. Serve with sour cream as a garnish.

Variation: Add a peeled, cored, grated Granny Smith apple with the sauerkraut.

- - - - - - - - - - - - - - - - - -

Yield: 6 servings
Serving size: 1 chicken breast

Calories: 249
Protein: 35 g
Carbohydrate: 5 g
Fat: 10 g
Cholesterol: 87 mg
Sodium: 948 mg   Dietary Fiber: 4 g
Calcium: 6 mg   Sugar: 0 g

WHITE WINE-RASPBERRY CHICKEN

4 boneless skinless chicken breasts
1 teaspoon cornstarch
¼ cup dry white wine or white cooking wine, divided
3 tablespoons seedless raspberry fruit spread

1. Place the chicken between pieces of wax paper or plastic wrap. Using a meat mallet or the edge of a saucer, pound thick areas lightly to even the thickness of the breasts. Season to taste with freshly ground black pepper and salt or salt substitute.

2. Preheat a sprayed large skillet over medium heat. Add chicken and cook about 10-12 minutes or until chicken is tender and lightly browned on each side. Remove chicken and keep warm.

3. Place cornstarch in a small bowl and gradually stir in 1 teaspoon wine until smooth. Set aside. Place remaining wine and fruit spread in the skillet over medium heat. Using a wire whisk, stir wine and fruit spread briskly until blended; bring to a boil.

4. Whisk in cornstarch-wine mixture and cook, stirring constantly, 2-3 minutes until sauce thickens and turns clear. Spoon the sauce over the chicken and serve immediately.

Flavor Perk: Add ¼ teaspoon lemon juice or grated lemon peel to the sauce.

- -

Yield: 4 servings
Serving size: 1 chicken breast

Calories: 213
Protein: 34 g
Carbohydrate: 8 g
Fat: 4 g
Cholesterol: 85 mg
Sodium: 411 mg
Calcium: 1 mg
Dietary Fiber: 0 g
Sugar: 6 g

SKILLET SAUSAGE AND VEGETABLES

Choose a light fruit or gelatin salad as an accompaniment to this hearty main dish.

**2 cups shredded green cabbage
1 (16 ounce) package frozen stir-fry vegetables, partially thawed
1 cup reduced sodium fat free chicken broth
1½ pounds precooked turkey sausage, diagonally sliced ¼-inch thick**

1. To a large skillet coated with non-stick cooking spray, add cabbage, mixed vegetables and broth. Cook on medium heat 10-12 minutes or until vegetables are crisp-tender.

2. Add sausage and stir until sausage is heated through, about 5 minutes. Season to taste with freshly ground black pepper.

Flavor Perk: Add 1 sliced onion and 1 finely minced or pressed garlic clove with vegetable mixture.

- - - - - - - - - - - - - - - - - - -

Yield: 6 servings
Serving size: About 1¼ cups

Calories: 228
Protein: 23 g
Carbohydrate: 8 g
Fat: 13 g
Cholesterol: 88 mg
Sodium: 797 mg
Calcium: 93 mg
Dietary Fiber: 1 g
Sugar: 2 g

EASY CHICKEN DIVAN

The combination of broccoli and chicken in a creamy sauce topped with cheese continues to be a favorite main-dish recipe.

**3 cups fresh broccoli florets, steamed until crisp-tender
2-3 boneless skinless chicken breasts, cooked, sliced
1 (10½ ounce) can reduced sodium fat free cream of chicken or mushroom soup
⅓ cup freshly grated reduced fat Parmesan or Romano cheese**

1. Preheat oven to 375°. Place broccoli florets in a sprayed shallow baking dish. Place the chicken on the broccoli. If desired, season chicken with salt or salt substitute and freshly ground black pepper.

2. Spoon soup evenly over chicken. Sprinkle with cheese and bake 15-20 minutes until thoroughly heated.

Flavor Perk: Add ¼ cup dry sherry to soup.
Variations: Substitute 1-2 (14 ounce) packages frozen baby broccoli florets, steamed lightly, for the fresh broccoli. Another variation is to use 1 pound steamed asparagus for the broccoli.

- - - - - - - - - - - - - - - - - - -

Yield: 4 servings
Serving size: About 1½ cups

Calories: 183
Protein: 24 g
Carbohydrate: 9 g
Fat: 6 g
Cholesterol: 54 mg
Sodium: 910 mg
Calcium: 135 mg
Dietary Fiber: 2 g
Sugar: 3 g

SPEEDY CHICKEN TETRAZZINI

Tetrazzini is a dish created nearly 100 years ago by the renowned French chef Escoffier in honor of Luisa Tetrazzini, a famous opera star. The combination of chicken, mushrooms and pasta in creamy sauce has not lost its appeal and popularity since.

1 (8 ounce) package fresh sliced mushrooms
2 (14 ounce) cans reduced fat cream of chicken
or cream of mushroom soup
2 cups cooked chicken or turkey, cubed
1 (7 ounce) package spaghetti, cooked, drained

1. Heat oven to 350°. In a Dutch oven sprayed with nonstick cooking spray, sauté mushrooms 3-4 minutes over medium heat. Add soup and heat 3-4 minutes. Stir in chicken or turkey and cooked spaghetti; heat through. Season to taste with freshly ground black pepper and salt or salt substitute.

2. Pour mixture into a sprayed 2-quart baking dish. Bake, uncovered, 30 minutes or until center is bubbly.

Flavor Perk: Add 2 tablespoons sherry or cooking sherry to spaghetti mixture. Before baking, top with ½ cup reduced fat grated Parmesan topping and 2 tablespoons toasted slivered almonds.

- -

Yield: 6 servings
Serving size: About ¾ cup

Calories: 222
Protein: 19 g
Carbohydrate: 24 g
Fat: 5 g
Cholesterol: 51 mg
Sodium: 566 mg
Calcium: 10 mg
Dietary Fiber: less than 1 g
Sugar: 3 g

DILLED CHICKEN SAUTE

3 teaspoons margarine or
vegetable oil
4 boneless skinless chicken breasts
½ cup light sour cream
½-1 teaspoon dried dill weed

1. Melt margarine or oil in skillet. Over medium heat, sauté chicken breasts on both sides until golden brown. Reduce heat and continue cooking 15-20 minutes or until chicken is tender.

2. Remove chicken from skillet and keep warm. Pour any remaining oil from the skillet; add sour cream and dill weed. Heat 2-3 minutes over low heat.

3. Spoon sauce over chicken to serve.

Variation: For Chive Chicken Sauté, substitute 2 teaspoons fresh or freeze-dried chives for the dill weed.

- - - - - - - - - - - - - - - -

Yield: 4 servings
Serving size: 1 chicken breast

Calories: 236
Protein: 35 g
Carbohydrate: 1 g
Fat: 10 g
Cholesterol: 97 mg
Sodium: 456 mg
Calcium: 34 mg
Dietary Fiber: 0 g
Sugar: 0 g

ORANGE-BROILED CHICKEN

Mustard and orange juice combine for a savory marinade and basting sauce for broiled chicken.

½ cup orange juice plus 2
tablespoons finely grated orange
peel
2 tablespoons vegetable oil
½ teaspoon ground mustard
4 boneless skinless chicken breasts
or 8 skinless chicken thighs

1. Mix orange juice, peel, oil and mustard. Add ¼ teaspoon salt or salt substitute. Place in bowl or resealable plastic bag and add chicken. Refrigerate about 15 minutes.

2. Remove chicken from marinade and place on broiler pan. Broil chicken 4-5 inches from heating element, basting frequently, 7-10 minutes on each side. Test for doneness by piercing thickest part of chicken to see if juices run clear.

Variation: Charcoal or gas-grill chicken about 15 minutes on each side.

- - - - - - - - - - - - - - - -

Yield: 4 servings
Serving size: 1 chicken breast

Calories: 188
Protein: 34 g
Carbohydrate: 4 g
Fat: 4 g
Cholesterol: 85 mg
Sodium: 410 mg
Calcium: 9 mg
Dietary Fiber: less than 1 g
Sugar: 3 g

"BEST" BROILED CHICKEN BREASTS

This is a no-nonsense, easy method for having deliciously-cooked chicken breasts on the dinner table in a hurry.

4 boneless skinless chicken breasts
Lemon-pepper seasoning or salt free seasoning blend of your choice

1. On a sheet of wax paper, spray both sides of chicken breasts with nonstick cooking spray. Sprinkle with seasoning blend or salt or salt substitute and freshly ground pepper.

2. Place chicken breasts on broiler pan 4-5 inches from heat element in oven. Broil each side 5-7 minutes or until golden brown. Check for doneness by piercing thickest part of breast for clear, not pink, juices.

Variation: Grill chicken breasts on charcoal or gas grill, following same preparation and cooking time.

- - - - - - - - - - - - - - - - - -

Yield: 4 servings
Serving size: 1 chicken breast

Calories: 170
Protein: 34 g
Carbohydrate: 0 g
Fat: 4 g
Cholesterol: 85 mg
Sodium: 410 mg
Calcium: 0 mg
Dietary Fiber: 0 g
Sugar: 0 g

BROILED CHICKEN KABOBS

Pineapple, bell pepper and chicken are a flavorful combination for these easy-to-make and fun-to-eat kabobs.

8-10 chicken breast strips, cut in 1-inch strips
⅓ cup light soy sauce
1 (8 ounce) can pineapple chunks in juice, drained
1 large red or green bell pepper, cut in 2-inch chunks

1. Place chicken strips in a large resealable plastic bag. Add soy sauce to coat; refrigerate at least 1 hour. Season chicken to taste with salt or salt substitute and freshly ground black pepper.

2. Thread chicken strips accordion or ribbon fashion on metal skewers, alternating with pineapple chunks and bell pepper. Leave small spaces between foods for even cooking. Place kabobs on broiler pan 4-5 inches from heating element. Broil 5 minutes on each side or until chicken is tender and no longer pink, and pineapple and bell pepper are lightly browned.

Flavor Perk: Add cherry tomatoes to the skewers.
- - - - - - - - - - - - - - - - - -
Yield: 4-5 servings
Serving size: 2 kabobs

Calories: 85
Protein: 8 g
Carbohydrate: 13 g
Fat: less than 1 g
Cholesterol: 16 mg
Sodium: 717 mg
Calcium: 7 mg
Dietary Fiber: 1 g
Sugar: 10 g

CRUNCHY "FRIED" CHICKEN

For those of us who crave fried chicken …

4 boneless skinless chicken breasts
1-2 cups buttermilk
1-1½ cups whole grain or whole wheat Melba toast crumbs
Salt free Creole seasoning or salt-free seasoning blend of your choice

1. Place chicken breasts in large resealable plastic bag. Cover with buttermilk and place in refrigerator overnight or at least 3-4 hours. When ready to cook, remove chicken breasts from bag and preheat oven to 375°.

2. Season Melba toast crumbs with your choice of seasoning blend. Place on pie plate and coat chicken breasts with crumbs, lightly pressing crumbs to the chicken with fingers. Let set 1 minute for crumbs to adhere.

3. Place chicken on lightly sprayed baking sheet, allowing space between each coated breast. Bake 20 minutes; then check for doneness by piercing the thickest part of the breast with a long fork. Look for clear, not pink, juices.

4. Serve hot.

Variation: Replace buttermilk with egg substitute and replace Melba toast crumbs with cornflake crumbs.

- -

Yield: 4 servings
Serving size: 1 chicken breast

Calories: 407
Protein: 43 g
Carbohydrate: 46 g
Fat: 5 g
Cholesterol: 87 mg
Sodium: 949 mg
Calcium: 96 mg
Dietary Fiber: 4 g
Sugar: 3 g

CRISPY BAKED DRUMSTICKS

Packaged drumsticks are economical and easy to prepare. They are particularly tasty as "fried" in this recipe. Removing skin from drumsticks reduces fat and calories. To remove slippery skin from a chicken drumstick, grasp the skin firmly with a paper towel and pull toward small end of drumstick.

**8 skinless chicken drumsticks
1-2 cups buttermilk
2-3 cups cornflake crumbs
Salt free herb seasoning blend or dried parsley to taste**

1. Place drumsticks in a deep bowl or resealable plastic bag. Pour buttermilk over drumsticks to cover. Cover bowl tightly or seal bag and place in refrigerator at least 3-4 hours.

2. Preheat oven to 375°. Remove drumsticks from refrigerator. Mix herb seasoning and cornflake crumbs and place on a pie plate. Place each drumstick on plate and coat with crumbs, pressing lightly with fingers.

3. Place coated drumsticks on a baking pan coated with nonstick cooking spray, arranging so that pieces do not touch. Wait about 1 minute before placing in oven. Bake 45 minutes and check for doneness by piercing thickest part of drumstick for clear, not pink, juices. When chicken is done, remove and serve.

Variation: Substitute fat free Italian salad dressing for the buttermilk.

- -

Yield: 4-6 servings
Serving size: 2 small or 1 large drumstick

Calories: 315
Protein: 45 g
Carbohydrate: 15 g
Fat: 7 g
Cholesterol: 159 mg
Sodium: 308 mg
Calcium: 93 mg
Dietary Fiber: less than 1 g
Sugar: 4 g

PANTRY CHICKEN TOSTADAS

Keep canned chicken, canned refried beans and boxed tostada shells handy to put this hearty dish together quickly.

1 (16 ounce) can fat free refried beans
1 (4.5 ounce) box tostada shells (flat tortillas)
2 (6 ounce) cans 98% fat free chunk breast of chicken
1 (8 ounce) package shredded reduced fat cheddar or mozzarella cheese

1. Preheat oven to 375°. Spread 2-3 tablespoons refried beans on 4 tostada shells. Add 2-3 tablespoons chicken, and sprinkle with 1 tablespoon cheese. Place on baking sheet and bake 10-12 minutes or until cheese melts and beans and chicken are heated through.

Flavor Perk: Garnish with salsa or reduced fat sour cream.

- - - - - - - - - - - - - - - - -

Yield: 4 servings
Serving size: 1 tostada

Calories: 200
Protein: 22 g
Carbohydrate: 12 g
Fat: 6 g
Cholesterol: 50 mg
Sodium: 625 mg
Calcium: 116 mg
Dietary Fiber: 3 g
Sugar: less than 1 g

MANDARIN CHICKEN TENDERS

1½-2 pounds chicken tenders (breast strips)
1 cup orange juice
2-3 teaspoons light (reduced sodium) soy sauce
1 (11 ounce) can mandarin oranges, drained

1. Preheat a sprayed skillet over medium heat. Season chicken tenders to taste with salt or salt substitute and freshly ground black pepper. Add tenders to the skillet and brown tenders lightly on both sides, checking for doneness.

2. Add orange juice and soy sauce to the skillet; cover and simmer about 10 minutes. Add mandarin orange sections and simmer an additional 5 minutes.

Flavor Perk: Add 2 tablespoons honey and ½ teaspoon ground ginger to soy sauce mixture.

- - - - - - - - - - - - - - - - -

Yield: 4 servings
Serving size: About 1 cup

Calories: 211
Protein: 35 g
Carbohydrate: 14 g
Fat: less than 1 g
Cholesterol: 99 mg
Sodium: 362 mg
Calcium: 16 mg
Dietary Fiber: less than 1 g
Sugar: 7 g

CHICKEN STRIPS WITH BROCCOLI

This recipe calls for blanched fresh broccoli spears. To blanch broccoli, pour boiling water over broccoli pieces in a colander. Rinse with cold water to retain crisp-tender texture and bright green color.

8-10 chicken breast strips, cut in 1-inch strips
8 fresh broccoli spears, blanched, cut in 1-inch pieces
1¼ cups canned reduced sodium fat free chicken broth, divided
4 teaspoons cornstarch, divided

1. In a large skillet coated with nonstick cooking spray, lightly brown chicken tenders; remove from skillet and keep warm. To the same skillet, add broccoli and cook about 1 minute until crisp-tender.

2. In a small bowl, combine ¼ cup broth and 3 teaspoons cornstarch, stirring to dissolve cornstarch. Add remaining broth and stir briskly until blended.

3. Place broth mixture in skillet with broccoli. Cook over low heat 5-10 minutes, stirring frequently, until sauce thickens and is translucent. If a thicker sauce is desired, stir 1 teaspoon cornstarch in 2 teaspoons water in a small bowl until blended; add to the skillet. Add cooked chicken and simmer an additional 3-4 minutes.

Flavor Perk: Add 2 minced garlic cloves and 1 teaspoon peeled, minced ginger root with broccoli.

Variation: Substitute 14 ounces frozen baby broccoli florets, partially thawed, for fresh broccoli. Do not blanch.

- -

Yield: 4 servings
Serving size: About 1 cup

Calories: 76
Protein: 14 g
Carbohydrate: 4 g
Fat: less than 1 g
Cholesterol: 37 mg
Sodium: 300 mg
Calcium: 9 mg
Dietary Fiber: 0 g
Sugar: less than 1 g

CHICKEN MEDLEY STIR-FRY

Chicken breast strips or tenders are ideal for stir-frying. For a more economical alternative, buy boned chicken breasts with skin and prepare your own.

6-7 chicken breast strips, cut in ¼-inch strips
3-4 tablespoons light soy sauce
1 carrot, peeled, shredded or grated
1 green bell pepper, cut in thin strips or slivers

1. Place chicken strips in bowl or resealable plastic bag. Cover with soy sauce and refrigerate at least 30 minutes. Preheat sprayed non-stick wok pan or skillet. Sauté shredded carrots 1 minute. Add green pepper and sauté an additional minute. Remove carrots and green pepper and set aside.

2. Add chicken strips to skillet and cook 2-3 minutes or until chicken turns white. Add cooked carrots, green pepper and remaining soy sauce to the skillet; heat through. Serve immediately.

Flavor Perk: Sauté ¼ cup sliced green onion and tops with the chicken strips; add 2 teaspoons cornstarch to soy sauce.

- -
Yield: 4 servings
Serving size: About 1½ cups

Calories: 71
Protein: 11 g
Carbohydrate: 5 g
Fat: less than 1 g
Cholesterol: 28 mg
Sodium: 527 mg
Calcium: 10 mg
Dietary Fiber: less than 1 g
Sugar: 4 g

CHICKEN-PARMESAN RICE

Add a fresh green salad and whole grain rolls to accompany this chicken-rice dish for a complete meal quickly prepared.

*8 boneless skinless chicken strips
1 (14 ounce) can 98% fat free seasoned chicken broth
¾ cup long grain white rice, uncooked
¼ cup reduced fat grated Parmesan topping

*Substitute 2 (6 ounce) packages cooked grilled chicken breast strips for fresh chicken strips.

1. Place chicken in a sprayed large skillet over medium heat and lightly brown strips on both sides. Check strips for doneness; remove from skillet and set aside. Add chicken broth and rice to the skillet; bring to boiling.

2. Reduce heat; then cover and simmer 25 minutes, adding 2-4 tablespoons water if needed to completely cook rice. Return chicken to skillet and heat through. Transfer to a serving dish and sprinkle with Parmesan topping.

- -
Yield: 4 servings
Serving size: 2 breast strips; ½ cup rice

Calories: 215
Protein: 15 g
Carbohydrate: 32 g
Fat: 2 g
Cholesterol: 33 mg
Sodium: 614 mg
Calcium: 10 mg
Dietary Fiber: less than 1 g
Sugar: less than 1 g

CHICKEN-BELL PEPPER STIR-FRY

Stir-frying, a healthful cooking technique, is a uniquely Chinese cooking method that has been adapted to cuisines throughout the world. By definition, stir-frying is quickly cooking and stirring foods in a tiny amount of oil over high heat. Foods are not "fried" but are tossed, cooked and seared. As a result, vegetables maintain crispness and meats become tender and flavorful, with juices sealed in.

A cardinal rule in stir-frying is to have all ingredients prepared and ready to cook before beginning, since stir-frying takes so little time from beginning to end. Wok pans are the best choice to use for stir-frying, but nonstick skillets can be successfully used. Electric woks have controls that help to monitor heating temperatures, important to the stir-frying technique. Both electric and well designed sturdy top-of-range woks are now available in nonstick finishes.

¼-½ cup stir-fry sauce or light soy sauce
6-8 chicken breast strips, rinsed, cut in ½-inch strips, patted dry
1 large red or green bell pepper, cut in ¼-inch strips
4-6 green onions and tops, sliced diagonally

1. Place stir-fry or soy sauce in a shallow bowl. Add chicken strips and turn to coat. Cover and refrigerate at least 15 minutes. Preheat nonstick wok or skillet over medium heat. Add pepper strips and sauté, stirring constantly, about 2 minutes or until pepper is crisp-tender. Add green onion and cook about 1-2 minutes, stirring constantly.

2. Remove pepper and onion from pan and set aside. Add marinated chicken strips and toss; cook until no longer pink. Return peppers and onions to pan and add additional soy sauce, if needed, to prevent sticking. Season to taste with freshly ground black pepper.

3. Serve immediately with brown or white cooked rice.

Flavor Perk: Sauté 1 finely minced garlic clove with green peppers.

- -

Yield: 4 servings
Serving size: About 1 cup

Calories: 68
Protein: 10 g
Carbohydrate: 6 g
Fat: less than 1 g
Cholesterol: 28 mg
Sodium: 160 mg
Calcium: 18 mg
Dietary Fiber: 1 g
Sugar: 2 g

GRILLED SOY-SAUCED CHICKEN

¼ cup light (reduced sodium) soy sauce
Sugar substitute equal to 1 tablespoon sugar
1 teaspoon ground ginger
4-5 boneless skinless chicken breasts

1. Combine soy sauce, sugar substitute, ground ginger, ¼ cup water and 1 teaspoon salt or salt substitute. Place marinade in bowl or resealable plastic bag; add chicken. Refrigerate 1-2 hours.

2. Prepare charcoal or gas grill according to manufacturer's instructions. Remove chicken from marinade and place on grill. Cook about 15 minutes on each side, basting frequently with marinade. When chicken juices are clear (not pink) and chicken is tender, remove and serve.

Flavor Perk: Sprinkle toasted sesame seeds over grilled chicken.

Variation: Broil chicken in oven, placing broiler pan 4-5 inches from heating element. Reduce cooking time to about 10 minutes for each side.

- - - - - - - - - - - - - - - - - - - -

Yield: 4 servings
Serving size: 1 chicken breast

Calories: 178
Protein: 35
Carbohydrate: 2 g
Fat: 4 g
Cholesterol: 85 mg
Sodium: 609 mg
Calcium: 9 mg
Dietary Fiber: 0 g
Sugar: less than 1 g

CHICKEN-GREEN BEAN CASSEROLE

4 boneless skinless chicken breasts
1 onion, peeled, sliced
1 cup reduced sodium fat free chicken broth, divided
½ pound fresh green beans, rinsed, tips removed, or 10 ounces frozen whole or cut green beans

1. Preheat oven to 300°. Place chicken breasts in Dutch oven. Add onion and ½ cup broth. Season to taste with salt or salt substitute and freshly ground black pepper. Cover tightly and bake 1 hour.

2. Add green beans and remaining broth; continue cooking 45-50 minutes or until chicken is done.

Flavor Perk: Add 2 tablespoons fresh chopped parsley or 1 tablespoon dried parsley flakes before baking.

Variation: Substitute ½ cup cooking sherry or white cooking wine for ½ cup of the chicken broth.

- - - - - - - - - - - - - - - - - - - -

Yield: 4 servings
Serving size: 1 chicken breast

Calories: 207
Protein: 36 g
Carbohydrate: 8 g
Fat: 4 g
Cholesterol: 85 mg
Sodium: 570 mg
Calcium: 29 mg
Dietary Fiber: 3 g
Sugar: 3 g

CHICKEN-TOMATO CASSEROLE

1 (2½-3 pound) chicken, skinned, cut in 8 pieces
2 tablespoons vegetable oil
½-¾ cup frozen seasoning blend (onion, celery, bell pepper and parsley), thawed
1½ cups canned no salt diced tomatoes

1. Preheat oven to 325°. Rinse chicken pieces and pat dry. Preheat oil in a large skillet over medium heat. Add chicken pieces a few at a time, and brown lightly on all sides. Place all chicken pieces in a sprayed baking pan, and season to taste with salt or salt substitute and freshly ground black pepper.

2. Add seasoning blend to the skillet and sauté 4-5 minutes, stirring constantly, to evaporate excess liquid. Add the tomatoes to the skillet and stir to combine with seasoning blend. Spoon tomato mixture over the chicken.

3. Cover and bake 45 minutes. Check for doneness by making a small slit in the thickest part of each chicken piece. If chicken is still pink, continue cooking until all pieces are done and tender. Serve chicken on a bed of rice with tomato sauce spooned over.

- -

Yield: 6 servings
Serving size: 1-2 pieces chicken

Calories: 342
Protein: 44 g
Carbohydrate: 4 g
Fat: 16 g
Cholesterol: 134 mg
Sodium: 158 mg
Calcium: 36 mg
Dietary Fiber: 1 g
Sugar: 2 g

OPEN-FACE TURKEY QUESADILLAS

4-6 (6 inch) whole wheat or flour tortillas
1 cup canned diced tomatoes and green chilies, drained
1-1½ cups cooked turkey breast, diced or in strips
1 (8 ounce) package finely shredded reduced fat or fat free cheddar
cheese

1. Preheat oven to 375°. Place tortillas on baking sheet and 2 tablespoons drained tomatoes on each. Add ¼ cup turkey and sprinkle 2-3 tablespoons cheese on top.

2. Place quesadillas in oven and check every five minutes. Bake only until cheese melts and quesadillas are heated through.

3. Serve immediately.

Flavor Perk: Add 1 teaspoon ground cumin and 2 tablespoons chopped fresh cilantro to drained tomatoes. Serve with light or fat free sour cream.

Variation: Substitute 1 cup salsa or fresh diced tomatoes for the tomatoes and green chilies.

- -

Yield: 4-6 servings
Serving size: 1 quesadilla

Calories: 255
Protein: 27 g
Carbohydrate: 11 g
Fat: 10 g
Cholesterol: 70 mg
Sodium: *590 mg
Calcium: 348 mg
Dietary Fiber: 7 g
Sugar: less than 1 g

Many pre-packaged deli meats are high in sodium. Nutritional analysis is calculated with fresh cooked turkey breast.

TURKEY ISLAND KABOBS

Skewers
4-6 slices turkey bacon
1 (8 ounce) can pineapple chunks
in juice

1. Soak skewers in water 10-15 minutes. Thread turkey bacon, ribbon style, and pineapple chunks between each fold of bacon.

2. Place skewers on broiler pan 4-5 inches from heat element. Broil kabobs about 4-5 minutes on each side until bacon is crisp and pineapple is lightly browned.

Variation: Bake kabobs at 400° for about 15-20 minutes, turning once, until bacon is crisp and pineapple lightly browned.

- - - - - - - - - - - - - - - - - - - -

Yield: 4-6 servings
Serving size: 1 kabob

Calories: 56
Protein: 10 g
Carbohydrate: 0 g
Fat: 13 g
Cholesterol: 50 mg
Sodium: 950 mg
Calcium: 0 mg
Dietary Fiber: 0 g
Sugar: 0 g

SILVER DOLLAR PATTIES

1 pound ground turkey
½ cup herb or Italian seasoned
bread crumbs
3 tablespoons minced onion
2 egg whites

1. In a mixing bowl, combine turkey, bred crumbs and minced onion until well blended. Season mixture to taste with salt or salt substitute and freshly ground black pepper. Add egg whites and stir to blend.

2. Form mixture into 8 small, thin patties. Over medium heat, preheat a skillet coated with nonstick cooking spray. Place patties in skillet and cook 4-5 minutes on each side or until no longer pink in middle. Do not overcook or patties will be dry.

Flavor Perk: Add 1 finely minced garlic clove to turkey mixture.

Variation: Substitute ½ cup egg substitute for the egg whites.

- - - - - - - - - - - - - - - - - - - -

Yield: 4 servings
Serving size: 2 patties

Calories: 236
Protein: 24 g
Carbohydrate: 11 g
Fat: 10 g
Cholesterol: 90 mg
Sodium: 505 mg
Calcium: 37 mg
Dietary Fiber: less than 1
Sugar: less than 1 g

SEAFOOD

If you are looking for healthier eating, find the fresh, canned, and frozen fish available in your supermarket. Nutritionally, fish is a bargain—low in overall calories, fat, saturated fat, and cholesterol, and high in quality protein. Broiling, grilling, and baking are healthy cooking methods for fish. Look in this section for simple, easy to prepare recipes for fish.

FRESH FLORIDA RED SNAPPER

1½ pounds red snapper fillets
1 teaspoon freshly grated nutmeg
or ground nutmeg
1½ teaspoons grated orange rind
1 teaspoon grapefruit rind (or a
combination of lemon and lime
rinds)

1. Preheat oven to 400°. Place fillets in a shallow sprayed baking dish. Season to taste with salt or salt substitute and freshly ground black pepper.

2. Sprinkle grated nutmeg over fillets. Place a portion of the grated rinds on each fillet.

3. Cover and bake 15 minutes or until fish flakes easily with a fork. Serve immediately.

4. Serve with lemon and lime wedges.

- - - - - - - - - - - - - - - - - - - -

Yield: 4 servings
Serving size: 1 fillet

Calories: 156
Protein: 34 g
Carbohydrate: less than 1 g
Fat: 2 g
Cholesterol: 41 mg
Sodium: less than 1 g
Calcium: 27 mg
Dietary Fiber: less than 1 g
Sugar: less than 1 g

CAJUN CATFISH

¼ cup flour
½-1 tablespoon no salt or lite
Cajun or Creole seasoning
¼ cup egg substitute
4 (6 ounce) catfish fillets

1. Combine flour and seasoning and place in a pie plate. Place egg substitute in another pie plate. Dip fillets in egg substitute, then in seasoned flour.

2. Cover fish and refrigerate 30 minutes. Spray a nonstick skillet with nonstick cooking spray and preheat over medium heat. Add fillets in batches and cook 5 minutes on one side; then turn and cook an additional 5 minutes. Spray skillet again as needed.

3. Fish is done when it is golden brown and flakes easily with a fork. Serve immediately.

Flavor Perk: Garnish with chopped fresh parsley and lemon wedges.

- - - - - - - - - - - - - - - - - - - -

Yield: 4 servings
Serving size: 1 fillet

Calories: 264
Protein: 29 g
Carbohydrate: 6 g
Fat: 13 g
Cholesterol: 79 mg
Sodium: 115 mg
Calcium: 21 mg
Dietary Fiber: less than 1 g
Sugar: less than 1 g

BROILED FLOUNDER

2 pounds flounder fillets
1-2 cups buttermilk
1 tablespoon chopped fresh dill weed or 1 teaspoon dried dill weed
4 tablespoons light mayonnaise

1. Place fillets in a 9 x 12-inch baking dish. Pour buttermilk over fillets to cover, and let set 15-20 minutes. Drain buttermilk; then sprinkle fillets with dill weed, salt or salt substitute and freshly ground black pepper to taste.

2. Spread mayonnaise on top of each fillet. Place fillets in a baking pan 4-6 inches from broiler element. Broil 10-15 minutes or until fish flakes easily with a fork. (If fillets are thick, bake at 400° for 7-8 minutes before broiling.)

Flavor Perk: Sprinkle Parmesan cheese on each fillet before broiling.

- - - - - - - - - - - - - - - - - - - -

Yield: 8 servings
Serving size: 1 (4 ounce) fillet

Calories: 278
Protein: 17 g
Carbohydrate: 18 g
Fat: 16 g
Cholesterol: 46 g
Sodium: 389 mg
Calcium: 36 mg
Dietary Fiber: 0 g
Sugar: 5 g

BROILED TROUT

4-6 trout, cleaned, heads and tails intact
4 sprigs fresh rosemary (optional)
Vegetable or olive oil cooking spray
Lemon wedges

1. Preheat oven broiler. Sprinkle the cavity of the fish with salt or salt substitute and freshly ground black pepper. Place a sprig of rosemary in the cavity of each trout. Spray the outside of the fish with nonstick cooking spray.

2. Place trout on a sprayed broiler pan about 5 inches below the broiler element. Broil 5 minutes on each side or until fish flakes easily with a fork. Serve with lemon wedges.

- - - - - - - - - - - - - - - - - - - -

Yield: 4 servings
Serving size: 1-2 trout, depending on size

Calories: 156
Protein: 24 g
Carbohydrate: 0 g
Fat: 6 g
Cholesterol: 67 mg
Sodium: 40 mg
Calcium: 77 mg
Dietary Fiber: 0 g
Sugar: 0 g

BROILED FISH WITH JALAPEÑO SAUCE

⅓ cup jalapeño jelly
1 tablespoon apple cider or white vinegar
4 fish fillets of your choice, rinsed, patted dry
Cilantro or parsley, coarsely chopped

1. Mix jelly and vinegar in a small saucepan and stir over low heat until jelly melts. Set aside.

2. Season fillets with salt or salt substitute and freshly ground black pepper. Place on a broiler pan sprayed with nonstick cooking spray. Place pan 4-6 inches from broiler element and broil 3-4 minutes on each side, or until fish flakes easily with a fork and is lightly browned.

3. To serve, drizzle the sauce over the fillets and sprinkle with cilantro or parsley. Serve with extra sauce.

- - - - - - - - - - - - - - - - - - -

Yield: 4 servings
Serving size: 1 fillet

Calories: 100
Protein: 20 g
Carbohydrate: 2 g
Fat: less than 1 g
Cholesterol: 48 mg
Sodium: 208 mg
Calcium: 20 mg
Dietary Fiber: 0 g
Sugar: 0 g

BRAISED FISH FILLETS

2 tablespoons stick margarine, divided
⅓ cup green onions and tops, chopped
1 tablespoon chopped fresh parsley
1½-2 pounds orange roughy or snapper

1. Heat 1 tablespoon margarine in a skillet; add onions and cook over medium heat 5-7 minutes until onions are tender. Stir in ¼ cup water and parsley. Bring water to a simmer and add fish fillets; then cover and cook about 3 minutes.

2. Turn the fillets and continue cooking for 3-4 minutes until fish flakes with a fork. Remove fillets and keep warm.

3. Whisk remaining tablespoon margarine into pan juices and pour over fillets. Serve immediately.

Flavor Perk: Serve with lemon or lime wedges.

- - - - - - - - - - - - - - - - - - -

Yield: 4 servings
Serving size: 1 (4 ounce) fillet

Calories: 171
Protein: 25 g
Carbohydrate: less than 1 g
Fat: 7 g
Cholesterol: 34 g
Sodium: 165 g
Calcium: 60 mg
Dietary Fiber: less than 1 g
Sugar: less than 1 g

ZAPPED FISH FILLETS

2 pounds fish fillets of your choice
Juice of 2 lemons, divided
1 cup Golden Cream Sauce (p. 253)

1. Clean and pat fillets dry. Place fillets in a microwave-safe dish. Squeeze lemon juice over, and spray with nonstick cooking spray. Cover dish with plastic wrap and cook on full power 6-8 minutes. Remove dish from microwave oven.

2. Pour sauce over fillets. Cover; return to microwave and cook on full power 6-8 more minutes.

3. Serve immediately.

- - - - - - - - - - - - - - - - - - - -

Yield: 8 servings
Serving size: ¼ pound or 1 fillet per person

Calories (with sauce): 270
Protein: 15 g
Carbohydrate: 18 g
Fat: 15 g
Cholesterol: 40 mg
Sodium: 348 mg
Calcium: 36 mg
Dietary Fiber: 0 g
Sugar: 2 g

GOLDEN CREAM SAUCE

This sauce is excellent for baked fish.

1 cup light sour cream
1 teaspoon Dijon-style mustard
Juice of 1 lemon
1 teaspoon Worcestershire sauce

1. Combine all ingredients. Spread on flounder or other fish fillets before baking.

- - - - - - - - - - - - - - - - - - - -

Yield: 4 servings (About 1 cup)
Serving size: ¼ cup

Calories: 91
Protein: 2 g
Carbohydrate: 5 g
Fat: 7 g
Cholesterol: 23 mg
Sodium: 70 mg
Calcium: 65 mg
Dietary Fiber: less than 1 g
Sugar: less than 1 g

SHRIMP FLORENTINE

2 (10 ounce) bags fresh spinach, rinsed, drained
2-3 teaspoons cornstarch
2 pounds frozen medium shrimp (cooked, peeled, deveined), partially thawed
Lemon-pepper seasoning to taste

1. In a sprayed large skillet, cook spinach 3-5 minutes over medium heat or until limp.

2. Mix cornstarch with equal amount of water and stir until dissolved. Add cornstarch mixture to the skillet and bring to a boil to thicken the liquid.

3. Add shrimp and lemon-pepper seasoning. Cook over low heat until shrimp are heated through.

4. Serve immediately.

- - - - - - - - - - - - - - - - - - -

Yield: 8 servings
Serving size: About 1 generous cup

Calories: 140
Protein: 25 g
Carbohydrate: 4 g
Fat: 2 g
Cholesterol: 172 mg
Sodium: 338 mg
Calcium: 130 mg
Dietary Fiber: 1 g
Sugar: 0 g

QUICK SHRIMP SCAMPI

2 pounds uncooked shrimp, peeled, deveined
Scampi Marinade (p. 255)
¼ cup finely chopped green onions and tops

1. Place shrimp and marinade in a shallow bowl. Let stand 15-20 minutes. Heat a large nonstick skillet over medium heat; add oil. Add shrimp and marinade to heated oil.

2. Cook until shrimp turn pink, stirring frequently. Stir in green onions and heat through.

3. Serve immediately.

4. Serve with lemon wedges.

- - - - - - - - - - - - - - - - - - -

Yield: 4 servings
Serving size: About 1 cup

Calories: 242
Protein: 46 g
Carbohydrate: 3 g
Fat: 4 g
Cholesterol: 345 mg
Sodium: 337 mg
Calcium: 122 mg
Dietary Fiber: less than 1 g
Sugar: less than 1 g

SCAMPI MARINADE

3 tablespoons fresh lemon juice
⅓ cup olive or vegetable oil
1 teaspoon Dijon-style mustard
1 clove garlic, finely minced or
    pressed

- - - - - - - - - - - - - - - - -

Yield: 5 servings
Serving size: 2 tablespoons

Calories: 130
Protein: 0 g
Carbohydrate: less than 1 g
Fat: 14 g
Cholesterol: 0 mg
Calcium: 2 mg
Dietary Fiber: 0 g
Sugar: less than 1 g

EASY BAKED SHRIMP

3 pounds jumbo
    or medium fresh shrimp
3 tablespoons fresh lemon juice
¼ cup olive or vegetable oil
1 teaspoon Dijon-style mustard

1. Preheat oven to 325°. Peel and devein shrimp, leaving tails intact. Combine lemon juice, oil and mustard in a large mixing bowl. Add shrimp, stirring well.

2. Pour shrimp and salad dressing mixture into a 13 x 9 x 2-inch baking dish. Stirring occasionally, bake uncovered 25 minutes or until shrimp turn pink.

3. Garnish each serving with fresh parsley sprigs.

- - - - - - - - - - - - - - - - - - -

Yield: 6-8 servings
Serving size: 4-5 shrimp

Calories: 277
Protein: 40 g
Carbohydrate: 2 g
Fat: 11 g
Cholesterol: 295 mg
Sodium: 304 mg
Calcium: 102 mg
Dietary Fiber: 0 g
Sugar: 0 g

GRILLED SHRIMP KABOBS

Bamboo or metal skewers
2 pounds uncooked jumbo
shrimp, peeled, deveined, tails
intact
2-3 tablespoons olive oil
2 fresh lemons

1. If using bamboo skewers, soak in water at least 15 minutes. Prepare charcoal grill, or preheat gas grill to medium heat. Thread 4-5 shrimp on each skewer. Avoid overcrowding. Brush shrimp with olive oil and sprinkle fresh lemon juice over each shrimp.

2. Place skewers on grill 4-6 inches from heating element or hot coals. Basting occasionally with oil and lemon juice, grill 3-4 minutes; then turn skewer over and cook an additional 2-3 minutes or until shrimp turn pink.

3. Serve immediately.

- - - - - - - - - - - - - - - - - - -

Yield: 4 servings
Serving size: 4-5 shrimp

Calories: 300
Protein: 46 g
Carbohydrate: 2 g
Fat: 11 g
Cholesterol: 345 mg
Sodium: 336 mg
Calcium: 118 mg
Dietary Fiber: 0 g
Sugar: 0 g

CRAB MORNAY

2 (6 ounce) cans crabmeat,
drained, bones and cartilage
removed
1 cup medium white sauce
¼ cup reduced fat Swiss cheese,
shredded
¼ cup herb seasoned bread
crumbs

1. Preheat oven to 350°. Combine crabmeat, sauce and cheese. Pour into a sprayed 1½-quart casserole dish; sprinkle with bread crumbs.

2. Bake, uncovered, 30 minutes or until soup mixture bubbles and bread crumbs are lightly browned.

- - - - - - - - - - - - - - - - - - - -

Yield: 4 servings
Serving size: ½-¾ cup

Calories: 234
Protein: 23 g
Carbohydrate: 11 g
Fat: 10 g
Cholesterol: 88 g
Sodium: 724 mg
Calcium: 245 mg
Dietary Fiber: less than 1 g
Sugar: less than 1 g

SEAFOOD CASSEROLE

1 (6 ounce) can shrimp, drained
1 (6 ounce) can crabmeat, drained
1½ cups homemade white or
   cheese sauce
¼ cup seasoned bread crumbs,
   divided

1. Preheat oven to 350°. Mix shrimp, crabmeat, sauce and half the bread crumbs. Place in a sprayed 1½-quart casserole dish.

2. Sprinkle casserole with remaining bread crumbs. Bake, uncovered, 30 minutes or until casserole bubbles and bread crumbs are lightly browned.

- - - - - - - - - - - - - - - - - - - -

Yield: 4 servings
Serving size: About ¾ cup

Calories: 207
Protein: 20 g
Carbohydrate: 13 g
Fat: 8 g
Cholesterol: 119 mg
Sodium: 877 mg
Calcium: 168 mg
Dietary Fiber: less than 1 g
Sugar: less than 1 g

SEARED SEA SCALLOPS

20 fresh sea scallops
1 teaspoon canola or olive oil
Lemon wedges

1. Rinse scallops and pat dry between paper towels. Heat oil in a large nonstick skillet over medium-high heat.

2. Sprinkle scallops, salt or salt substitute and freshly ground black pepper to taste. Add scallops to the hot skillet and cook, stirring constantly, 3-5 minutes on each side.

3. Serve immediately with lemon wedges.

Flavor Perk: Garnish with fresh chopped parsley or parsley sprigs.

- - - - - - - - - - - - - - - - - - - -

Yield: 4 servings
Serving size: 5 scallops

Calories: 79
Protein: 11 g
Carbohydrate: 1 g
Fat: 3 g
Cholesterol: 21 mg
Sodium: 280 mg
Calcium: 16 mg
Dietary Fiber: 0 g
Sugar: 0 g

SILVER DOLLAR SALMON CROQUETTES

1 (7 ounce) package skinless and boneless pink salmon, flaked
¼ cup egg substitute
⅓ cup horseradish sauce or chili sauce
½ cup plain or seasoned bread crumbs, divided

1. In a large mixing bowl, combine salmon, egg substitute, horseradish or chili sauce and ½ cup bread crumbs. Season to taste with salt or salt substitute and freshly ground black pepper.

2. Use about 2 tablespoons mixture to form small patties. If the mixture is too dry to form, add ¼ teaspoon water at a time. Place remaining bread crumbs on wax paper and lightly coat patties.

3. Using a spatula, place patties in a skillet sprayed with nonstick cooking spray. Cook patties over medium heat until lightly brown.

4. Serve with extra horseradish or chili sauce.

- - - - - - - - - - - - - - - - - - - -

Yield: 4 servings
Serving size: 2 patties

Calories: 170
Protein: 14 g
Carbohydrate: 11 g
Fat: 8 g
Cholesterol: 34 mg
Sodium: 233 mg
Calcium: 71 mg
Dietary Fiber: less than 1 g
Sugar: less than 1 g

TUNA CROQUETTES

2 (6 ounce) cans reduced sodium white albacore tuna in water, drained
24 reduced sodium saltine crackers, crushed
½ cup egg substitute
½ cup skim milk

1. Combine all ingredients and shape into small patties. Season to taste with freshly ground black pepper.

2. In a sprayed skillet over medium heat, lightly brown patties on both sides.

Flavor Perk: Add 2 teaspoons fresh chopped parsley and 2 tablespoons minced onion.

- - - - - - - - - - - - - - - - - - - -

Yield: 4 servings
Serving size: 3-4 patties

Calories: 200
Protein: 25 g
Carbohydrate: 15 g
Fat: 3 g
Cholesterol: 38 mg
Sodium: 232 mg
Calcium: 50 mg
Dietary Fiber: less than 1 g
Sugar: 2 g

SAUCES

Characteristically, a sauce is any liquid or thickened liquid that enhances, gives moisture to or adds richness to the food it accompanies. Along with the basic and traditional sauces in this section are several salsa recipes, plus savory sauces from different international cuisines.

ALL-PURPOSE RED CHILE SAUCE

This versatile sauce can be used as an enchilada sauce or as a red sauce for Mexican dishes. Use it to season lean ground beef or turkey for tacos, enchiladas or burritos. Using chili powder instead of making a paste from dried chiles shortens preparation time.

1 onion, minced
2 finely minced or pressed garlic cloves
3½ cups no salt tomato sauce
2-4 tablespoons chili powder, divided

1. Sauté onion and garlic 1-2 minutes in a large saucepan coated with non-stick cooking spray. If needed, spray again after 1 minute. Add tomato sauce; then bring to a boil and gradually stir in 2 tablespoons chile powder.

2. Reduce heat and simmer (covered or uncovered) 15 minutes. Add additional chile powder to taste. Continue simmering at least 15 minutes, and season to taste with salt or salt substitute.

3. Serve as is or strain through a wire mesh strainer. For a smoother sauce, place in food processor and puree. Refrigerate or freeze in small amounts for later use.

Flavor Perk: Add ½ teaspoon ground cumin and ¼ teaspoon dried oregano, crumbled.

Variation: Sauté onion and garlic in 1-2 tablespoons vegetable oil.

- -

Yield: 12 servings (About 3 cups: enough sauce for 20 enchiladas)
Serving size: About ¼ cup

Calories: 31
Protein: less than 1 g
Carbohydrate: 6 g
Fat: less than 1 g
Cholesterol: 0 mg
Sodium: 36 mg
Calcium: 6 mg
Dietary Fiber: 2 g
Sugar: 5 g

QUICK GREEN CHILE SAUCE

Use in making chicken enchiladas or as a sauce over Mexican dishes.

1 tablespoon light butter or light stick margarine
1½ tablespoons flour
1½ cups reduced sodium fat free chicken broth
1 (4 ounce) can chopped green chilies, undrained

1. Melt butter in a heavy saucepan over medium heat. Add flour and whisk or stir until flour is blended with butter. When mixture bubbles, continue to cook and stir about 1 minute.

2. Gradually stir in broth and cook until thickened. Add green chilies and salt or salt substitute to taste. Simmer 15-20 minutes.

Flavor Perk: Sauté ½ cup finely chopped onion and 1 finely minced garlic clove in the butter before adding flour. Add pinch of ground cumin.

- - - - - - - - - - - - - - - - - -

Yield: 5-6 servings (About 1½ cups)
Serving size: ¼ cup

Calories: 25
Protein: 1 g
Carbohydrate: 3 g
Fat: 1 g
Cholesterol: 4 mg
Sodium: 228 mg
Calcium: 16 mg
Dietary Fiber: less than 1 g
Sugar: less than 1 g

DIJON MUSTARD SAUCE

This sauce is a nice complement to ham and broiled fish.

2 tablespoons light butter or margarine
2 tablespoons flour
1¼ cups skim milk
2-4 tablespoons Dijon-style mustard

1. Melt butter in a heavy saucepan. Whisk in flour and cook about 2 minutes, stirring constantly until the mixture cooks and bubbles. Do not brown. Add milk and stir until sauce thickens.

2. Bring to a boil and add mustard and salt or salt substitute to taste. Reduce heat and cook, stirring, 2-3 minutes.

3. Remove from heat and cover with plastic wrap or wax paper (to prevent skin from forming) for later use.

- - - - - - - - - - - - - - - - - -

Yield: 4 servings (About 1 cup)
Serving size: ¼ cup

Calories: 77
Protein: 3 g
Carbohydrate: 7 g
Fat: 3 g
Cholesterol: 12 mg
Sodium: 299 mg
Calcium: 95 mg
Dietary Fiber: less than 1 g
Sugar: 3 g

ROASTED RED PEPPER SAUCE

1 cup roasted red peppers
¼ cup plain nonfat yogurt
1 tablespoon red wine vinegar
2-3 teaspoons Dijon-style mustard

1. Place all ingredients in a blender or food processor; add freshly ground black pepper to taste. Process until smooth.

2. Serve or keep refrigerated up to 3 days.

Flavor Perk: Add 1 teaspoon dried oregano leaves to ingredients in the blender.

- - - - - - - - - - - - - - - - - - - -

Yield: 4 servings (About 1 cup)
Serving size: ¼ cup

Calories: 21
Protein: 1 g
Carbohydrate: 4 g
Fat: 0 g
Cholesterol: less than 1 mg
Sodium: 70 mg
Calcium: 34 mg
Dietary Fiber: less than 1 g
Sugar: less than 1 g

FRESH PESTO

Pesto can be tossed with cooked pasta, served as a sandwich spread, mixed into salads or spooned as a topping on cooked meat or vegetables. If fresh basil is not available, buy prepared basil in the refrigerator or produce section of the supermarket.

2 cups lightly packed fresh basil leaves, washed, dried in salad spinner or patted dry with paper towels
½ cup grated reduced fat Parmesan topping
⅓ cup olive oil
1-2 garlic cloves, finely minced or pressed

1. Place all ingredients in a blender or food processor and pulse until basil is finely chopped and ingredients are well blended. Use in recipes or serve immediately.

1. Store in an airtight container with a thin layer of olive oil to prevent darkening.

3. Refrigerate 2-3 days or freeze.

Flavor Perk: Add ¼ cup toasted pine nuts to blender.

- - - - - - - - - - - - - - - - - - - -

Yield: 4 servings (About 1 cup)
Serving size: ¼ cup

Calories: 224
Protein: 2 g
Carbohydrate: 7 g
Fat: 21 g
Cholesterol: 0 mg
Sodium: 226 mg
Calcium: 34 mg
Dietary Fiber: less than 1 g
Sugar: 0 g

CITRUS-OLIVE OIL SAUCE

Serve with grilled foods, especially fish.

2 fresh navel oranges
1 small fresh lemon
2-4 tablespoons extra-virgin olive
oil

1. Remove peel and white membrane from oranges. Over a mixing bowl, cut the orange and lemon sections, with sections and juice going into the bowl.

2. Stir in olive oil, salt or salt substitute and freshly ground pepper to taste. Serve immediately or cover and refrigerate.

3. Sauce stays fresh about 1 day.

- - - - - - - - - - - - - - - - - - - -

Yield: 4 servings (About ½ cup)
Serving size: 2 tablespoons

Calories: 98
Protein: 1 g
Carbohydrate: 11 g
Fat: 7 g
Cholesterol: 0 mg
Sodium: 2 mg
Calcium: 44 mg
Dietary Fiber: 3 g
Sugar: 7 g

HEARTY TOMATO SAUCE

Here is a quick and easy all-purpose tomato sauce.

¾ cup no salt tomato paste
2½ cups no salt diced canned
tomatoes
1 carrot, grated
1 tablespoon dried basil leaves,
crushed

1. Preheat a heavy saucepan over medium heat. Add tomato paste, tomatoes, carrot and basil; simmer 30 minutes. If sauce becomes too thick, stir in 1 tablespoon water at a time until of desired consistency. Cook an additional 15 minutes.

2. Season to taste with salt or salt substitute and freshly ground black pepper. Serve with cooked pasta or refrigerate for later use.

Variation: Sauté 1 finely chopped onion and 2 finely minced garlic cloves in saucepan before adding tomato mixture.

- - - - - - - - - - - - - - - - - - - -

Yield: 8 servings (4 cups)
Serving size: ½ cup

Calories: 39
Protein: 2 g
Carbohydrate: 9 g
Fat: less than 1 g
Cholesterol: 0 mg
Sodium: 56 mg
Calcium: 24 mg
Dietary Fiber: 3 g
Sugar: 4 g

FRESH TOMATO SAUCE

Serve this delicious, fresh-tasting sauce with your favorite pasta.

7 cups (about 8 large) ripe tomatoes
1 tablespoon olive or vegetable oil
6 cloves garlic, finely minced or pressed
½ cup dry white wine or white cooking wine

1. To peel tomatoes, carefully drop into a large pot of boiling water. When skins begin to split, remove tomatoes and place in cold water. Peel and dice tomatoes and set aside.

2. In a large saucepan or Dutch oven, heat oil and add garlic. Sauté garlic 3-4 minutes or until fragrant and tender. Add tomatoes and bring to a boil; then reduce heat to a simmer. Simmer 20-25 minutes; then stir in wine and simmer 5 minutes.

3. Season to taste with salt or salt substitute and freshly ground black pepper.

Flavor Perk: *Add 2 tablespoons chopped fresh basil or 1-2 teaspoons dried basil leaves, crushed.*

- - - - - - - - - - - - - - - - - - -

Yield: 8 servings
About ½ cup

Calories: 70
Protein: 2 g
Carbohydrate: 10 g
Fat: 2 g
Cholesterol: 0 mg
Sodium: 19 mg
Calcium: 15 g
Dietary Fiber: 2 g
Sugar: 6 g

TOMATO-GREEN CHILE SALSA

Also known as Salsa Cruda, this colorful fresh sauce is served at the table, to spoon onto food to suit taste.

6 tomatoes
1 (4 ounce) can diced green chiles, undrained
⅓ cup finely minced onion
Fresh jalapeño or Serrano pepper, seeded, finely minced (amount to suit taste)

1. Add tomatoes to a large pot of boiling water. When skins begin to split, remove tomatoes and plunge into cold or ice water. When cool, peel tomatoes and finely chop.

2. Stir together tomatoes, green chiles, onion, fresh pepper to taste and 1 teaspoon salt or salt substitute.

Variation: *Use canned or pickled jalapeños instead of fresh. Substitute 2-3 cups canned petite diced tomatoes for fresh tomatoes. Drain tomatoes and reserve tomato juice to add as needed for desired consistency.*

- - - - - - - - - - - - - - - - - - -

Yield: 12 servings (About 3 cups)
Serving size: ¼ cup

Calories: 17
Protein: less than 1 g
Carbohydrate: 4 g
Fat: less than 1 g
Cholesterol: 0 mg
Sodium: 33 mg
Calcium: 11 mg
Dietary Fiber: less than 1 g
Sugar: 2 g

FRESH TOMATILLO SALSA

Used primarily for hot or cold sauces in Mexican cooking, tomatillos look like small green tomatoes encased in parchment-paper husks. They have a lemony tang as compared to the sharp flavor of green tomatoes.

8 ounces fresh tomatillos, husked, rinsed, coarsely chopped
½ cup coarsely chopped white or red onion
***3-5 fresh jalapeño or Serrano peppers, seeded, coarsely chopped**
3-4 tablespoons fresh cilantro sprigs or leaves

*Use caution in seeding and chopping hot peppers with your hands; rubber gloves are recommended.

1. Add all ingredients to a blender or food processor container. Pulse until salsa is coarsely pureed, leaving some small chunks. Transfer to a mixing bowl, adding just enough cold water to make a sauce-like consistency.

2. Season to taste with salt or salt substitute. Serve immediately.

3. Salsa will stay fresh about 1 hour.

Flavor Perk: Add 1 peeled garlic clove to blender or food processor. Add sugar substitute to equal ½ teaspoon sugar.

- -

Yield: 4 servings
Serving size: ¼ cup

Calories: 29
Protein: less than 1 g
Carbohydrate: 6 g
Fat: less than 1 g
Cholesterol: 0 mg
Sodium: 1 mg
Calcium: 9 mg
Dietary Fiber: 2 g
Sugar: less than 1 g

SALSA FRESCA OR PICO DE GALLO

*3-5 fresh jalapeño or Serrano
 peppers, seeded, minced
½ cup white or red onion, finely
 chopped, rinsed, drained
3-4 plum (Roma) or 2 large ripe
 tomatoes, finely diced
¼-½ cup snipped fresh cilantro
 sprigs or leaves

*Use caution in seeding and mincing
 hot peppers with your hands; rubber gloves are recommended.

1. Stir all ingredients together in a
 mixing bowl. Add 2 tablespoons
 cold water and salt or salt substitute to taste.

2. Serve immediately.

*Flavor Perk: Substitute 2 tablespoons fresh lime
 juice for the cold water; add 1 finely
 minced garlic clove.*

- - - - - - - - - - - - - - - - - -

Yield: 4 servings (About 1 cup)
Serving size: ¼ cup

Calories: 30
Protein: 1 g
Carbohydrate: 7 g
Fat: less than 1 g
Cholesterol: 0 mg
Sodium: 8 mg
Calcium: 10 mg
Dietary Fiber: 2 g
Sugar: 3 g

ROASTED TOMATILLO SALSA

1 pound fresh tomatillos, husked,
 rinsed
3 fresh jalapeño or Serrano
 peppers, seeded, chopped
½ cup white onion, finely
 chopped, rinsed, drained
3-4 tablespoons fresh snipped
 cilantro leaves or sprigs

1. Preheat oven broiler. Cover a baking sheet with aluminum foil and
 place tomatillos in a single layer
 on the sheet. Broil tomatillos
 about 4 minutes until softened.
 Turn over and broil other side
 about 5 minutes. Cool completely.

2. Add cooled tomatillos and the
 peppers to a blender or food processor. Pulse until coarsely pureed.
 Transfer to a mixing bowl; stir in
 onion and cilantro. Add about ¼
 cup water and salt or salt substitute to taste.

3. Let salsa stand a few minutes for
 the flavors to blend; then serve.

*Flavor Perk: Add 1 finely minced garlic clove
 and sugar substitute to taste.*

- - - - - - - - - - - - - - - - - -

Yield: 6 servings (About 1½ cups)
Serving size: ¼ cup

Calories: 31
Protein: less than 1 g
Carbohydrate: 6 g
Fat: less than 1 g
Cholesterol: 0 mg
Sodium: 1 mg
Calcium: 9 mg
Dietary Fiber: 2 g
Sugar: less than 1 g

MANGO SALSA

Raw onion can overpower other flavors. To tone down an onion's strong flavor, simply rinse in cold water and drain before adding other ingredients.

¼-½ cup red onion, chopped, rinsed, drained
⅛-¼ cup fresh lime juice
1-2 large ripe mangos, peeled, diced, drained, juice reserved
1 fresh jalapeño or Serrano pepper, seeded, finely chopped

1. Stir onion and lime juice in mixing bowl. Add diced mango and pepper; stir to mix. Optional: add reserved mango juice to desired consistency; season to taste with salt/salt substitute.

2. Serve immediately or cover tightly and serve within a few hours.

Flavor Perk: Add 1 finely minced garlic clove and ¼ cup fresh chopped cilantro.

- - - - - - - - - - - - - - - - - - -

Yield: 4 servings (About 1 cup)
Serving size: ¼ cup

Calories: 44
Protein: less than 1 g
Carbohydrate: 12 g
Fat: less than 1 g
Cholesterol: 0 mg
Sodium: 2 mg
Calcium: 10 mg
Dietary Fiber: 1 g
Sugar: 9 g

CANTALOUPE SALSA

Salsas are now being made with a variety of fruits. Try this recipe with cantaloupe, or even honeydew melon.

¼-½ cup red onion, chopped, rinsed, drained
⅛-¼ cup fresh lime juice
1-2 cups fresh diced cantaloupe, undrained, juice reserved
1 fresh jalapeño or Serrano pepper, seeded, finely chopped (amount to suit taste)

1. Stir onion and lime juice together in mixing bowl. Add diced cantaloupe and pepper; stir to mix. (Optional: add reserved cantaloupe juice to desired consistency; season to taste with salt/salt substitute.)

2. Serve immediately or cover tightly and serve within a few hours.

Flavor Perk: Add ¼ cup fresh chopped parsley and 1 finely minced garlic clove.

- - - - - - - - - - - - - - - - - - -

Yield: 4 servings (About 1 cup)
Serving size: ¼ cup

Calories: 25
Protein: less than 1 g
Carbohydrate: 6 g
Fat: less than 1 g
Cholesterol: 0 mg
Sodium: 4 mg
Calcium: 9 mg
Dietary Fiber: less than 1 g
Sugar: 4 g

CHEESE OR MORNAY SAUCE

Combine this versatile sauce with other ingredients, or use as a topping.

1 cup medium white sauce made with skim milk and reduced fat margarine or butter (no seasonings)
¼ cup reduced fat cheese (Swiss, Parmesan, cheddar, Monterey Jack or mozzarella)
Pinch ground red pepper (cayenne)
Few grains nutmeg

1. In a heavy saucepan over low heat, add ¼ cup reduced fat cheese of your choice to the fully cooked, heated white sauce.

2. Heat, stirring, just until cheese melts. Season to taste with salt or salt substitute, red pepper and nutmeg.

Note: If the sauce is overheated and the cheese becomes stringy, heat just to a simmer; then whisk in a few drops of lemon juice. Remove from heat.

- -

Yield: 4 servings (About 1 cup)
Serving size: ¼ cup

Calories: 137
Protein: 6 g
Carbohydrate: 6 g
Fat: 10 g
Cholesterol: 14 mg
Sodium: 239 mg
Calcium: 199 mg
Dietary Fiber: less than 1 g
Sugar: 0 g

COTTAGE CHEESE TOPPING

Serve this creamy sauce over baked potatoes or cooked noodles, or even as a low calorie salad dressing.

1 cup reduced fat cottage cheese
1 tablespoon lemon juice
1 tablespoon snipped chives or green onion tops

1. Place cottage cheese and lemon juice in blender. Slowly add 3-4 tablespoons water, blending until mixture reaches desired consistency.

2. Stir in chives.

- -

Yield: 4 servings (About 1 cup)
Serving size: ¼ cup

Calories: 42
Protein: 7 g
Carbohydrate: 2 g
Fat: less than 1 g
Cholesterol: 2 mg
Sodium: 229 mg
Calcium: 35 mg
Dietary Fiber: 0 g
Sugar: 2 g

COTTAGE-SWISS CHEESE SAUCE

1 cup buttermilk
1 tablespoon cornstarch
½ cup reduced fat small curd
cottage cheese
¼ cup grated or shredded reduced
fat Swiss cheese

1. In a medium saucepan, heat buttermilk and cornstarch to boiling, stirring constantly. Reduce heat to simmer to smooth and thicken. Stir in cheeses.

Flavor Perk: Add 1 tablespoon chopped parsley.

Variation: Substitute shredded reduced fat cheddar cheese for the Swiss cheese.

- - - - - - - - - - - - - - - - - - - -

Yield: 6 servings (About 1½ cups)
Serving size: ¼ cup

Calories: 65
Protein: 6 g
Carbohydrate: 4 g
Fat: 3 g
Cholesterol: 9 mg
Sodium: 131 mg
Calcium: 143 mg
Dietary Fiber: 0 g
Sugar: 2 g

CREAMY CHICKEN BROTH SAUCE

In classic French cuisine, this is known as Velouté Sauce.

2 tablespoons light butter or light
stick margarine
2 tablespoons flour
1 cup reduced sodium fat free
chicken broth
⅛ teaspoon nutmeg

1. Melt butter in a saucepan over low heat. Use a wire whisk to stir in flour; then continue cooking at least 1 minute, stirring constantly until mixture bubbles and is smooth.

2. Add broth gradually, stirring constantly. Heat sauce to boiling and cook 1 minute, continuing to use the wire whisk to stir.

3. Stir in nutmeg and salt or salt substitute to taste.

- - - - - - - - - - - - - - - - - - - -

Yield: 4 servings (About 1 cup)
Serving size: ¼ cup

Calories: 43
Protein: 1 g
Carbohydrate: 3 g
Fat: 3 g
Cholesterol: 10 mg
Sodium: 155 mg
Calcium: less than 1 mg
Dietary Fiber: less than 1 g
Sugar: less than 1 g

WHITE SAUCE BASICS

In classic French cuisine, medium white sauce is known as a Mother Sauce,
since the sauce serves as a base for many other sauces.
When combining with other ingredients, use 1 cup for every 2 cups
of solid ingredients, such as vegetables, fish, or poultry.

2 tablespoons light butter or light stick margarine
2 tablespoons flour
1¼ cups skim milk

1. Melt butter in a heavy saucepan. Stirring or whisking constantly, add flour and cook about 2 minutes until the mixture bubbles. Do not brown. Add milk and whisk or stir constantly until sauce thickens.

2. Bring to a boil; then reduce heat and cook, stirring, 2-3 minutes. If the sauce is to be used as a base for adding other ingredients, do not add salt or pepper. If the sauce is to be used as is, season to taste with salt or salt substitute and freshly ground pepper.

3. Remove from heat and use immediately or cover with plastic wrap or wax paper (to prevent skin from forming) for later use.

Flavor Perk: Add dash freshly grated or ground nutmeg.

Variation: For a thicker sauce, use 3 tablespoons flour and 1 cup skim milk. For a thinner sauce, use 1 tablespoon flour and 1 cup skim milk.

- -

Yield: 4 servings (About 1 cup)
Serving size: ¼ cup

Calories: 66
Protein: 3 g
Carbohydrate: 7 g
Fat: 3 g
Cholesterol: 12 mg
Sodium: 40 mg
Calcium: 95 mg
Dietary Fiber: less than 1 g
Sugar: 3 g

TARTAR SAUCE

½ cup light or fat free mayonnaise
2 tablespoons dill pickle relish
2 teaspoons Dijon-style mustard
2 tablespoons fresh chopped parsley or 2 teaspoons dried parsley flakes, crumbled

1. Combine all ingredients in a small bowl. Use immediately or cover and refrigerate.

- - - - - - - - - - - - - - - - - - -

Yield: 8 servings
Serving size: About 1 tablespoon

Calories: 53
Protein: 0 g
Carbohydrate: 2 g
Fat: 5 g
Cholesterol: 5 mg
Sodium: 179 mg
Calcium: 1 mg
Dietary Fiber: less than 1 g
Sugar: less than 1 g

YOGURT-DILL SAUCE FOR FISH

1 (8 ounce) carton nonfat plain yogurt
1 teaspoon dried dill weed or 1 tablespoon fresh dill, snipped
¼ teaspoon finely grated lemon peel
1 garlic clove, minced

1. Stir all ingredients together and add ¼ teaspoon freshly ground black pepper.

2. Serve immediately or cover and refrigerate.

- - - - - - - - - - - - - - - - - - -

Yield: 4 servings (About 1 cup)
Serving size: ¼ cup

Calories: 34
Protein: 3 g
Carbohydrate: 5 g
Fat: less than 1 g
Cholesterol: 1 mg
Sodium: 44 mg
Calcium: 119 mg
Dietary Fiber: 0 g
Sugar: 3 g

SAUCE FOR MUSHROOM LOVERS

This sauce has the wonderful flavor and aroma of cooked fresh mushrooms.

1-2 tablespoons light butter or light stick margarine
8 ounces sliced fresh mushrooms
¼ cup finely chopped onion
1¼ cups reduced sodium fat free chicken, vegetable or beef broth

1. Melt butter in a heavy saucepan. Over medium-low heat, add mushrooms and onion and sauté about 10 minutes until soft.

2. Add broth and cook uncovered 20-30 minutes until sauce thickens. Season to taste with freshly ground black pepper.

Flavor Perk: To thicken the sauce, stir 2-3 teaspoons cornstarch into 2-3 teaspoons water. Bring sauce to boiling and stir in the cornstarch mixture. Boil 2-3 minutes, stirring constantly.

- - - - - - - - - - - - - - - - - -

Yield: 4 servings (About 1 cup)
Serving size: ¼ cup

Calories: 37
Protein: 3 g
Carbohydrate: 3 g
Fat: 3 g
Cholesterol: 5 mg
Sodium: 196 mg
Calcium: 4 mg
Dietary Fiber: less than 1 g
Sugar: 2 g

CURRY CREAM SAUCE

Curry powder is actually a blend of several spices including turmeric, cumin and coriander. Use this sauce to perk up leftovers or accent chicken or fish.

2 tablespoons light butter or light stick margarine
2 tablespoons flour
1 teaspoon curry powder
1¼ cups skim milk

1. Melt butter in a heavy saucepan. Stirring or whisking constantly, add flour and curry powder and cook about 2 minutes until mixture bubbles. Do not brown. Add milk and whisk or stir constantly until sauce thickens.

2. Bring to a boil; then reduce heat. Cook, stirring, 2-3 minutes. Season to taste with salt or salt substitute.

3. Remove from heat and use immediately or cover with plastic wrap or wax paper (to prevent skin from forming) for later use.

Flavor Perk: Add ¼ teaspoon ground ginger with the curry powder.

- - - - - - - - - - - - - - - - - -

Yield: 4 servings (About 1 cup)
Serving size: ¼ cup

Calories: 66
Protein: 3 g
Carbohydrate: 7 g
Fat: 3 g
Cholesterol: 12 mg
Sodium: 40 mg
Calcium: 95 mg
Dietary Fiber: less than 1 g
Sugar: 3 g

CREAMY ONION SAUCE

This sauce complements main-dish vegetables and fish.

2 tablespoons light butter or light stick margarine
1 cup finely chopped onion
2 tablespoons flour
1¼ cups skim milk

1. Melt butter in a heavy saucepan. Add onion, and sauté until soft. Add flour and cook about 2 minutes until the mixture bubbles, stirring constantly. Do not brown.

2. Add milk and stir until sauce thickens. Bring to a boil; then reduce heat. Cook, stirring, 2-3 minutes. Season to taste with salt or salt substitute and freshly ground black pepper.

3. Remove from heat and use immediately or cover with plastic wrap or wax paper (to prevent skin from forming) for later use.

Flavor Perk: Add ¼ teaspoon ground nutmeg with onions.

- -

Yield: 4 servings (About 1 cup)
Serving size: ¼ cup

Calories: 66
Protein: 3 g
Carbohydrate: 7 g
Fat: 3 g
Cholesterol: 12 mg
Sodium: 40 mg
Calcium: 95 mg
Dietary Fiber: less than 1 g
Sugar: 3 g

ZESTY SAUCE FOR GREEN VEGETABLES

1 red onion, thinly sliced, separated into rings
2 tablespoons fresh chopped parsley
Hot pepper sauce to taste

1. Preheat a sprayed skillet over medium heat. Add onion rings; cover and cook until tender and clear.

2. Add parsley, hot sauce and freshly ground black pepper to taste.

- -

Yield: 4 servings (About 1 cup)
Serving size: ¼ cup

Calories: 11
Protein: less than 1 g
Carbohydrate: 2 g
Fat: 0 g
Cholesterol: 0 mg
Sodium: 2 mg
Calcium: 8 mg
Dietary Fiber: less than 1 g
Sugar: 2 g

PEANUT SAUCE

Full-bodied and surprisingly good, this sauce made with creamy peanut butter tastes great with grilled poultry or meats.

½ cup reduced fat creamy peanut
butter
2 tablespoons lime juice
2 cloves garlic, minced
½ teaspoon ground coriander or
ground cumin

1. Mix all ingredients and 1 cup water in medium saucepan with wire whisk. Over medium heat, cook and stir until sauce is smooth and heated through. If not served immediately, cover and refrigerate 2-3 days or freeze.

Flavor Perk: Use both ground coriander and cumin.

- - - - - - - - - - - - - - - - - - - -

Yield: 5-6 servings (About 1½ cups)
Serving size: ¼ cup

Calories: 141
Protein: 6 g
Carbohydrate: 12 g
Fat: 9 g
Cholesterol: 0 mg
Sodium: 182 mg
Calcium: 10 mg
Dietary Fiber: 2 g
Sugar: 3 g

NOTES

_____

_____

_____

_____

_____

_____

_____

_____

_____

_____

_____

_____

_____

_____

_____

_____

_____

_____

_____

_____

Cakes, Pies, and Desserts

A Healthful Dessert's Cool Secret – Frozen Whipped Toppings

Many of the dessert, cake and pie recipes in this cookbook include "lite" or fat free frozen whipped toppings. These creamy toppings are a great solution for people who love desserts, but are trying to reduce fat, cholesterol and overall calories in the foods they eat.

Two tablespoons of "lite" frozen whipped topping have 20 calories, 1 gram of fat and 0 milligrams cholesterol. The same amount of heavy whipping cream contains 100 calories, 10 grams of fat and 40 milligrams cholesterol.

Nutritionally speaking, it is no wonder that frozen whipped toppings can be found in many of today's home freezers.

FOR CHEESECAKE LOVERS

2 cups reduced fat cottage cheese
8 ounces reduced fat cream cheese
Sugar substitute equal to 1 cup sugar
2 teaspoons vanilla

1. Place cottage cheese in a strainer placed over a large bowl. Place in refrigerator for 30 minutes.

2. Preheat oven to 350°. Remove cottage cheese from refrigerator and place in food processor. Process 2-3 minutes, scraping sides as necessary, until the cheese is very smooth.

3. Microwave cream cheese on full power for 30 seconds; add cream cheese to food processor bowl with the cottage cheese. Add sugar substitute and vanilla and pulse 2-3 times; then scrape the bowl and pulse again. (Overprocessing will thin the cheese mixture.)

4. Pour batter into a prepared 8-inch springform pan; place pan on a large piece of aluminum foil. Carefully fold foil up over the edges of the pan so that water will not leak into the pan. Place the pan in a large baking dish, and set in the oven. Pour boiling water to reach halfway up the side of the springform pan.

5. Bake about 45 minutes or until the edges are puffed, but the center is still moist. Cool completely before removing from pan.

6. Serve with fresh crushed or pureed berries.

- -

Yield: 10-12 servings

Calories: 108
Protein: 9 g
Carbohydrate: 5 g
Fat: 6 g
Cholesterol: 20 mg
Sodium: 281 mg
Calcium: 80 mg
Dietary Fiber: 0 g
Sugar: 2 g

APPLE-SPICE BUNDT CAKE

Bundt cakes are usually baked in a 12-cup Bundt pan, a tube pan with fluted sides and a nonstick finish, which allows for easy cleaning. Although the terms "Bundt pan" and "Bundt cake" are commonplace today, Bundt is actually a registered trademark of Northland Aluminum Products, Inc.

The 10-inch tube pan, or angel food pan, may also be used for Bundt cakes if a recipe specifies a Bundt pan.

1 box spice cake mix
1 (20 ounce) can lite no sugar added apple pie filling
½ cup egg substitute
2 tablespoons chopped walnuts (optional)

1. Preheat oven to 350°. Place cake mix in mixing bowl, and break up lumps. Add apple pie filling, egg substitute and walnuts, if desired. Mix thoroughly with a spoon.

2. Pour into a greased and floured 12-cup Bundt pan.

3. Bake 50 minutes. Cake is done when a toothpick is inserted in the center and comes out clean. Cool for 20 minutes; then invert onto cake rack or serving plate.

Flavor Perk: Dust cooled cake with sifted powdered sugar.

Variation: Substitute no sugar added cherry, peach, blueberry or other pie fillings for the apple pie filling.

- -

Yield: 12 servings

Calories: 171
Protein: 2 g
Carbohydrate: 34 g
Fat: 3 g
Cholesterol: 0 mg
Sodium: 242 mg
Calcium: 71 mg
Dietary Fiber: 0 g
Sugar: 20 g

TRIMMED DOWN "POUND" CAKE

1 (18.25 ounce) package yellow cake mix with pudding
1¼ cups buttermilk
⅓ cup unsweetened applesauce
1 cup egg white substitute or 4 egg whites

1. Preheat oven to 350°. Place mix, buttermilk, applesauce and egg whites in electric mixer bowl. Beat 1 minute on low speed and scrape sides and bottom of bowl. Beat 2 minutes on medium speed.

2. Pour batter into a sprayed 12-cup Bundt pan, and bake 35-40 minutes. Cake is done when a toothpick is inserted in the center and comes out clean. Place pan on rack, and cool 20 minutes before removing from pan.

3. Serve with fresh crushed fruit or canned lite pie filling.

Flavor Perk: Add 1 teaspoon vanilla.

- - - - - - - - - - - - - - - - - - - -

Yield: 16 servings

Calories: 142
Protein: 2 g
Carbohydrate: 28 g
Fat: 2 g
Cholesterol: less than 1 mg
Sodium: 237 mg
Calcium: 84 mg
Dietary Fiber: 0 g
Sugar: 16 g

SPICED PEAR BUNDT CAKE

1 (15 ounce) can pears in light syrup, undrained
1 white cake mix
¼ cup plus 2 tablespoons egg substitute
2 teaspoons pumpkin pie spice

1. Preheat oven to 350°. Drain pears and reserve liquid; chop pears.

2. Place pears and reserved juice in a mixing bowl; add cake mix, egg substitute and pie spice. Beat on low speed for 30 seconds, scraping sides and bottom of bowl as necessary. Beat on high for 4 minutes.

3. Grease and flour a 10-12 inch Bundt pan. Pour in batter.

4. Bake at 350° about 45 minutes. Cake is done when a toothpick is inserted in the center and comes out clean. Cool in pan for 20 minutes; then invert onto cake rack or serving plate.

Flavor Perk: Dust cooled cake with sifted powdered sugar.

- - - - - - - - - - - - - - - - - - - -

Yield: 12 servings

Calories: 207
Protein: 3 g
Carbohydrate: 40 g
Fat: 4 g
Cholesterol: 0 mg
Sodium: 305 mg
Calcium: 44 mg
Dietary Fiber: less than 1 g
Sugar: 23 g

SPICED ANGEL CAKE

1 (16 ounce) angel food cake mix
1 teaspoon cinnamon
½ teaspoon nutmeg
¼ teaspoon cloves

1. Preheat oven to 350°, and remove top oven rack. Move remaining rack to lowest position. Wash electric mixer bowl, beaters and spatula to remove any grease. Place cake mix in electric mixer bowl. Add spices and 1¼ cups water or amount specified by mix instructions.

2. Blend mix and water about 30 seconds on low speed. Add spices; increase speed to medium and beat 1 minute, scraping sides of bowl as necessary. Pour into an ungreased 10-inch tube pan with removable bottom.

3. Place pan on lowest oven rack, and bake about 35-40 minutes. Cake is done when a toothpick is inserted in the center and comes out clean, and top is cracked and golden brown. Do not underbake.

4. Remove cake from oven. Invert tube pan over a bottle neck, or rest the tube pan upside down on 4 glasses.

5. Cool 1½ hours before serving.

6. Serve with Creamy Coffee Topping (p. 283).

- -

Yield: 10 servings

Calories: 169
Protein: 4 g
Carbohydrate: 39 g
Fat: less than 1 g
Cholesterol: 0 mg
Sodium: 334 mg
Calcium: 55 mg
Dietary Fiber: less than 1 g
Sugar: 0 g

To Unmold Angel Cake:
Gently slide a thin spatula between the cake and the pan to avoid tearing the cake. Pull the tube upward, and slide spatula under the cake. Slide cake off tube upside down onto a rack; then invert right side up onto another rack or serving plate.

COFFEE-FLAVORED ANGEL CAKE

This is a cake for coffee lovers.

1 (16 ounce) angel food cake mix
3 tablespoons instant crushed decaffeinated coffee granules or finely
ground coffee beans

1. Preheat oven to 350°, and remove top oven rack. Move remaining rack to lowest position. Wash electric mixer bowl, beaters and spatula to remove any grease. Place cake mix in electric mixer bowl, and add 1¼ cups water or amount specified by mix instructions.

2. Blend mix and water about 30 seconds on low speed. Add coffee granules; increase speed to medium and beat for 1 minute, scraping sides of bowl as necessary. Pour into an ungreased 10-inch tube pan with removable bottom; place on lowest rack and bake about 35-40 minutes. Cake is done when a toothpick is inserted in the center and comes out clean, and top is cracked and golden brown. Do not underbake.

3. Remove cake from oven and invert tube pan over a bottle neck or rest the tube pan on 4 glasses.

4. Cool 1½ hours before unmolding.

5. Serve with Creamy Coffee Topping (p. 283).

- -

Yield: 12 servings

Calories: 144
Protein: 4 g
Carbohydrate: 33 g
Fat: less than 1 g
Cholesterol: 0 mg
Sodium: 279 mg
Calcium: 48 mg
Dietary Fiber: less than 1 g
Sugar: 0 g

MOCHA ANGEL CAKE

1 teaspoon instant decaffeinated coffee granules
1 (16 ounce) angel food cake mix
¼ cup unsweetened cocoa

1. Preheat oven to 350°, and remove top oven rack. Move remaining rack to lowest position. Wash electric mixer bowl, beaters and spatula to remove any grease.

2. Dissolve coffee granules in 1¼ cups water or amount specified by mix instructions. Place cake mix and coffee-flavored water in electric mixer bowl; blend about 30 seconds on low speed. Add cocoa, increase speed to medium and beat for 1 minute, scraping sides of bowl as necessary.

3. Pour batter into an ungreased 10-inch tube pan with removable bottom. Place on lowest oven rack and bake about 35-40 minutes. Cake is done when a toothpick is inserted in the center and comes out clean, and top is cracked and golden brown. Do not underbake.

4. Remove cake from oven, and invert tube pan over a bottle neck or rest the tube pan on 4 glasses.

5. Cool 1½ hours before unmolding*.

6. Serve with fat free or reduced fat whipped topping, thawed, garnished with finely chopped or grated semisweet or unsweetened chocolate.

- -

Yield: 10 servings

Calories: 174
Protein: 4 g
Carbohydrate: 40 g
Fat: less than 1 g
Cholesterol: 0 mg
Sodium: 335 mg
Calcium: 58 mg
Dietary Fiber: less than 1 g
Sugar: 0 g

COCONUT ANGEL CAKE

Although coconut is high in saturated fat, this recipe uses flaked coconut sparingly, and adds coconut extract for extra flavor.

To toast flaked coconut, preheat oven to 350°. Spread coconut on baking sheet and bake, checking and stirring frequently, about 5 minutes or until coconut is evenly golden brown.

1 (16 ounce) angel food cake mix
1 teaspoon coconut extract
1 (8 ounce) fat free or lite frozen whipped topping, thawed
¼ cup flaked sweetened dried coconut, toasted

1. Preheat oven to 350°, and remove top oven rack. Move remaining rack to lowest position. Wash electric mixer bowl, beaters and spatula to remove any grease. Place cake mix, extract and 1¼ cup water (or amount specified by mix instructions) in electric mixer bowl. Blend about 30 seconds on low speed. Increase speed to medium and beat for 1 minute, scraping sides of bowl as necessary.

2. Pour batter into ungreased 10-inch tube pan with removable bottom. Place on lowest rack, and bake about 35-40 minutes. Cake is done when a tooth-pick is inserted in the center and comes out clean, and top is cracked and golden brown. Do not underbake.

3. Remove cake from oven, and invert tube pan over a bottle neck or rest the tube pan on 4 glasses. Cool 1½ hours; then unmold.

4. Top cake slices with whipped topping sprinkled with toasted coconut.

- -

Yield: 12 servings

Calories: 189
Protein: 3 g
Carbohydrate: 37 g
Fat: 3 g
Cholesterol: 0 mg
Sodium: 279 mg
Calcium: 46 mg
Dietary Fiber: less than 1 g
Sugar: 2 g

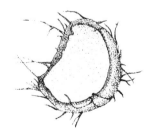

CREAMY COFFEE TOPPING

1 (8 ounce) carton lite or fat free frozen whipped topping, thawed
1-2 teaspoons instant decaffeinated coffee granules or finely ground coffee beans

1. Fold granules into whipped topping. Serve as a topping or frosting. Store in refrigerator.

- - - - - - - - - - - - - - - - - - -

Yield: 16 ounces (1 cup)
Serving size: 1 tablespoon

Calories: 42
Protein: 0 g
Carbohydrate: 4 g
Fat: 2 g
Cholesterol: 0 mg
Sodium: 0 mg
Calcium: less than 1 mg
Dietary Fiber: 0 g
Sugar: 2 g

PINEAPPLE ANGEL CAKE

1 (1-step) angel food cake mix
1 (20 ounce) can crushed pineapple in juice, undrained
Lite frozen whipped topping, thawed

1. Preheat oven to 350°. Place cake mix in mixing bowl and add pineapple and juice. Beat as directed on cake mix box, scraping sides of bowl as necessary.

2. Pour into an ungreased 9 x 13-inch baking pan. Bake 30 minutes.

3. Serve chilled with lite or fat free whipped topping. Store in refrigerator.

- - - - - - - - - - - - - - - - - - -

Yield: 10 servings

Calories: 202
Protein: 4 g
Carbohydrate: 47 g
Fat: less than 1 g
Cholesterol: 0 mg
Sodium: 339 mg
Calcium: 55 mg
Dietary Fiber: less than 1 g
Sugar: 7 g

ORANGE ANGEL CAKE

1 (16 ounce) angel food cake mix
1 teaspoon orange extract
2 tablespoons finely grated orange peel

1. Preheat oven to 350°, and remove top oven rack. Move remaining rack to lowest position. Wash electric mixer bowl, beaters and spatula to remove any grease. Place cake mix in electric mixer bowl, and add 1¼ cups water or amount specified by mix instructions.

2. Blend mix and water about 30 seconds on low speed. Add orange extract and peel; then increase speed to medium and beat for 1 minute, scraping sides of bowl as necessary.

3. Pour batter into an ungreased 10-inch tube pan with removable bottom. Place on lowest rack and bake about 35-40 minutes. Cake is done when a toothpick is inserted in the center and comes out clean, and top is cracked and golden brown. Do not underbake.

4. Remove cake from oven and invert tube pan over a bottle neck, or rest the tube pan on 4 glasses. Cool 1½ hours before unmolding*.

5. Serve with fat free or reduced fat thawed whipped topping, or drizzle Lemon Glaze (p. 286) or Orange Glaze (p. 286) on top of cake.

- -

Yield: 12 servings
Serving size: 1 slice

Calories: 142
Protein: 3 g
Carbohydrate: 32 g
Fat: less than 1 g
Cholesterol: 0 mg
Sodium: 279 mg
Calcium: 47 mg
Dietary Fiber: less than 1 g
Sugar: less than 1 g

*To unmold: Gently slide a thin spatula between the cake and the pan to avoid tearing the cake. Pull the tube upward, and slide spatula under the cake. Slide cake off tube upside down onto a rack; then invert right side up onto another rack or serving plate.

LEMON ANGEL CAKE

1 (16 ounce) angel food cake mix
1 teaspoon lemon extract
2 tablespoons lemon zest (finely grated lemon peel)

1. Preheat oven to 350°, and remove top oven rack. Move remaining rack to lowest position. Wash electric mixer bowl, beaters and spatula to remove any grease. Place cake mix in electric mixer bowl, and add 1¼ cups water or amount specified by mix instructions.

2. Blend mix and water about 30 seconds on low speed. Add lemon extract and zest; then increase speed to medium and beat for 1 minute, scraping sides of bowl as necessary. Pour into an ungreased 10-inch tube pan with removable bottom. Place on lowest oven rack, and bake about 35-40 minutes. Cake is done when a toothpick is inserted in the center and comes out clean, and top is cracked and golden brown. Do not underbake.

3. Remove from oven and invert tube pan over a bottle neck, or rest the tube pan on 4 glasses. Cool 1½ hours.

4. Serve with reduced fat free or fat free whipped topping, thawed; or drizzle Lemon Glaze (p. 286) or Orange Glaze (p. 286) on top of cake.

- -

Yield: 10 servings

Calories: 170
Protein: 4 g
Carbohydrate: 39 g
Fat: less than 1 g
Cholesterol: 0 mg
Sodium: 334 mg
Calcium: 56 mg
Dietary Fiber: less than 1 g
Sugar: less than 1 g

ORANGE GLAZE OR DESSERT SAUCE

2 tablespoons margarine
¾ cup sifted powdered sugar or
sugar substitute
1-2 tablespoons fresh orange juice
and 1 tablespoon finely grated
orange peel

1. In a small saucepan, melt margarine. Add sugar substitute, orange juice and grated peel. Bring to a boil and boil 1 minute. Remove from heat and cool.

2. Beat with a small wire whisk every few minutes until glaze reaches desired consistency. Drizzle glaze over cake or other dessert.

- - - - - - - - - - - - - - - - - - - -

Yield: 16 servings (about 1 cup)
Serving size: 1 tablespoon

Calories: 32
Protein: 0 g
Carbohydrate: 5 g
Fat: 1 g
Cholesterol: 0 mg
Sodium: 17 g
Calcium: 1 mg
Dietary Fiber: 0 g
Sugar: 4 g

LEMON GLAZE OR DESSERT SAUCE

2 tablespoons margarine
¾ cup sifted powdered sugar or
sugar substitute
1 tablespoon lemon juice and 1
tablespoon finely grated lemon
peel

1. Place margarine in a microwave-safe bowl. Cover with plastic wrap and heat on full or 50% power in microwave oven about 10 seconds, or just until melted.

2. Stir in sugar, lemon juice and peel; cover and cook 1 minute on 50% power. Remove and beat with a spoon until cooled and of desired consistency. Drizzle on top of cake or dessert.

- - - - - - - - - - - - - - - - - - - -

Yield: 16 servings (1 cup)
Serving size: 1 tablespoon

Calories: 32
Protein: 0 g
Carbohydrate: 5 g
Fat: 1 g
Cholesterol: 0 mg
Sodium: 17 mg
Calcium: 1 mg
Dietary Fiber: 0 g
Sugar: 4 g

ANGEL TUNNEL CAKE

This is a fun and different way to serve angel food cake.

1 (15 ounce) prepared angel food cake
3 cups fruit sherbet of your choice
¼ cup frozen juice concentrate, thawed
1 cup lite or fat free frozen whipped topping, thawed

1. Slice angel food cake in half horizontally. Pull out pieces of cake to leave two 1-inch thick cake shells. Spoon sherbet into bottom shell. Set top half, hollow side down, over bottom.

2. Poke holes in top of cake, and drizzle with juice concentrate. Top or frost cake with whipped topping.

3. Serve immediately or freeze. If frozen, let stand 10 minutes before serving.

- - - - - - - - - - - - - - - - -

Yield: 10 servings

Calories: 198
Protein: 3 g
Carbohydrate: 42 g
Fat: 2 g
Cholesterol: 3 mg
Sodium: 339 mg
Calcium: 86 mg
Dietary Fiber: less than 1 g
Sugar: 14 g

QUICK PINEAPPLE CAKE

1 yellow cake mix
1 cup egg substitute
¾ cup unsweetened applesauce
½ (20 ounce) can crushed pineapple in juice, ½ juice reserved

1. Preheat oven to 350°. In mixing bowl, beat cake mix, egg substitute, applesauce and pineapple with juice for 4 minutes, scraping sides and bottom of bowl as necessary.

2. Pour into a greased and floured 9 x 13-inch baking pan.

3. Bake for 30-35 minutes. Cake is done when a toothpick is inserted in the center and comes out clean.

4. Cool.

5. Serve with Lemon-Pineapple Topping, (p. 288).

- - - - - - - - - - - - - - - - -

Yield: 12 servings

Calories: 207
Protein: 3 g
Carbohydrate: 42 g
Fat: 3 g
Cholesterol: 0 mg
Sodium: 304 mg
Calcium: 92 mg
Dietary Fiber: less than 1 g
Sugar: 25 g

LEMON-PINEAPPLE CAKE

1 (16.5 ounce) package lemon
    cake mix
¾ cup egg substitute
⅓ cup unsweetened applesauce
1 (20 ounce) can crushed
    pineapple in juice, undrained

1. Preheat oven to 350°.

2. In mixing bowl, combine cake
   mix, egg substitute, applesauce
   and pineapple with juice.

3. Blend on low speed, scraping bottom and sides of bowl; then beat
   on medium for 2 minutes.

4. Pour batter into a greased and
   floured 9 x 13-inch baking dish.

5. Bake 30-35 minutes. Cake is done
   when a toothpick is inserted in the
   center and comes out clean.

6. Serve with Lemon-Pineapple Topping (p. 288).

- - - - - - - - - - - - - - - - - -

Yield: 12 servings

Calories: 191
Protein: 2 g
Carbohydrate: 39 g
Fat: 3 g
Cholesterol: 0 mg
Sodium: 274 mg
Calcium: 78 mg
Dietary Fiber: less than 1 g
Sugar: 24 g

LEMON-PINEAPPLE TOPPING

1 (14 ounce) can fat free sweet-
    ened condensed milk
¼ cup lemon juice
1 (8 ounce) carton lite frozen
    whipped topping, thawed

1. Blend all ingredients, mixing well.
   Spread over cake. Store in refrigerator.

- - - - - - - - - - - - - - - - - -

Yield: 24 servings
Serving size: About 2 tablespoons

Calories: 86
Protein: 2 g
Carbohydrate: 16 g
Fat: 1 g
Cholesterol: 2 mg
Sodium: 23 mg
Calcium: less than 1 mg
Dietary Fiber: 0 g
Sugar: 15 g

EASY ORANGE CAKE

In this recipe, applesauce is a healthful substitute for vegetable oil.

1 (16.5 ounce) package orange cake mix
1 cup egg substitute
⅔ cup unsweetened applesauce
½ cup water

1. In mixing bowl, combine all ingredients.

2. Beat on low speed 1 minute to blend. Scrape bottom and sides of bowl; then beat on medium speed for 2 minutes. Pour into a greased and floured 9 x 13-inch baking pan.

3. Bake at 350° for about 30 minutes. Cake is done when a toothpick is inserted in the center and comes out clean.

4. Cool before serving.

5. Serve with Easy Orange Topping (p. 289).

Variation: Add 2 tablespoons poppy seeds.

- - - - - - - - - - - - - - - - - -

Yield: 12 servings

Calories: 179
Protein: 3 g
Carbohydrate: 34 g
Fat: 4 g
Cholesterol: 0 mg
Sodium: 287 mg
Calcium: 7 mg
Dietary Fiber: less than 1 g
Sugar: 19 g

EASY ORANGE TOPPING

1 (14 ounce) can low fat sweetened condensed milk
⅓ cup lemon juice
1 (8 ounce) carton lite frozen whipped topping
2 (11 ounce) cans mandarin oranges, drained, halved, chilled

1. In a large bowl, blend condensed milk and lemon juice and mix well.

2. Fold in whipped topping until blended. Fold in orange slices.

3. Pour mixture over cooled cake. Store in refrigerator.

- - - - - - - - - - - - - - - - - -

Yield: 30 servings
Serving size: About 2 tablespoons

Calories: 80
Protein: 2 grams
Carbohydrate: 15 grams
Fat: 2 grams
Cholesterol: 0 milligrams
Sodium: 1 milligram
Calcium: 2 milligrams
Dietary Fiber: 0 grams
Sugar: less than 1 gram

CHERRY-ANGEL TRIFLE

Using a large crystal bowl or footed crystal trifle bowl spotlights this cherry-cranberry dessert.

1 prepared angel food cake, torn into bite-size pieces
½ cup reduced calorie cranberry juice cocktail
1 cup lite or fat free frozen whipped topping, thawed
1 (6 ounce) carton low fat cherry-vanilla yogurt

1. In a crystal or trifle bowl, place cake pieces and drizzle with juice. Stir together whipped topping and yogurt; spoon onto cake.

2. Refrigerate up to 2 hours before serving.

Flavor Perk: Garnish with fresh Bing cherries, pitted and halved, or chopped maraschino cherries.

- - - - - - - - - - - - - - - - - -

Yield: 8 servings

Calories: 152
Protein: 3 g
Carbohydrate: 31 g
Fat: 2 g
Cholesterol: less than 1 mg
Sodium: 335 mg
Calcium: 88 mg
Dietary Fiber: less than 1 g
Sugar: 5 g

PINEAPPLE-LEMON TRIFLE

1 (18.25 ounce) reduced fat white cake mix
3 egg whites
1½ cups pineapple chunks in juice, drained
1 (22 ounce) can prepared lemon pie filling

1. Preheat oven to 350°. Prepare cake mix according to package instructions, using 1¼ cups water and egg whites. Pour batter into a sprayed 9 x 13-inch baking pan. Bake about 30 minutes. Cake is done when a toothpick is inserted in the center and comes out clean.

2. Cool cake on wire rack; then cut cake into 1-inch cubes. In a trifle bowl, layer ⅓ cake cubes, pineapple chunks and lemon pie filling. Repeat for two more layers.

Flavor Perk: Garnish with whipped topping sprinkled with lemon zest (finely grated lemon peel).

- - - - - - - - - - - - - - - - - -

Yield: 12 servings

Calories: 243
Protein: 3 g
Carbohydrate: 54 g
Fat: 2 g
Cholesterol: 0 mg
Sodium: 338 mg
Calcium: 67 mg
Dietary Fiber: less than 1 g
Sugar: 20 g

STRAWBERRY-ANGEL TRIFLE

1 (5 ounce) package sugar free
instant vanilla pudding mix
2 cups skim milk
3 cups fresh strawberries, divided
1 prepared angel food cake or
reduced fat white cake

1. Prepare pudding with skim milk according to package directions. Stem and slice 2 cups strawberries. Crush 1 cup sliced strawberries.

2. Tear or cut cake into bite-size pieces. Place a layer of cake in a crystal or trifle bowl. Spoon ½ cup crushed strawberries over cake. Spread on 1 cup vanilla pudding, followed by a layer of sliced strawberries. Repeat layers, ending with sliced strawberries.

3. Refrigerate several hours or overnight.

Flavor Perk: Top with lite or fat free frozen whipped topping, thawed.

- - - - - - - - - - - - - - - - - - -

Yield: 12 servings

Calories: 103
Protein: 4 g
Carbohydrate: 22 g
Fat: less than 1 g
Cholesterol: less than 1 mg
Sodium: 268 mg
Calcium: 105 mg
Dietary Fiber: 1 g
Sugar: 4 g

MINI-FRUITCAKE CONFECTIONS

Serve these delicious mini-fruitcakes for morning coffee, brunch, receptions or a family dessert.

½ cup self-rising flour
½ cup brown sugar substitute
2 cups dried tropical fruit mix or
any dried fruit or combination
½ cup egg substitute

1. Preheat oven to 300°. Sift together flour and sugar substitute; set aside. Placed mixed fruit in a food processor and pulse 15-30 seconds. Add flour-sugar mixture and egg substitute. Pulse until mixture is well blended. Spoon 1 tablespoon into each cup of two mini-muffin pans. Spread batter evenly in each cup with back of spoon.

2. Place muffin pans in the center of the oven. Bake 20 minutes and test one confection for doneness. The confection should be shiny on top and slightly golden on the bottom. If needed, continue cooking and checking every few minutes. Remove from oven. Remove confections and place on racks to cool.

3. Serve immediately or store in an airtight container.

- - - - - - - - - - - - - - - - - - -

Yield: 24 servings (About 50 fruitcakes)
Serving size: 2 confections

Calories: 58
Protein: 1 g
Carbohydrate: 14 g
Fat: less than 1 g
Cholesterol: 0 mg
Sodium: 45 mg
Calcium: 18 mg
Dietary Fiber: 2 g
Sugar: less than 1 g

VERY BERRY-LEMON SHORTCAKE

4 reduced fat biscuits,
  freshly baked
⅓ cup low fat lemon pie yogurt
2 cups frozen mixed berries,
  thawed, crushed
1 cup fat free or lite frozen
  whipped topping, thawed

1. Split biscuits horizontally. Spread biscuit bottoms with yogurt; replace tops. Place on dessert plates and spoon berries over biscuits. Garnish with whipped topping.

- - - - - - - - - - - - - - - - - -

Yield: 8 servings
Serving size: ½ biscuit

Calories: 144
Protein: 3 g
Carbohydrate: 22 g
Fat: 5 g
Cholesterol: less than 1 mg
Sodium: 319 mg
Calcium: 45 mg
Dietary Fiber: 1 g
Sugar: 8 g

ZESTY ORANGE TOPPING

1 (8 ounce) carton lite frozen
  whipped topping, thawed
½ teaspoon orange extract
2 tablespoons finely grated
  orange peel

1. Fold extract and grated peel into whipped topping. Serve as a topping or frost a cake, as desired.

2. Refrigerate.

- - - - - - - - - - - - - - - - - -

Yield: 16 servings (1 cup)
Serving size: 1 tablespoon

Calories: 32
Protein: 0 g
Carbohydrate: 3 g
Fat: 2 g
Cholesterol: 0 mg
Sodium: 0 mg
Calcium: less than 1 mg
Dietary Fiber: 0 g
Sugar: 2 g

BANANA-STRAWBERRY CREAM PIE

To prevent banana slices from browning, sprinkle with lemon juice or fruit preservative.

1 (9 inch) reduced fat graham
    cracker crust
1 cup fresh sliced strawberries,
    divided
2 bananas, sliced, divided
2 cups prepared fat free vanilla
    pudding

1. Place strawberries in bottom of crust, reserving 4-6 slices. Arrange banana slices, reserving ¼ cup slices, on top of strawberries. Top with vanilla pudding, and garnish with reserved banana and strawberry slices.

2. Serve immediately or cover tightly with plastic wrap and refrigerate.

- - - - - - - - - - - - - - - - - - -

Yield: 6-8 servings

Calories: 194
Protein: 2 g
Carbohydrate: 37 g
Fat: 4 g
Cholesterol: 0 mg
Sodium: 194 mg
Calcium: 33 mg
Dietary Fiber: 1 g
Sugar: 22 g

ORANGE-PINEAPPLE CREAM PIE

1 cup orange sherbet, softened
1 cup lite frozen whipped topping,
    thawed
¼ cup crushed pineapple, well-
    drained
1 (9 inch) reduced fat graham
    cracker crumb crust

1. Fold together sherbet, whipped topping and pineapple. Place in pie crust and refrigerate 6-8 hours, or freeze until firm.

Variation: Substitute strawberry sherbet for the orange sherbet.

- - - - - - - - - - - - - - - - - - -

Yield: 8 servings

Calories: 135
Protein: less than 1 g
Carbohydrate: 24 g
Fat: 4 g
Cholesterol: 1 mg
Sodium: 99 mg
Calcium: 29 mg
Dietary Fiber: 0 g
Sugar: 12 g

COOK'S CHOICE CREAM PIE

½ cup frozen juice concentrate of your choice, thawed
1 (6 ounce) carton fat free vanilla yogurt
1 cup lite or fat free frozen whipped topping, thawed
1 (9 inch) reduced fat graham cracker crumb crust

1. In a mixing bowl, stir juice concentrate and yogurt until well blended. Fold in whipped topping.

2. Spoon mixture into the graham cracker crust. Refrigerate 6-8 hours or until firm

- -

Yield: 8 servings

Calories: 190
Protein: 1 g
Carbohydrate: 29 g
Fat: 7 g
Cholesterol: 0 mg
Sodium: 101 mg
Calcium: 99 mg
Dietary Fiber: 0 g
Sugar: 12 g

STRAWBERRY SHERBET PIE

1 cup strawberry sherbet, softened
1 cup lite frozen whipped topping, thawed
¾ cup fresh strawberries, sliced; and ¼ cup fresh strawberries, unsliced
1 (9 inch) reduced fat graham cracker crumb crust

1. Fold together sherbet, whipping topping and ¾ cup strawberries. Spoon mixture into the pie crust, and refrigerate 6-8 hours or until firm.

2. Garnish with ¼ cup unsliced strawberries.

- -

Yield: 8 servings

Calories: 141
Protein: less than 1 g
Carbohydrate: 23 g
Fat: 5 g
Cholesterol: 1 mg
Sodium: 94 mg
Calcium: 13 mg
Dietary Fiber: less than 1 g
Sugar: 13 g

FAVORITE FROZEN LIME PIE

2 (6 ounce) cartons fat free no sugar added key lime pie yogurt
1 (3 ounce) package sugar free lime gelatin
1 (8 ounce) carton lite frozen whipped topping, thawed
1 (9 inch) reduced fat graham cracker crust

1. In a mixing bowl, combine yogurt and lime gelatin; mix well to moisten gelatin.

2. Fold in whipped topping and spread mixture in pie crust. Freeze.

3. Remove from freezer 20 minutes before slicing.

- - - - - - - - - - - - - - - - - - - -

Yield: 8 servings

Calories: 178
Protein: 3 g
Carbohydrate: 24 g
Fat: 7 g
Cholesterol: 1 mg
Sodium: 138 mg
Calcium: 0 mg
Dietary Fiber: 0 g
Sugar: 11 g

CHERRY-KEY LIME PIE

2 (6 ounce) cartons fat free no sugar added key lime pie yogurt
⅓ cup chopped fresh cherries or maraschino cherries, divided
1 (8 ounce) carton lite frozen whipped topping, thawed
1 (9 inch) reduced-fat graham cracker crust

1. In a mixing bowl, stir yogurt and ¼ cup cherries until well blended. Fold in whipped topping.

2. Spoon pie mixture into graham cracker crust and garnish with remaining chopped cherries. Refrigerate 6-8 hours or until firm.

- - - - - - - - - - - - - - - - - - - -

Yield: 8 servings

Calories: 178
Protein: 2 g
Carbohydrate: 25 g
Fat: 7 g
Cholesterol: 1 mg
Sodium: 108 mg
Calcium: 1 mg
Dietary Fiber: less than 1 g
Sugar: 12 g

COOKIE CRUST FRUIT PIE

1¾ cups sugar free or fat free cookies of your choice, crumbed, divided
⅓ cup melted margarine
1 cup sherbet of your choice, softened
1 (8 ounce) carton fat free frozen whipped topping, thawed

1. Preheat oven to 350°. Mix 1½ cups cookie crumbs with the margarine, and pat evenly into a 9-inch pie plate. Bake 10 minutes; remove and cool.

2. Fold together sherbet and whipped topping. Spoon into crumb crust and sprinkle ¼ cup cookie crumbs on top. Refrigerate 6-8 hours or until firm.

- - - - - - - - - - - - - - - - - - - -

Yield: 8 servings

Calories: 254
Protein: 3 g
Carbohydrate: 45 g
Fat: 9 g
Cholesterol: 1 mg
Sodium: 244 mg
Calcium: 33 mg
Dietary Fiber: 4 g
Sugar: 4 g

PINEAPPLE ICE

Ices and sorbets have become a popular ending to a hearty meal.

2 cups fresh or canned crushed unsweetened pineapple, drained
Sugar substitute equal to ¾ cup sugar
½ cup fresh lemon juice

1. Drain pineapple and reserve juice. In a large saucepan, place reserved juice and enough water to equal 2 cups. Stir in sugar substitute. Bring to a boil; stir in crushed pineapple and lemon juice.

2. Cool; then freeze in electric ice cream freezer according to manufacturer's instructions. (Alternate method: Pour mixture into a 9 x 13-inch baking pan and place in refrigerator freezer. Partially freeze; then place in blender or food processor and pulse 2-3 times or until smooth and frothy. Return to freezer and freeze until firm.)

Variation: Orange Ice – Substitute 3 cups orange juice and zest of 2 oranges for ½ cup lemon juice.

- - - - - - - - - - - - - - - - - - - -

Yield: 4 servings
Serving size: About 1 cup

Calories: 69
Protein: less than 1 g
Carbohydrate: 18 g
Fat: 0 g
Cholesterol: 0 mg
Sodium: 8 mg
Calcium: 101 mg
Sodium: 8 mg
Calcium: 101 mg
Dietary Fiber: 1 g
Sugar: 10 g

VERY BERRY SORBET

Remember those berries saved in the freezer for a special occasion? This is it – a "company best" dessert that will be a sensation every time.

2 pints fresh or frozen unsweetened berries (raspberries, blueberries)
Sugar substitute equal to 1 cup sugar
Zest of one lemon (about 1 tablespoon)

1. Place berries, sugar substitute, zest and 1½ cups water in a medium saucepan. Bring to a boil and boil gently, uncovered, about 10 minutes. Remove from heat and cool 20 minutes.

2. Process berry mixture in food processor 3 minutes; then pour into a cheesecloth placed in a wire mesh strainer over a large bowl. Press the berry mixture with the back of a spoon to press through the cheesecloth and strainer. If the mixture is too thick to strain, return to saucepan and add ½-1 cup water and bring to boil. Then press mixture again through strainer to separate juice from seeds and skins.

3. Pour strained mixture into a 9 x 13-inch pan or dish; freeze at least 4 hours. Remove from freezer; then break into chunks and place in food processor. Pulse 1-2 minutes; then spoon ½ cup each into 6 goblets or dessert dishes and serve immediately.

Flavor Perk: Garnish with fresh mint leaves.

- -

Yield: 6 servings
Serving size: ¾ cup

Calories: 44
Protein: less than 1 g
Carbohydrate: 11 g
Fat: less than 1 g
Cholesterol: 0 mg
Sodium: 4 mg
Calcium: 95 mg
Dietary Fiber: 2 g
Sugar: 6 g

THREE FRUIT SHERBET

By definition, sherbet may contain only sweetened fruit juice and water, but milk and other ingredients may also be added. Compared to other similar desserts, sherbet is richer than an ice, but lighter than ice cream.

1½ cups fresh-squeezed orange juice
½ cup frozen lemonade concentrate
1½ cups bananas (about 3), cut in 1-2 inch chunks
2 cups skim milk

1. Mix orange juice, lemonade and bananas in blender or food processor and process about 1 minute or until smooth. Transfer to a large mixing bowl. Stir in skim milk and 3 cups water.

2. Freeze in electric ice cream freezer according to manufacturer's instructions. (Alternate method: Pour mixture into a 9 x 13-inch baking pan and place in freezer. Partially freeze; then place in blender or food processor and process until smooth and frothy. Place in one container or in individual molds; return to freezer until frozen.)

- - - - - - - - - - - - - - - - - - -

Yield: 8 servings
Serving size: About ½ cup

Calories: 116
Protein: 3 g
Carbohydrate: 27 g
Fat: less than 1 g
Cholesterol: 1 mg
Sodium: 33 mg
Calcium: 84 mg
Dietary Fiber: 1 g
Sugar: 17 g

COOL LEMON SHERBET

This sherbet is cooling and refreshing on a hot summer day.

4 cups buttermilk
¾ cup lemon juice (6 lemons) plus 6 tablespoons finely grated lemon peel
1 cup light corn syrup
Sugar substitute to taste

1. Mix all ingredients and sweeten to taste with sugar substitute.

2. Freeze in electric ice cream freezer according to manufacturer's instructions. (Alternate method: Pour mixture into a 9 x 13-inch baking pan and place in freezer. Partially freeze; then place in blender or food processor and process until smooth and frothy. Place in one container or in individual molds; return to freezer until frozen.)

Variation: Decrease lemon juice to ¼ cup, and add 1 cup fresh pureed strawberries or peaches.

- - - - - - - - - - - - - - - - - - -

Yield: 8 servings
Serving size: About ½ cup

Calories: 170
Protein: 4 g
Carbohydrate: 39 g
Fat: 1 g
Cholesterol: 4 mg
Sodium: 178 mg
Calcium: 153 mg
Dietary Fiber: less than 1 g
Sugar: 27 g

KAHLÚA ANGEL PARFAIT

Kahlúa is a popular liqueur with the concentrated flavors of roasted coffee, vanilla bean and semisweet chocolate.

2 tablespoons decaffeinated instant coffee granules
1 cup lite or fat free frozen whipped topping, thawed
½ prepared angel food cake
⅓ cup Kahlúa chocolate liqueur

1. Fold instant coffee granules into whipped topping. Cut or tear cake into bite-size pieces and place about 4-5 pieces in 4 parfait or stemmed glasses. Drizzle cake pieces lightly with Kahlúa; cover with about 1 tablespoon whipped topping.

2. Repeat layers; top with a light drizzle of Kahlúa. Refrigerate 1-2 hours before serving.

Variation: Substitute almond-flavored amaretto liqueur for the Kahlúa.

- - - - - - - - - - - - - - - - - - - -

Yield: 4 servings

Calories: 233
Protein: 3 g
Carbohydrate: 40 g
Fat: 2 g
Cholesterol: 0 mg
Sodium: 321 mg
Calcium: 64 mg
Dietary Fiber: less than 1 g
Sugar: 2 g

CHOCOLATE-VANILLA PARFAITS

A parfait is a layered dessert using several kinds of ice cream or other smooth treat, garnished and served in a tall glass. This one is a people-pleasing combination of creamy chocolate and vanilla pudding.

¼ cup slivered almonds
4 cups skim milk, divided
1 small box sugar free instant chocolate pudding mix
1 small box sugar free instant vanilla pudding mix

1. Place almonds in a dry skillet over medium heat. Stir and heat until almonds are evenly browned; set aside. In a blender or food processor, add 2 cups skim milk and chocolate pudding mix. Blend thoroughly and pour pudding into a medium bowl.

2. Wash blender or food processor; then add remaining 2 cups skim milk and vanilla pudding mix. Blend thoroughly. In parfait or stemmed glasses, spoon ¼ cup chocolate pudding, then ¼ cup vanilla pudding. Repeat.

3. Sprinkle parfaits with toasted almonds and refrigerate until serving time.

4. Garnish with whipped topping.

- - - - - - - - - - - - - - - - - - - -

Yield: 4 servings
Serving size: 1 parfait
(1 cup pudding plus almonds)

Calories: 268
Protein: 12 g
Carbohydrate: 45 g
Fat: 5 g
Cholesterol: 5 mg
Sodium: 1642 mg
Calcium: 322 mg
Dietary Fiber: 2 g
Sugar: 11 g

APRICOT-ALMOND MOUSSE

This light and creamy dessert gets its smooth texture from a surprising ingredient – pureed baby food!

1 (4 ounce) jar infant food pureed apricots or apricots with pears and apples
½-1 teaspoon almond extract
1 (8 ounce) carton lite frozen whipped topping, thawed
1-2 tablespoons brown sugar substitute

1. Combine apricots and almond extract. Fold apricots into whipped topping. Stir in sugar substitute to taste.

2. Spoon into 4 goblets or dessert dishes. Refrigerate at least 1-2 hours before serving.

Flavor Perk: Garnish with sprigs of fresh mint.

- -

Yield: 4 servings
Serving size: About ⅓ cup

Calories: 141
Protein: 0 g
Carbohydrate: 16 g
Fat: 6 g
Cholesterol: 0 mg
Sodium: less than 1 mg
Calcium: 2 mg
Dietary Fiber: less than 1 g
Sugar: 9 g

APRICOT-PINEAPPLE SUNDAES

When counting calories and fat grams becomes rather dreary, treat yourself with this tempting yogurt sundae. Two grams of fat and 10 milligrams cholesterol make this one practically guilt-free.

8 teaspoons low sugar apricot preserves
1 teaspoon ground cinnamon
2 cups reduced fat frozen vanilla yogurt
4 tablespoons pineapple tidbits in juice, drained

1. Place preserves and cinnamon in glass measuring cup. Cover and place in microwave oven on 50% power until almost melted, about 30 seconds. Cool slightly.

2. Spoon ½ cup each frozen yogurt into 4 dessert dishes. Top with 1 tablespoon pineapple tidbits. Spoon 2 teaspoons warmed preserves on each; serve immediately.

- -

Yield: 4 servings

Calories: 147
Protein: 4 g
Carbohydrate: 29 g
Fat: 2 g
Cholesterol: 10 mg
Sodium: 76 mg
Calcium: 157 mg
Dietary Fiber: less than 1 g
Sugar: 26 g

RASPBERRY-YOGURT CHIFFON

Chiffon describes a light and smooth dessert made with gelatin or egg whites and beaten until fluffy. This recipe is another "company-best" dessert that makes an elegant presentation.

1 (3 ounce) package sugar free raspberry or mixed berry gelatin
1 (8 ounce) carton light or fat free French vanilla yogurt
1¼ cups fresh or frozen raspberries, thawed, drained, divided

1. In electric mixer bowl, dissolve gelatin in 1 cup boiling water. Add 1 cup cold water and chill until partially set, about 35-40 minutes.

2. Remove from refrigerator; add yogurt and beat 1-2 minutes with a spoon or wire whisk until light and foamy. If mixture does not mound when spooned, refrigerate. Into 6 dessert dishes or stemmed goblets, place about 1 tablespoon raspberries followed by ½ cup gelatin mixture, then about 2 tablespoons raspberries on top.

3. Refrigerate at least 30 minutes before serving.

Flavor Perk: Garnish with fresh mint leaves.

- - - - - - - - - - - - - - - - - - - -

Yield: 6 servings
Serving size: About ⅓ cup

Calories: 49
Protein: 1 g
Carbohydrate: 10 g
Fat: less than 1 g
Cholesterol: 2 mg
Sodium: 18 mg
Calcium: 45 mg
Dietary Fiber: less than 1 g
Sugar: 8 g

PEACHY CHIFFON SQUARES

1 (3 ounce) package sugar free peach or lemon gelatin
1 (4 ounce) jar infant food pureed peaches
1 teaspoon almond extract
1 (8 ounce) carton fat free whipped topping

1. In a medium bowl, pour 1 cup boiling water over gelatin and stir until dissolved. Add 1 cup cold water; refrigerate until partially set.

2. Fold in pureed peaches, almond extract and whipped topping. Pour mixture into a 9 x 9-inch square dish. Refrigerate 3-4 hours; cut into squares to serve.

Flavor Perk: Drizzle individual servings with crushed or pureed raspberries or strawberries.

- - - - - - - - - - - - - - - - - - - -

Yield: 9 servings
Serving size: 1 square

Calories: 62
Protein: less than 1 g
Carbohydrate: 7 g
Fat: 3 g
Cholesterol: 0 mg
Sodium: less than 1 mg
Calcium: less than 1 mg
Dietary Fiber: less than 1 g
Sugar: 4 g

FROZEN PINEAPPLE-GRAPE KABOBS

These kabobs keep well in the freezer, but may be eaten before they can be stored!

½ cup flaked sweetened coconut, toasted
1 (20 ounce) can pineapple chunks in juice, drained, juice reserved
1½ cups green or red grapes
5-6 inch long wooden skewers

1. To toast coconut, spread in a single layer on a baking pan. Bake at 350° about 5-10 minutes, stirring frequently. Check for brownness every few minutes, as coconut will easily burn.

2. Place cooled coconut on wax paper or a pie plate. Place juice from pineapple in a separate pie plate. Thread pineapple chunks and grapes alternately on skewers. Roll in juice; then roll in toasted coconut.

3. Place kabobs on baking sheet; then cover with foil and freeze. To serve, remove from freezer, thaw 3-5 minutes and serve immediately.

- - - - - - - - - - - - - - - - - - -

Yield: 8 servings (About 16 kabobs)
Serving size: 2 kabobs

Calories: 94
Protein: less than 1 g
Carbohydrate: 18 g
Fat: 3 g
Cholesterol: 0 mg
Sodium: 23 mg
Calcium: 206 mg
Dietary Fiber: less than 1 g
Sugar: 17 g

FLAVORFUL FRUIT MÉLANGE

This mélange, or "mixture," consists of strawberries, pineapple and bananas in a smooth cherry pie filling.

1 quart (32 ounces) fresh strawberries, stemmed, halved or quartered
1 (20 ounce) can pineapple chunks in juice, well drained
2 bananas, sliced
1 (20 ounce) can lite no sugar added cherry pie filling

1. In large bowl, gently mix strawberries, pineapple chunks and bananas. Fold in pie filling and chill.

- - - - - - - - - - - - - - - - - - -

Yield: 10 servings
Serving size: About 1 cup

Calories: 88
Protein: less than 1 g
Carbohydrate: 22 g
Fat: less than 1 g
Cholesterol: 0 mg
Sodium: less than 1 mg
Calcium: 171 mg
Dietary Fiber: 2 g
Sugar: 18 g

CINNAMON BROILED GRAPEFRUIT

Grapefruit isn't just for breakfast anymore. This is a quick and satisfying dessert.

2 grapefruits, halved
Cinnamon to taste

1. Preheat oven to 300°. With a sharp or serrated knife, separate sections of each grapefruit half. Sprinkle each half with cinnamon to taste. Place halves on foil-covered baking sheet and bake 10 minutes. Remove.

2. Preheat broiler; broil grapefruit until edges are lightly brown and the sections are puffed.

- -

Yield: 4 servings
Serving size: ½ grapefruit

Calories: 37
Protein: less than 1 g
Carbohydrate: 9 g
Fat: less than 1 g
Cholesterol: 0 mg
Sodium: 0 mg
Calcium: 14 mg
Dietary Fiber: 2 g
Sugar: 8 g

GOLDEN RICE PUDDING

⅓ cup packaged dried golden raisin-cranberry mix, divided
2 cups skim milk
1 (3 ounce) package sugar free instant vanilla pudding
½ cup cooked rice

1. Pour 1 cup boiling water over ¼ cup raisin-cranberry mix. Let stand until plumped, about 10-15 minutes; then drain.

2. In a blender, place skim milk and instant pudding. Pulse about 30 seconds or until thoroughly mixed; place in mixing bowl. Add rice and raisin-cranberry mix to pudding. Cover top with plastic wrap and refrigerate.

3. At serving time, spoon into small bowls and sprinkle reserved raisin-cranberry mix on top.

Variation: Substitute dried tropical fruit mix for the raisin-cranberry mix.

- -

Yield: 4 servings
Serving size: About ¾ cup

Calories: 175
Protein: 5 g
Carbohydrate: 38 g
Fat: less than 1 g
Cholesterol: 2 mg
Sodium: 1018 mg
Calcium: 159 mg
Dietary Fiber: less than 1 g
Sugar: 14 g

BROWN RICE PUDDING

This is a healthful version of old-fashioned rice pudding.

1½ cups cooked brown rice, cold
½ cup raisins or other dried fruit
2 tablespoons brown sugar substitute
1 cup nonfat plain yogurt

1. Mix all ingredients and refrigerate.

2. Spoon ½ cup each into 6 dessert dishes. Serve cold.

Flavor Perk: Add 2 teaspoons lemon juice and ⅛ teaspoon cinnamon.

- - - - - - - - - - - - - - - - -

Yield: 6 servings
Serving size: ½ cup

Calories: 118
Protein: 4 g
Carbohydrate: 25 g
Fat: less than 1 g
Cholesterol: less than 1 mg
Sodium: 36 mg
Calcium: 93 mg
Dietary Fiber: 1 g
Sugar: 11 g

DESSERT WAFFLES WITH BERRY SAUCE

This special dessert is a good ending to a light meal.

1 (10 ounce) carton frozen unsweetened raspberries, strawberries or mixed berries in syrup, thawed
¼ cup sugar substitute
4 frozen reduced fat square waffles
2 cups frozen fat free vanilla yogurt

1. To make berry sauce, press berries and syrup through a cheesecloth in a fine wire strainer set over a large bowl. Discard seeds and pulp. Place berry juice in a small bowl and stir in sugar substitute.

2. Toast waffles and cut each in half diagonally. For each serving, place 2 waffle halves on a dessert dish or plate. Place ½ cup frozen yogurt on each plate and drizzle with berry sauce.

3. Serve immediately.

- - - - - - - - - - - - - - - - -

Yield: 4 servings
Serving size: 1 waffle

Calories: 200
Protein: 6 g
Carbohydrate: 42 g
Fat: 1 g
Cholesterol: 0 mg
Sodium: 256 mg
Calcium: 480 mg
Dietary Fiber: 3 g
Sugar: 21 g

RASPBERRY DESSERT SAUCE

This is a versatile and appealing sauce that can be used as a coulis to decorate dessert plates or as a topping for a variety of desserts.

2 cups fresh or frozen raspberries, thawed
Sugar substitute to equal 1 tablespoon sugar
1 teaspoon fresh orange juice plus 1 teaspoon grated orange peel

1. Place all ingredients in a blender or food processor, and puree. Strain through cheesecloth placed inside a mesh strainer. After sauce has been strained, cover and refrigerate until serving time.

2. To use as a coulis to decorate dessert plates, place sauce in a squeeze bottle or plastic bag with a corner snipped. Drizzle in an attractive design on the plate before adding sliced cake or pastry.

3. Serve with low fat frozen vanilla yogurt, buttermilk sherbet or angel food cake.

- - - - - - - - - - - - - - - - - -

Yield: 8 servings (About 2 cups)
Serving size: ¼ cup

Calories: 11
Protein: less than 1 g
Carbohydrate: 2 g
Fat: 0 g
Cholesterol: 0 mg
Sodium: less than 1 mg
Calcium: 11 mg
Dietary Fiber: 2 g
Sugar: 2 g

BLUEBERRY DESSERT SAUCE

Be sure to prepare this delicious sauce when fresh blueberries are available, or prepare anytime with frozen blueberries.

1 tablespoon cornstarch
Sugar substitute equal to 2 tablespoons sugar
2 teaspoons lemon juice
1 cup fresh blueberries or thawed frozen blueberries

1. Combine cornstarch and ½ cup water in saucepan. Stir until cornstarch dissolves. Bring to boiling and cook, stirring constantly, about 1 minute or until mixture turns clear and thickens.

2. Reduce heat; add sugar substitute and lemon juice and cook 1 minute. Add blueberries and cook about 4 minutes. Mash blueberries slightly.

3. Serve warm or at room temperature.

4. Serve with fat free frozen vanilla yogurt or vanilla ice cream.

- - - - - - - - - - - - - - - - - -

Yield: 4 servings (About 1 cup)
Serving size: ¼ cup

Calories: 29
Protein: less than 1 g
Carbohydrate: 7 g
Fat: less than 1 g
Cholesterol: 0 mg
Sodium: 1 mg
Calcium: 18 mg
Dietary Fiber: 2 g
Sugar: 3 g

STRAWBERRY DESSERT SAUCE

1 teaspoon cornstarch
Sugar substitute to equal ¼ cup sugar
1 (16 ounce) package frozen unsweetened strawberries, thawed

1. Combine cornstarch and sugar in a saucepan. Add strawberries. Cook and stir over medium heat until mixture boils; then cook and stir 2 more minutes.

2. Pour sauce in a bowl; cover and chill at least 1 hour.

3. Serve with low fat frozen vanilla or strawberry yogurt or angel food cake.

- - - - - - - - - - - - - - - - - - -

Yield: 8 servings (About 2 cups)
Serving size: ¼ cup

Calories: 24
Protein: less than 1 g
Carbohydrate: 6 g
Fat: 0 g
Cholesterol: 0 mg
Sodium: 2 mg
Calcium: 24 mg
Dietary Fiber: 1 g
Sugar: 4 g

PEACH CRISP

To substitute for brown sugar, a granular brown sugar replacement (brown sugar substitute) is now available. The replacement works well in baked goods or sauces and is easy to use and store. Since it is dry and granular and does not melt like brown sugar, it does not work as well for recipes such as streusels or baked apples.

5 cups peeled and sliced fresh peaches or frozen unsweetened peach slices, thawed
1½ cups reduced fat granola
2 tablespoons brown sugar substitute
3 tablespoons margarine, melted

1. Preheat oven to 350°. Place sliced fruit in a sprayed 9 x 9-inch pan.

2. Mix granola, brown sugar substitute and margarine until sugar substitute is moistened. Crumble granola mixture over peaches and bake, uncovered, 30-35 minutes or until fruit is tender.

3. Serve warm.

- - - - - - - - - - - - - - - - - - -

Yield: 12 servings
Serving size: About ½ cup

Calories: 104
Protein: 2 g
Carbohydrate: 18 g
Fat: 4 g
Cholesterol: 0 mg
Sodium: 63 mg
Calcium: 11 mg
Dietary Fiber: 3 g
Sugar: 12 g

BROWN SUGAR BAKED APPLES

Rome Beauty apples are thought by many to be the best baking apples.

½ cup unsweetened apple juice
¼ teaspoon cinnamon, divided
4 small red baking apples
¼ cup brown sugar

1. Preheat oven to 350°. Mix apple juice and ⅛ teaspoon cinnamon in small bowl. Spoon juice into 4 custard cups.

2. Core apples and remove peel from the top of each. Set an apple in each of the custard cups and place cups in a shallow baking pan. Combine brown sugar and remaining cinnamon; sprinkle over apples.

3. Bake, covered with foil, about 30-40 minutes or until apples are tender.

- - - - - - - - - - - - - - - - - -

Yield: 4 servings
Serving size: 1 apple

Calories: 130
Protein: less than 1 g
Carbohydrate: 34 g
Fat: less than 1 g
Cholesterol: 0 mg
Sodium: 4 mg
Calcium: 21 mg
Dietary Fiber: 4 g
Sugar: 30 g

APPLESAUCE

For best sauce, look for tart, juicy apples such as Granny Smith.

4 cooking apples, peeled, cut into fourths
¼ teaspoon ground cinnamon
⅛ teaspoon ground nutmeg
White or brown sugar substitute to equal 3 tablespoons sugar

1. Heat apples to boiling in ½ cup water in a 2-quart saucepan over medium heat, stirring occasionally. Reduce heat and simmer uncovered 5-10 minutes until tender, stirring occasionally.

2. Add cinnamon and nutmeg; cook 1 minute and stir to break up apples. Remove from heat and add sugar substitute.

- - - - - - - - - - - - - - - - - -

Yield: 6 servings
Serving size: About ½ cup

Calories: 52
Protein: less than 1 gCarbohydrate: 14 g
Fat: less than 1 g
Cholesterol: 0 mg
Sodium: less than 1 mg
Calcium: 20 mg
Dietary Fiber: 2 g
Sugar: 11 g

GOLDEN APPLESAUCE

Use as a substitute for oil in muffins and cakes.

2 pounds Golden Delicious apples, peeled, cored, cut into chunks
½ cup unsweetened apple juice concentrate, thawed
2 tablespoons lemon juice
½ teaspoon ground cinnamon

1. Place apples, concentrate and ¼ cup water in a large saucepan. Bring to boil over high heat.

2. Reduce heat to medium; then cover and cook about 15 minutes or until apples are soft. Add lemon juice and cinnamon. Mash until as smooth as desired.

3. Serve hot or cold. Refrigerate up to 4 days.

- -

Yield: 6 servings (3 cups)
Serving size: ½ cup

Calories: 130
Protein: less than 1 g
Carbohydrate: 33 g
Fat: less than 1 g
Cholesterol: 0 mg
Sodium: 6 mg
Calcium: 17 mg
Dietary Fiber: 4 g
Sugar: 20 g

RED WINE-POACHED ANJOU PEARS

In the fall months, choose Anjou pears with unblemished, smooth yellow to yellow-green skins. This dessert is a delicious combination of cooked, sweet pears enhanced with cinnamon and red wine.

¼ cup red wine or red cooking wine
1-inch piece cinnamon stick
Sugar substitute
4 whole ripe Anjou pears, peeled, stems intact

1. Bring ¾ cup water to boiling in a large saucepan. Add wine, cinnamon stick and pears. Reduce heat and simmer until pears are soft; remove from heat. Add sugar substitute to taste, and boil 1-2 minutes.

2. Pour syrup over pears and serve immediately or chill.

Flavor Perk: Add 1 tablespoon grated lemon peel to the wine mixture when adding sugar substitute.

- -

Yield: 4 servings
Serving size: 1 pear

Calories: 110
Protein: less than 1 g
Carbohydrate: 25 g
Fat: less than 1 g
Cholesterol: 0 mg
Sodium: 2 mg
Calcium: 19 mg
Dietary Fiber: 4 g
Sugar: 18 g

COOKING HEALTHY

C

Grandmother's Cucumbers 37
Granny's Tidbits 99
Green Bean Casserole 163
Green Bean -Mushroom Saute 164
Green Beans and Zucchini 165
Green Beans Medley 80
Green Bean-Tomato Salad 80
Green Bell Pepper Chop 34
Green Chile Dunk 26
Green Chile-Cheese Squares 18
Green Chili-Artichoke Scoop 30
Grilled Portobello Burgers 65
Grilled Shrimp Kabobs 256
Grilled Soy-Sauced Chicken 245
Grilled Squash-Mushroom Kabobs 174
Grilled Turkey-Salsa Burgers 65
Grilled Vegetable Kabobs 152

H

Healthy Wrap Ideas 66
Hearty Mushroom Sauce 219
Hearty Beef Noodles 217
Hearty Chicken Soup 141
Hearty Tomato Sauce 263
Hearty Tomato-Pasta Soup 145
Herbed Onion Soup 147
Herbed Pork Chop Skillet 222
Herb-Marinated Tomatoes 79
Hi-O Silver Vegetable Dip 27
Hollandaise Sauce 198
Holy Guacamole 26
Homemade Chicken Noodle Soup 146
Honey Blue Nana Medley 41
Honey-Mustard Dressing 118
Hot Cheezy Crab Dip 24
Hot Pumpkin Soup 137
Hot Shrimp Canapes 15
Huevos Rancheros (Ranch-Style Eggs) 195

I

Iced Coffee 55
Island Smoothie 47
Italian Asparagus Spears 94

J

Just The Beef Fajitas 204
Just-The Beef Pot Roast 214

K

Kahlua Angel Parfait 299
Kid-Pleasing Turkey Toms 64

L

Lacey Melon Salad 110
Lazy Pita Crisps 21
Lemon Angel Cake 285
Lemon Glaze Or Dessert Sauce 286
Lemon-Bell Pepper Dressing 120
Lemon-Garlic Baked Chicken 231

Lemon-Lime Tea 52
Lemon-Orange tea 52
Lemon-Pineapple Cake 288
Lemon-Pineapple Punch 53
Lemon-Pineapple Topping 288
Lemon-Sesame Chicken 232
Lemony Linguine 181
Lime-Cilantro Dressing 120
Lime-Honey Salad Dressing 83
Lite Biscuit Mix 74
Lite Buttermilk Dressing 123
Lite Cornbread Mix 76
Lite Muffin Mix 75
Lite Pancake Mix 73
Lentil Soup 136
London Broil 210
Lunchbox Turkey Rollups 68

M

Man "N" Cheese 180
Mandarin Chicken Tenders 241
Mandarin Spinach Salad 90
Mango Salsa 267
Mango-Banana Smoothie 48
Marinated Brussels Sprouts 78
Marinated Cucumber Slices 78
Marinated Shrimp Teasers 15
Meatball Gravy 224
Melon Boat Pleasure 109
Merry Berry Banana Smoothie 46
Mexi-Eggs 196
Mini-Fruitcake Confections 291
Mixed Fruit Gingerbread 61
Mocha Angel Cake 281
Mocha Yummy 54
Mushroom Empanadas 197
Mushroom-Cheese Omelet 194

N

New Red Potatoes With Rosemary 169
Noodles Parmesan 182
Nutty Bing Cherry Dunk 42

O

Old Southern Black-Eyed Pea Soup 132
Olive-Onion Spread 33
Open-Face Turkey Quesadillas 247
Orange Angel Cake 284
Orange Glaze Or Dessert Sauce 286
Orange Marmalade Delight 42
Orange Slush 50
Orange Vinaigrette Dressing 115
Orange-Asparagus Skillet 153
Orange-Basil Dressing 117
Orange-Broiled Chicken 237
Orange-Pineapple Cream Pie 293
Orange-Pineapple Gingerbread 61
Orzo And Sun-Dried Tomatoes 182
Oven-Roasted Pork Tenderloin 221

BOOKS PUBLISHED BY COOKBOOK RESOURCES

Easy Cooking With 5 Ingredients
The Ultimate Cooking With 4 Ingredients
The Best of Cooking With 3 Ingredients
Easy Gourmet Cooking With 5 Ingredients
Healthy Cooking With 4 Ingredients
Easy Slow-Cooker Cooking With 4 Ingredients
Easy Desserts With 5 Ingredients
Quick Fixes With Mixes
Casseroles To The Rescue
Kitchen Keepsakes/More Kitchen Keepsakes
Mother's Recipes
Recipe Keepsakes
Cookie Dough Secrets
Gifts For The Cookie Jar
Cookbook 25 Years
Pass The Plate
Texas Longhorn Cookbook
Mealtimes and Memories
Holiday Treats
Homecoming
Cookin' With Will Rogers
Best of Lone Star Legacy Cookbook
Little Taste of Texas
Little Taste of Texas II
Southwest Sizzler
Southwest Ole
Classroom Treats
Leaving Home

www.cookbookresources.com